THE CHARTED MIRROR

THE CHARTED MIRROR

Literary and Critical Essays

by

JOHN HOLLOWAY

HORIZON PRESS

NEW YORK

First American edition 1962
Published by Horizon Press, New York
© *John Holloway 1960*

Library of Congress Catalog Card No. 62-8197

Printed in Great Britain

CONTENTS

PREFACE

THE PARTS OF THIS BOOK are intended to make a balanced
collection as between criticism of verse, criticism of prose, and
discussion of some of the guiding ideas of criticism itself. A consequence of this is that most of the essays in Part One and Part
Two put into practice ideas which are advanced more generally in
Part Three; or conversely, mark out in a given case the limitations
of ideas which are called into question in that Part. It would be
wrong, however, to look for more than a certain definite though
limited degree of connexion between the two sides of the book.
The multiplicity of tasks which critical discussion can undertake, and the always decisive importance of what is distinctive
in the particular instance, mean that to think of 'putting theories
into practice' would be out of place. Rather, it is a question of
exploring, in particular or in general, how any guiding idea
with which the critic may equip himself, any question which he
comes recurrently to ask about what he reads, is likely to open
up certain parts of his particular subject, but certain parts only.
Illumination is always from a certain angle, and of a certain
kind. It cannot easily throw one thing into relief, without throwing another into shadow. In part, the mirror which the critic
must 'chart' is that in himself which forms an image of the work
he studies. It is no unrelieved or flawless plane, but complex and
partly personal, both magnifying and diminishing, in accordance with all that makes up his outlook, guiding ideas, and
general approach.

More important than this, though, it is the work as a mirror of life (though in being so, it is also a new and precious reality in itself) that the critic must chart; and I speak of such a patient and modest activity as charting with a particular fact in mind. This is, that although critics have learnt over the past generation to discuss literary works (or at least the texture of their language) in remarkable detail, a difference remains between discussing something in detail and revealing the detail which it has. The former need not lead to the latter, but may well do the opposite; and the essays in this book have the common ground that they seek to explore their subject from the standpoint of a guiding idea which is often neglected. This is an idea of the *variety* in the questions which a critic may put about a work: the variety, on different occasions, of the paths he must pursue, or the factors he must consider, if the final picture is to emerge truly into focus. His task may be to locate the deeper qualities of something which could be praised or condemned for what it seems on the surface: the reader will find attempts of this kind in Chapters I and IV. It may be to trace closely how what can be known of a writer's life lights up the exact feature and quality of what he wrote (Chapter III). It may be to see how the literary interest of a work is made clearer when its reflection of an age, or resumption of an historical continuity, is also made clearer (Chapters VIII to X). It may be to bear in mind (Chapter VI) that in a distinctive kind of writing like irony, the local texture of language may operate quite differently from what we have learnt to look for in 'practical criticism' of lyrical verse (that erstwhile adventure that is now so often a routine).

Chapter V explores a related problem. It discusses the kind of literary significance which deliberately avoids those complexities of language upon which practical criticism characteristically seizes. Chapters II, VII, and IX all explore, in concrete cases, something which has also been given too little attention over the last generation: how the local features of a work have their meaning only in the context of its longer contours; in the case of a fiction, its developing situation and the whole movement and curve of its narrative. Then in Part Three these matters are examined more generally; examined, now, in the context of recent or current criticism.

Preface

This book is therefore no mere aggregation of pieces which throw no light on each other. But the essays in it have been written at various times, and were not written as parts of a single enterprise, that of illustrating their author's theories. Nor should they have been. This point goes deeper than may appear at first. There are, and have been in the past, certain writers of distinction whose work is most naturally called criticism, but who at least in part, or from time to time, have taken the works they discuss less as an end in themselves than as a means; a means, by using which these writers may express not only their most general literary preferences, but also their first-hand sense of life and its values. In employing the works of others for this purpose they have sometimes greatly illuminated them, and sometimes held them up before the distorting mirror of a powerfully and interestingly subjective vision. Such critics come near, in fact, to the creative writer himself. They are inclined to treat their subject, books, with a masterful self-assurance not unlike that with which he sometimes treats his, reality; and what they write must in part be seen and judged as a distinctive kind of contribution to original literature. There are many ways of contributing to this coveted field, and no reason why this way should be less judged on its merits than another. But for my part, I should prefer to avoid it, and to keep in mind the idea of criticism as an activity which works—though sometimes through the medium of condemnation—in the service of another activity, original writing, of which the status is intrinsically higher. Therefore, in the first two Parts of the present book, it is the work of the authors discussed, as these change from chapter to chapter, which should remain the reader's prime object of interest; and in Part Three, the general exploration of guiding ideas only as preliminary to their use in the service of creative literature. If the other kind of criticism is exhilarating, it is also heady, and perhaps predatory. To see himself as in the service of another kind of writing is in the end, I believe, the best way for a critic to serve the reader.

J. H.

Cambridge,
November 1959

ix

ACKNOWLEDGEMENT

ACKNOWLEDGEMENT IS GRATEFULLY made to the following periodicals and other bodies, in or through which the pieces contained in this book were originally printed or delivered: The British Academy (for permission to reprint the Chatterton Lecture, 1957, on Skelton); *Northern Miscellany* (II); *The Cambridge Journal* (III); *The Hudson Review* (VI, IX, X, XII); *From Jane Austen to Joseph Conrad* (James Hillhouse Memorial Essays, edited by Robert C. Rathburn and Martin Steinmann, jr., Minnesota, 1959) in which 'Hardy's Major Fiction' first appeared; *Essays in Criticism* (XI, XIII); the B.B.C. (IV, V, VIII, and sections 1 and 3 of XIV); and *The Listener*, in which several of these broadcasts were reprinted. The pieces included in this book have been revised, some in matters of detail and others substantially. I should also like to record thanks to the University Librarians at Aberdeen and Cambridge, and to those many others who have helped me at various times with discussion and suggestions.

J. H.

PART ONE

I

SKELTON

TO DISCUSS SKELTON EFFECTIVELY is to do more than elucidate the past on its own terms, and for its own sake. There is no
constraint on anyone to do more than this, and to think that
there is, is to think like a barbarian. But if a critic finds that his
subject empowers him to do more, he ought to say so. Although
Skelton was writing more than 450 years ago, there are certain
respects in which his poetry offers us enlightenment and guidance in the literary and cultural problems which confront us today. To seize on the essence of his poetry is to be wiser for our
own time. Were that not so, I should perhaps have left the subject of Skelton to others, because I find it congenial but do not
find it reassuringly easy.

The problems of today upon which this poet casts light may
be indicated by two quotations: one from Mr Robert Graves
and one from Bernard Berenson. Mr Graves, writing in 1943 on
the development of modern prose, referred to the 'eccentrically
individual styles' of Meredith, Doughty, James, and others, and
added, 'many more styles were invented as the twentieth century advanced and since there was keen competition among
writers as to who should be "great" and since it was admitted
that "greatness" was achieved only by a highly individual style,
new tricks and new devices multiplied'.[1] Forty years before this,
Berenson in his essay on the decline of art pointed out how

[1] *The Reader over Your Shoulder* (1943), p. 120.

3

modern European culture, 'mad for newness' as he put it, has committed itself to a ritual of unremitting dynamism. 'We are thus perpetually changing: and our art cycles, compared to those of Egypt or China, are of short duration, not three centuries at the longest; and our genius is as frequently destructive as constructive.'[1]

Modern English literature surely illustrates what Berenson referred to. The unremitting search for a new way with words, a new kind of hero, a new device for carrying matters a stage further, a new model from some past writer or some foreign literature—these features of the scene are familiar. The search for newness is not itself new, and probably no age has been quite without it. Naturalizing foreign models was an integral part of Chaucer's achievement (though very far of course from the whole of it). But the question is not one merely of innovation; it is of a growing need for constant innovation, and a sense that however often the game of change is played, we are always soon back with what is played out and old-fashioned.

This attitude to writing seems to have become established in England in the course of the sixteenth century. There is a well-known passage in Bacon's *De Augmentis Scientiarum*, written towards the close of his life, in which he adverts to the playing-out first of the vogue for Cicero, then of the vogue for Seneca, shortly before, and shortly after, 1600. More to our immediate purpose is a passage from Puttenham's *Art of English Poetry* of 1589. Puttenham was himself the author of the best and best known manual of a new poetry, which was learning amply from ancient and from foreign models, and which had for many years been coming to dominate the English literary scene. The following passage not only illustrates how Puttenham saw Skelton as the last of the bad old days, and Skelton's immediate successors as those who laid the foundations for the new and stylish; it also points unconsciously forward, in several turns of phrase, to the derivativeness, the vacuous grandiosity, the empty ingenuity, which have plagued us intermittently ever since:

Skelton (was) a sharp satirist, but with more rayling and scoffery than became a Poet Lawreat, such among the Greeks were called

[1] *Italian Painters of the Renaissance* (1938 edition), p. 331.

Pantomimi, with us Buffons, altogether applying their wits to scurrilities and other ridiculous matters. *Henry* Earle of Surrey and Sir *Thomas Wyat*, betweene whom I find very littel difference, I repute them ... for the two chief lanternes of light to all others that have since employed their pennes upon English Poesie, their conceits were loftie, their stiles stately, their conveyance cleanely, their termes proper, their meetre sweete and well proportioned, in all imitating very naturally and studiously their Maister *Francis Petrarcha*.[1]

Ever since the time of these two indistinguishable lanterns of light, imitating one's master naturally and studiously, or finding a new master, or going one better than the old master, have figured prominently, in English verse; and whether the end sought has been stateliness and loftiness, or cleanness and propriety, or sweetness and naturalness, the underlying ideas of a regulation of poetry or a reform of poetry have seldom been far distant.

To take Skelton as representative of something different from this tradition, and as instructive on account of the difference, is not to see him merely as an illiterate extemporising buffoon. He has been seen in these terms in the past, but modern scholarship has made the view quite untenable. Skelton was one of a group of Latinists—the proto-humanists we might call them—whom Henry VII drew into his service, and of whom Polydore Vergil is perhaps the best known.[2] He was an accomplished rhetorician, and his employment of the figures of rhetoric is as deliberate (if somewhat more intelligent) as that of his contemporary Stephen Hawes.[3] His best known poem, *Phyllyp Sparowe*, is a kind of reverent burlesque of the ritual of the Mass in accordance with established medieval convention;[4] and in the description of his heroine in this poem, we can recognize the two places, and no more, where Skelton the poet abandoned the literary model, for the sake one supposes of the real girl.[5] That model was the first specimen *descriptio* in Geoffrey de Vinsauf's *Poetria Nova*, and this work was as much the medieval poetic handbook

---

[1] *op. cit.*, I. xxxi; ed. G. D. Willcock and A. Walker, 1936, p. 62.
[2] W. Nelson, *John Skelton* (1939), pp. 4–59.
[3] V. L. Rubel, *Poetic Diction in the English Renaissance* (1941), pp. 37–9.
[4] See, e.g., Ian A. Gordon, *John Skelton* (1943), pp. 122 *et seq.*
[5] See the introduction to Skelton's translation of the *Bibliotheca Historica* of Diodorus Siculus (ed. F. M. Salter and H. H. L. Edwards, 1956; E.E.T.S. original series 229, p. xxxix).

as Puttenham's work was the Elizabethan one. Skelton's own disclaimer 'though my rhyme be ragged',[1] is itself something of a literary convention: his first modern editor, in 1843, pointed out that Sir David Lindsay and Spenser say the same of their own verse. William Caxton notices that in his translation of Diodorus Siculus Skelton wrote 'not in rude and old language but in polished and ornate terms craftily', and it is essentially the same kind of compliment as Caxton pays elsewhere, justly, to Chaucer ('crafty and sugared eloquence'), and as Spenser's spokesman E. K. was later to pay to the 'well trussed up' verse of Spenser. Skelton was a learned, a professional writer, conversant with his craft and art, an aureate poet as well as a laureate one.

There is always a danger, however, that in registering the qualities of a poem which have been laboriously and scrupulously brought into focus by scholarship, we become blind to the qualities which were never in need of such focusing, because they sprang off the page at us. This is a vital point for Skelton. One of his shorter poems, which begins: *Knolege, aquayntance, resort, fauour with grace*, has been described as 'an ecphrasis in the aureate manner of Lydgate'[2] so it is: we can easily see that it conforms to a literary recipe, and there is little to see in it besides. A companion piece is in part very similar. Also an address to a woman, it closes with an appeal to her to observe the conventional courtly code. It opens with the literary convention at its limpest and most stilted:

> The auncient acquaintance, madam, betwen vs twayn,
>   The famylyaryte, the formar dalyaunce,
> Causyth me that I can not myself refrayne
> But that I must wryte for my plesaunt pastaunce

But Skelton's tongue is in his cheek; this poem is rapidly transformed; its subject—a wife who has been playing fast and loose with her husband—turns into a hectic stable-yard scene, and a horseman struggling with a mare that has the devil in her, 'ware, ware, the mare wynsyth wyth her wanton hele!', 'Haue in sergeaunt ferrour (farrier)'. The violence and confusion veritably explode what was only a mock-decorous poem. It is not, of

---

[1] *Colyn Cloute*, l. 83.   [2] Salter and Edwards, *ed. cit.* p. xxxvii.

course, the first English poem to explode the convention in which it is ostensibly written; but to explode a literary convention it is necessary to obtain a powerful charge drawn from outside convention.

What this is may be seen, perhaps, by turning to the most misjudged of all Skelton's poems, *The Tunnying of Elynour Rummyng*. To say that the tradition of this rough, vernacular poetry has been lost, is not to say everything about it; but is certainly to point towards the difficulty which this poem has created for one critic after another. Henry Morley saw it as 'a very humble rendering to simple wits of the repulsive aspects of intemperance in women';[1] Miss E. P. Hammond refers to its wallowing coarseness;[2] even Professor Lewis seems to see the problem as one of tolerating ugliness for the sake of the liveliness, and expresses his preference for the Scottish poem *Christis Kirk on the Grene*, which he praises for melody, gaiety, and orderliness, and which attracts him through its occasional underlying lyricism.[3]

To experience these feelings about *Elynour Rummyng* is to wish that it were different in kind from what it is, rather than better in quality. This picture of a morning in a low country ale-house is if anything less coarse than Langland's superb account of Gluttony in the ale-house, in *Piers Plowman*,[4] and melody and gaiety are as far from Skelton's purpose as they were from Langland's. Indeed, to mention Langland is at once to become aware that Skelton's piece is no thoughtless extemporisation, but has its literary antecedents. Its subject, and its attitude to that subject, were both recurrent in medieval writing;[5] and it is possible that Skelton's poem, with its old and ugly ale-wife whose customers are all old and ugly women, is even a kind of calculated counterpart to a poem by Lydgate, the *Ballade on an Ale-Seller*, in which (to express oneself in modern terms) a bold and handsome barmaid attracts an exclusively male clientele.

[1] *English Writers*, Vol. 7 (1891), p. 190.
[2] *English Verse between Chaucer and Surrey* (1927), p. 337.
[3] C. S. Lewis, *English Literature in the Sixteenth Century* (1954), p. 138; p. 106.
[4] C Text, Passus VII, ll. 349–441.
[5] Cf. R. L. Greene, *Early English Carols* (1935), No. 419 ('The Gossips' Meeting'); Greene compares this with the 'Good Gossippes Songe' in the Chester play of the Deluge, but this is too short and slight to have much in common with Skelton's poem.

7

In Lydgate's poem, we certainly have orderliness, the order of the ballade; and we have a literary, even sometimes a lofty diction. But they are quite out of key with the subject; and

> With your kissyng thouh that ye do plesaunce
> It shall be derrer, er thei do ther way
> Than al ther ale, to them I dar wel say

—that is perhaps the best that Lydgate's poem can do: a hasty glimpse of fact, a trite moral, a reader nonplussed with tedium.

The ugly side of *Elynour Rummyng* is simply an honest reflection of the poverty and primitiveness which were the staple of life for a rural peasantry in England at that time, as they doubtless are still for rural peasants over most of the planet. If we find coarseness, it is not through identifying what Skelton is trying to make of his material, but through plain unfamiliarity with the material itself. In a now almost unknown poem of just after Skelton's time (happily almost unknown, for in the main it is very bad), we can glimpse those same conditions, but they peer through despite the poet's almost admitted inability to render them. The poem is Copland's *Hie Waie to the Spitale Hous*, and the passage is that which describes the beggars and vagrants as the Watch sees them at night:

> But surely, every night here is found
>   One or other lying by the pound
> In the sheep cotes or in the hay loft
> And at Saint Bartholomew's church door full oft
> And even here alway by this brick wall
>   We do them find, that do both chide and brawl
> And like as beasts together they be throng
>   Both lame and sick and whole them among,
> And in many corners where that we go,
> Whereof I greatly wonder that they do so.[1]

Copland virtually confesses, with that disastrous last line, how his facts defeat him. Skelton's poem is in another world; or rather, his ale-wife with her skin that is 'grained lyke a sacke', her customers who tie their hair up in a shoe-rag when they come to pawn their crocks for ale, her pigs that wander in and

---

[1] Quoted from A. V. Judges, *The Elizabethan Underworld* (1930), pp. 4-5.

out of the bar and scratch themselves on the furniture, take us back with exuberant vitality into the real world.

This extraordinary vividness, where many find vividness an embarrassment, has prevented readers from grasping the full range of the poem, as a record of fact. *Elynour Rummyng* is not, as it has been called, a 'purely objective' record of peasant reality.[1] It is not a moralizing poem, but it is full of an awareness of the essential humanity of the scene it depicts, and of a such comprehension of this (a comprehension neither harsh nor slack and casual) as is the only foundation for significant moralizing. It is easy to miss this subtler side to the poem; but it is there, in the customers who

> lothe to be espyde,
> Start in at the backe syde,
> Ouer the hedge and pale,
> And all for the good ale.

It is there in those who sit glumly because they have nothing to barter for ale, and can only drink as much as they can chalk up on the beam. It shows in the differences among what customers bring to barter: some the reasonable merchandise of the prosperous peasant, some the last thing in the house or the last thing that they ought to part with. Once we are conscious of these aspects of the poem, even the character of Elynour herself takes on a new light. Her shocked indignation when one of the customers falls over and lets her skirts fly up is a genuine and convincing turn of peasant character. Some of the customers ask for drink and have no money. Skelton writes:

> Elynour swered, Nay,
> Ye shall not beare away
> My ale for nought,
> *By hym that me bought!*

This does not merely contrast the bargains which men and women strike, with that which Christ struck: it brings them disquietingly, revealingly together. With these things in mind, one can see that the opening description of Elynour herself has a somewhat similar deeper significance. It clearly resembles one of

[1] W. L. Renwick and H. Orton, *The Beginnings of English Literature to Skelton* (second ed., 1952), p. 114.

9

the most humane and moving passages in the whole of Chaucer's writings, the *Reve's Prologe*:

> For sikerly, whan I was bore, anon
> Deeth drough the tappe of lyf and leet it gon;
> And ever sithe hath so the tappe yronne
> Til that almoost al empty is the tonne.

Incidentally, the elderly Reeve's 'grene tayl' may have its connexion with 'Parot hath a blacke beard and a fayre grene tale' in Skelton's *Speke, Parot*, a poem which I shall discuss later. But there is a clear detailed link with *Elynour Rummyng* too. Chaucer's Reeve says:

> But ik am oold, me list not for pley for age;
> Gras tyme is doon, my fodder is now forage
> This white top writeth myne old yeris.

Skelton uses just this idea of fresh plants and dead forage, and when he does so, it is difficult not to see both Chaucer's direct influence, and the general quality of his insight into human transience:

> Her eyen . . .
> . . . are blered
> And she gray hered . . .
> Her youth is farre past:
> Foted lyke a plane
> Leged lyke a crane;
> And yet she wyll iet,
> Lyke a jolly fet . . .
> Her huke of Lyncole grene,
> It had been hers, I wene,
> More then fourty yere;
> And so doth it apere,
> For the grene bare thredes
> Loke lyke sere *wedes*,
> Wyddered lyke *hay* . . .

As against this poem, *Christis Kirk on the Grene* is gay boisterous comedy with something even of slapstick; and to compare it with Skelton's poem is to bring out not the defects, but the distinctiveness, and the depth of the latter.

Miss M. M. Gray has pointed out that the spirit of poems like

Christis Kirk on the Grene is not typical of the Scottish poetry of its period.[1] If *The Tunnyng of Elynour Rummyng* is related instead to such poems as *Tydingis fra the Sessioun*, which is by Dunbar, or *The Devillis Inquest*, which is almost certainly not so, a quite new kind of difference emerges. In *The Devillis Inquest* we find:

> 'Be Goddis blud,' quod the taverneir,
> 'Thair is sic wyine in my selleir
> Hes never come in this cuntrie.'
> 'Yit,' quod the Devill, 'thou sellis our deir,
> With thy fals met cum downe to me.'

This is not a Chaucerian movement of thought; it is a vision which concentrates on the evil in the fact, sees it intensely, and is directed by uncompromising though sternly controlled indignation. One side of reality is brought into a clear focus by a cold and masterly economy of language. This is still a link with Chaucer, but it is not Skelton's kind of link. With rare exceptions, Chaucer's firm linguistic line, his masterly economy, do not serve purposes like these, but less severe ones. Dr Edwards, discussing Skelton's lyrics, wrote: 'He possessed none of Chaucer's smiling acceptance of men and women as they are.'[2] Even as an account of Chaucer, that might need a little amendment; but what is relevant for the moment is that it distinguishes too sharply between Chaucer and Skelton.

In my view *Elynour Rummyng* is the most significant of the poems which Skelton wrote in the short metre which has been named after him. *Philip Sparow* has great grace and charm, but its chief character is to be an endearing poem, and one which deserves a rather higher place in our affections than it does in our minds as a whole. What may be found in it is not far from what may readily be found elsewhere, and its principle of organization lacks the vitality and distinctiveness of what integrates *Elynour Rummyng*, the single scene of the poem itself as that is brought progressively into focus.

[1] M. M. Gray, *Scottish Poetry from Barbour to James VI*, Introduction (1935 edition, p. xvii); these remarks relate specifically to another similar work, *Peblis to the Play*, but also generally to the humourous poems in the Bannatyne and Maitland MSS. which stand out (like *Christis Kirke on the Grene*) for their 'boisterous merriment and rough-and-tumble'.

[2] H. L. R. Edwards, *Skelton* (1949), p. 53.

Colyn Cloute and *Why Come Ye Nat to Courte* can by no means be passed over altogether, and if I pass them over for the moment, it is in order to give emphasis to a more general point. The poems which Skelton wrote in short lines, rhyming consecutively—in 'Skeltonics'—are usually thought of as his most distinctive and most interesting ones. Long ago, this idea supplied Isaac D'Israeli with a cumbrous joke and a mixed metaphor: 'Whenever (Skelton's) muse plunges into the long measure of heroic verse, she is drowned in no Heliconian stream.'[1] The idea reappears implicitly in what has surely been the most influential of recent pronouncements on Skelton, Mr Graves' poem *John Skelton*,[2] which is itself written in a kind of Skeltonics, and which catalogues most of 'helter-skelter John's' short-line poems, without any reference to his other works. And when Professor Lewis writes[3] 'the things that Mr Graves gets out of Skelton's work are much better than anything Skelton put in', he is clearly not taking issue with this conception of Skelton, even if it is not entirely clear that he is endorsing it.

This notion of what most distinguishes Skelton is erroneous; the Skeltonics are what stand out if we survey only the externals of his work, if our findings are a little too much like what a computer could find if Skelton's poems were fed into it. Some of the most remarkable qualities of Skelton's work are obscured and concealed by his short line. It is in what D'Israeli misleadingly called 'the long measure of his heroic verse' that these qualities are most abundantly manifested; and when this is realized, Mr Graves's

> What could be *dafter*
> Than John Skelton's laughter?
> What sound more *tenderly*
> Than his *pretty* poetry?

falls short of adequacy.

Skelton's *The Bouge of Court* is widely recognized as a poem which gives a new individuality to a conventional form, that of the dream-poem; but this is perhaps to praise that work on too easy terms. References to Skelton's avoidance of 'the conven-

---

[1] *Amenities of Literature* (1841), Vol. II, p. 69.
[2] *Poems (1914–26)*, pp. 6–8. [3] *op. cit.*, p. 143.

tional arbor'[1] or statements like 'for the first time the medieval
vision is given a strictly local habitat'[2] ignore such things as the
opening of the *Kingis Quair*: King James of Scotland's sleepless
night, with his book at his bedside and the matins bell to disturb
him. With this, one might perhaps take Henryson in his study
mending the fire and taking strong drink to keep out the cold
before he settles down to write *The Testament of Cresseid*. The distinction of Skelton's poem lies less in any simple change in its
mechanical organization, than in something which is woven intimately into its texture. Among the various allegorical figures
whom Skelton meets as passengers when he boards the ship,
from which the poem takes its title, that of *Riot* is perhaps the
best known.

> Wyth that came Ryotte, russhynge all at onces,
>   A rusty gallande, to-ragged and to-rente;
> And on the borde he whyrled a payre of bones,
>   Quater treye dews he clatered as he wente;
> Now haue at all, by saynte Thomas of Kente!
> And euer he threwe and kyst I wote nere what:
> His here was growen thorowe oute his hat.
>
> Thenne I behelde how he dysgysed was:
>   His hede was heuy for watchynge ouer nyghte;
> His eyen blereed, his face shone lyke a glas;
>   His gowne so shorte that it ne couer myghte
>   His rumpe, he wente so all for somer lyghte;
> His hose was garded wyth a lyste of grene,
> Yet at the knee they were broken, I wene.

This account, as a whole, is more than 'a brilliant sketch of
the seedy, jazz-humming early Tudor roué' as it has been
called;[3] and it displays more than 'a genius for satirical por-
traiture'[4] *tout court*. The affinity with Chaucer's *Pardoner's Tale*
may be partial, but it is unmistakable. The note of pathos, of
tragedy in Riot's high spirits and gay tatters is not, surely, the
mere interpolation of a modern mind. 'Counter he coude *O lux*
vpon a potte,' Skelton writes: it is the medieval hymn *O lux*

[1] Nelson, *op. cit.*, p. 78. [2] Edwards, *op. cit.*, p. 62.
[3] Edwards, *op. cit.*, p. 63. [4] Nelson, *op. cit.*, p. 82.

beata trinitas that Riot counters. We are never—even if only
through the oaths that come incessantly throughout this poem—
allowed to forget the religious dimension in which all these
essentially human and mortal figures have their being. '. . . by
that Lorde that bought dere all mankynde, I can not flater, I
muste be playne to thẽ'; 'by that Lorde that is one, two, and
thre, I haue an errande to rounde in your ere' (an echo of
Chaucer echoing Dante). This note might not be clear as irony,
were it not for the constantly scriptural note, also sounding
ironically, of the rest:

> Loo, what it is a man to haue connynge!
> All erthly tresoure it is surmountynge.

and

> Nay, naye, be sure, whyles I am on your syde,
> Ye may not fall, truste me, ye may not fayle

and

> Maystress, quod I, I haue none aquentaunce,
> That wyll for me be medyatoure and mene

—all these illustrate something which is sustained so much without intermission through the poem, that in the end it is quite
inescapable. Skelton is leading us to see these figures—figures
'for whome Tybourne groneth both daye and nyghte'—as err-
ing mortal creatures in the fullest sense; in fact his compassionate comprehension is if anything more in evidence here, and
more sombrely and solemnly in evidence, than it was in *Elynour
Rummyng*.

Something else is in evidence also. Skelton's insight into
men's behaviour, exact and humane as it was, could not but
equip him with real power for dramatization. English literature
seems to have reached fully dramatic writing only with difficulty: perhaps because this demands a sense of realistic detail, a
power of comprehension and selection which is more than realism, and also (if it is to be in verse) an appropriately developed
metrical vehicle. Chaucer mastered it even as early as the *Hous
of Fame*; most English medieval plays only strive towards it. In
The Bouge of Court it is otherwise. Dyssymulation, for example,
tells the poet that the people in the court are all malicious gossips. Then he makes an exception of himself:

For all be it that this longe not to me,
  Yet on my backe I bere suche lewde delynge:
Ryghte now I spake with one, I trowe, I see;
  But, what, a strawe! I maye not tell all thynge.
By God, I saye there is grete herte brennynge
Betwene the persone ye wote of, (and) you.

These lines are typical, and to read them is to find oneself in
almost total contact with the movement of a living mind as it
works its way from word to word.

Contrast that moment in Stephen Hawes' *Example of Vertue*
when the poet meets Dame Sensuality riding on a goat. If we
have any hopes that her arrival will infuse a little vitality into
the poem, the poet extinguishes those hopes with stunning
celerity:

'Nay,' said Discretion, 'that may nat be'
'No,' said I, 'in no maner of wise
To her request will I now agree
But evermore her foul Lust despise . . .'

'So forth I went . . .' Hawes' next stanza baldly opens. That is a
phrase which recurs throughout his poem: each time it marks
an evasion of reality, a giving up by the poet before material he
cannot handle.

By contrast, the personifications of *The Bouge of Court* have a
vivid vernacular life. So have those in *Magnyfycence*. Among
Skelton's works for acting, this is the only one (apart, probably,
from a recently discovered and uninspired fragment) which sur-
vives.[1] For all that it is too intricate and much too long, some of
the dialogue of this play is remarkable for the period in which
it was written or indeed for long after. One example is the scene
in which three of the characters in the play recognize a fourth
through his disguise, and then pretend that he is a priest, and
maul at his clothes:

Cloked Colusyon: Knowe they not me, they are to blame
              Knowe you not me, syrs?
Fancy: No, in dede.
Crafty Conveyaunce: Abyde, lette me se, take better hede:
              Cockes harte, it is Cloked Colusyon

[1] See the article by G. L. Frost and Ray Nash, *'Good Order': A Morality Fragment*, S.P., 1944, p. 483.

Cl. Col.:	A, syr, I pray God gyve you confusyon!
Fan.:	Cockes armes, is that your name?
C. Count.:	Ye, by the masse, this is euen the same,
	That all this matter must vnder grope.
Cr. Con.:	What is this he wereth, a cope?
Cl. Co.:	Cappe, syr; I say you be to bolde.
Fan.:	Se, howe he is wrapped for the colde:
	Is it not a vestment?
Cl. Col.:	A, ye wante a rope.
C. Count.:	Tushe, it is Syr Johnn Double cloke
Fan.:	Syr, and yf ye wolde not be wrothe——
Cl. Col.:	What sayst?
Fan.:	Here was to lytell clothe.

This is essentially—a point to which my argument will revert—a colloquial, a vernacular kind of drama. But it is written with a fine sense of action upon the stage, and with real shrewdness and insight into how men can behave.

Yet vivid dialogue is not what gives *Magnyfycence* its essential significance. After all, the most that can be said of it on that score is that it points forward, hesitantly and intermittently, to the comic dialogue of Shakespeare. In some other qualities also (its overtly political setting, and perhaps its emphasis on Aristotelian ideas of the good ruler and of virtue) this work looks forward; but in its most deeply significant qualities it does not. Miss Dodds has pointed out that although the moral of the play for Magnyfycence himself is Measure, the Aristotelian Golden Mean, it is not that for the audience.[1] For the audience the moral is the more deeply traditional idea of universal Mutability:

> A myrrour incleryd is this interlude,
> This lyfe inconstant for to beholde and se;
> Sodenly riches, and sodenly pouerty,
> Sodenly comfort, and sodenly adversyte . . .

With these lines, and the quite new note that they strike, we reach the core of Skelton's achievement. The idea is that upon which Chaucer ends his *Troilus and Criseyde*, and the lines are from a rhyme-royal stanza, which is Chaucer's metre in *Troilus*

[1] Madeleine Hope Dodds, 'Early Political Plays' (*Library*, Series III, Vol. 4, p. 393).

also. But what Skelton writes in the two whole stanzas which follow is a collection of gnomic sayings, having the structure of thought and the rhythm of language of an essentially proverbial wisdom—in this case, the basic idea, that life is suddenly one thing, and then suddenly its opposite.

I have not seen any explicit recognition of how much Skelton's work owes to proverbial language, and in doing so, to the whole way of life and cast of mind which finds its expression in proverbial language; although the first modern edition of his work is full of information on this very subject. Here the short line poems are relevant once again. 'Such apple-tree, such fruit'; 'loth to hang the bell / About the cattes neck'; 'hearted like an hen'; 'not worth a leek'; 'as wise as Waltham's calfe'; 'all is fish that cometh to net'; 'we may blow at the coal'; 'Mock hath lost her shoe'; '. . . . it is a wily mouse / That can build hys dwellyng house / Within the cat's ear'—it is not a matter merely of Skelton's using proverbial wise sayings. His verse draws on the proverbial kind of expression for a good deal of its vivid metaphorical wealth, and for something of its whole attitude to its subject—bold yet unassuming, essentially down-to-earth. It uses the clichés of ordinary people (which are not clichés at all, because instead of making the mind gloss over the plain facts, they bring it abruptly up against them) but it is using these in order to assimilate the whole idea which ordinary people form of reality. To notice Skelton's reliance on the proverbial expression is not to notice a literary trick or a literary routine, but to notice, at its most easily recognizable point, the essential quality of what was creative in his mind. It is the same quality which shows, if we consider the use that he made of the authors on whose work he draws. Juvenal in his eighth satire, for example, had written:

> quo, si nocturnus adulter
> Tempora Santonico velas adoperta cucullo

Skelton almost certainly has this passage in mind when he attacks Wolsey in *Why Come Ye Nat to Courte*. But what he writes is:

> Ye may weare a cockes come;
> Your fonde hed in your furred hood,
> Holde ye your tong, ye can no goode:

17

Juvenal's line embodies penetrating diagnosis of a fact, and an attitude of angry superiority to it; Skelton replaces this by the common sense, and the impudence towards the great, of the plain man.¹ In the *Garlande of Laurell* there is an account of how the Phoenix consumes itself in the fire. Skelton probably had a passage from Ovid's *Metamorphoses*, Book XV, in mind. But he adds something of his own about this Phoenix:

> her wynges betwene
> She *bet vp a fyre* with the sparkis full kene.

Perhaps it is not fanciful to suggest that this comes nearer to an early morning scene in Skelton's own Norfolk parsonage, than it does to Ovid. Again, when Skelton in the same poem describes the bard Iopas singing his song in the garden of the Muses, he follows the closing lines of the first book of the Aeneid; but there is nothing in Virgil which corresponds to the lively turn of thought, humorous rather than witty, whereby Skelton's Iopas, in his songs about the constellations, includes

> that pole artike which doth remayne
> *Behynde the taile* of Vrsa so clere

and there is nothing in Virgil, beyond a plain 'rainy Hyades', which could produce the vividness in Skelton's homely touch of the Hyades' 'misling eye'.

Thus, Skelton's manner of drawing on proverbial language and of drawing away from literary models both show the essential quality of his mind. So, more important perhaps, do his rhythms. Dr Nelson argues that of all the various progenitors which have been suggested for Skelton's short-line verse, the brief chiming cadences of Latin rhyming prose are the most likely.² In this he seems clearly right. It is much more open to question, though, whether he is right in suggesting that the transition from prose to verse was, in Skelton's case, one towards smoothness and regularity. Across Skelton's short lines there seems often to be an irregular longer rhythm; one which

---

¹ Juvenal, *Satires*, VIII, 144–5; *Why Come Ye Nat to Courte*, ll. 1232–4. It should be noticed that at l. 1224 Skelton has quoted *verbatim* part of l. 140 of the Eighth Satire.
² *op. cit.*, pp. 90 *et seq.*

is essentially a long spoken rhythm, the angry accelerating
tirade brought to a halt by an emphatic rallentando and
pause. *Why Come Ye Nat to Courte*, ll. 65–81, seem to be a good
illustration of this. If this is so, it is yet another example of
how Skelton adapts what is literary in origin to vehement
speech and to the cast of mind which lies behind that kind
of speech.

However this may be, a parallel trend is quite indisputable in
the case of Skelton's longer metre. His long lines, it is true, can
sometimes be seen almost as two short 'Skeltonic' lines combined into one: but that is by no means the whole of the story.
The convention that the poet should disparage his own work
may have been why Skelton makes one of the characters in
Magnyfycence say that his big speech—really a dramatic chorus—
will be 'In bastarde ryme after the dogrell gyse'. But again, that
is not the whole story. Ramsay, in his admirable Introduction
to *Magnyfycence*, made it clear that Skelton's long line, even in
the rhyme-royal sections of this poem, is not the regular five-
stress line of Chaucer at all, but a four-stress line, which never
carries the sense on from line to line; which is marked by constant alliteration; which may vary in length from seven to four-
teen syllables; and which (in its ampler forms) centres round a
very emphatic central pause. The result is a loose and exceedingly flexible verse form, which can vary from almost naïve
spareness to great amplitude and copiousness, which has as its
metrical unit not the foot at all, but the self-dependent phrase,
and which is such as we might expect, in fact, if the *sense* of
rhythm which we have in Langland were to be forced into expression through a Chaucerian rhythmic *form*. It is essentially a
metre dominated by the speaking voice, as against a metre
which dominates the voice. Here is one part of its connexion
with proverbial utterance, and the cast of mind which goes with
that. Another part is how it resists enjambement—each line
makes a separate statement—and how it naturally falls into two
parts around its central pause, for this is also common in proverbs. (Many hands, light work; if wishes were horses, beggars
would ride.)

Skelton may be the master of this metre, but he did not in-
vent it. A fifteenth-century poem like 'Lex is layde and lethyrly

lukys'[1] falls not only into the metre, but also into the gnomic quality, the macaronics, and the general attitudes, which are common in Skelton:

> Veritas is demytt to hange one the ruyde,
> Verecundia was drownytt at the laste fluyde,
> So that few freyndes may a man fynde,
> ffor rectum iudicium commys so farre be-hynde.
> ffraus is fykyll as a fox, and reuys in this lande
> ffuror is hys freynde, as I vnderstande . . .

Another poem of this general period is especially interesting, because it shows the attitude of mind which tended to force a poet into using the stress metre. Like Skelton's *Ancient Aqueyntaunce*, it begins as a deceptively decorous compliment to a lady, and turns into a ribald and telling palinode against her. As it makes this transition in attitude, its rhythm changes from smooth, regular rhythm by feet, to an abrupt Skeltonic rhythm of the half-line and the independent phrase.[2] The poem opens:

> O mosy Quince hangyng by your stalke
> The whyche no man may pluk away ner take

but by the time it is speaking out, as it were, we find lines like:

> My louely lewde masterasse take consideracion
> I am so sorrowfull there as yet be absent
> The flowre of the barkfate[3] the fowlyst of all the nacion
> To loue you but a lytyll hit myne entent.

Counterfeit Countenaunce's chorus speech, to which I referred just now, is essentially in this stress-rhythm also; and it is this which enables it to move, with great freedom and ease, out of abrupt and lively dialogue into what is almost a rhetoric of moral denunciation. It opens with a light rhythm like

> Fansy hath cachyd in a flye net
> This noble man Magnyfycence

---

[1] Carleton Brown, *Religious Lyrics of the Fifteenth Century* (1959), No. 176, p 269.
[2] Henry A. Person (ed.), *Cambridge Middle English Lyrics* (1953), No. 49, p. 40.　　　　　[3] Tanner's vat.

and little by little, in a kind of flux and reflux, it is amplified
into lines like

> Counterfet preaching and byleue the contrary
> Counterfet conscyence, peuysshe pope holy:
> Counterfet sadness, with delynge full madly;
> Counterfet holyness is called ypocrysy;
> Counterfet reason is not worth a flye;
> Counterfet wysdome, and workes of foly;
> Counterfet countenaunce every man doth occupy:

In fact, the general recurrent movement of this play is to modu-
late from dialogue to this kind of moralistic verse, solemn yet
essentially popular and traditional in both its style and its
attitudes.

This same kind of poetry is constantly breaking through the
'literary' tedium of *The Garlande of Laurell*:

> He is not wyse ageyne the streme that stryvith;
> Dun is in the myre, dame, reche me my spur;
> Nedes must he rin that the deuyll dryuith;
> When the stede is stolyn, spar the stable dur;
> A ientyll hownde shulde neuer play the kur;
> It is sone aspyed where the thorne prikketh;
> And wele wotith the cat whose berde she likketh.

But it is in *Speke, Parot* that these qualities of Skelton's work are
most important, for that extraordinary poem is surely his
masterpiece. Historically, this poem marks not only Skelton's
hostility to Wolsey, and those policies of Wolsey which were in-
escapably bringing the whole traditional order to an end, but
also Skelton's general hostility to the growing Erastianism of
the time,[1] and his now final abandonment of London and the
Court, for the great conservative family of the Earl of Surrey.
Indeed, everything which shows Skelton's place in the culture
of his time seems to converge in this poem. Morality based upon
the Bible and the people's proverbial wisdom goes here with an
essentially vernacular use of language throughout, with a distinctive development of the polyglot macaronic kind of writing
(a popular and goliardic mode rather than a literary one), and
with a structure, perhaps, somewhat like those commonplace

[1] See J. M. Berdan, 'Speke, Parrot'; MLN, Vol. 30 (1915), p. 140.

books which passed from hand to hand in the country houses of the time and contained, as Dr Person writes, 'poetry and prose, English, Latin, or French, long poems and scraps, religion and science, devotional and satiric works, riddles and proverbs'.[1] Yet out of this gallimaufry, Skelton has made a poem which (though a chaos from a mechanical standpoint) is imaginatively perhaps the most unified of his works. It is unified in the persistent vivid presence and exceedingly distinctive tone—the tone of one who threatens and is himself in danger—of the parrot itself. Above all it is unified in the gathering power and directness of the attack as this gradually breaks through the speaker's prudence, and at last converts his glancing blows into the finale: a fierce and solemn denunciation of Wolsey himself:

> So braynles caluys hedes, so many shepis taylys;
> So bolde a braggyng bocher, and flesshe sold so dere;
> So many plucte partryches, and so fat quaylles;
> So mangye a mastyfe curre, the grete grey houndes pere;
> So bygge a bulke of brow antlers cabagyd that yere;
> So many swannes dede, and so small revell;—
> Syns Dewcalyons flodde, I trow, no man can tell.

We scarcely need to trace Wolsey's father the butcher in these lines, nor the Tudor greyhound, nor the swan of the Duke of Buckingham. The passionate, unflinching, comprehensive grasp of reality, and embodiment of it in an idiom wholly the writer's own, are unmistakable. If we think that we are not in the presence here of poetic greatness, it is because there is a kind of poetic greatness which we have not learnt to know.

To make this claim is not to make every claim. Nothing in Skelton has the poignancy, strangeness, and deep compassion of the scene in Henryson's poem where Cressid the leper begs an alms of Prince Troilus, and his memory of her swims half way to the light, but then goes back into darkness. Skelton has nothing of the imaginative brilliance of Sir David Lindsay's *Ane Satire of the Thrie Estatis*, in the opening words of Sensualitie:

> Luifers awalk, behald the fyrie spheir,
> Behauld the naturall dochter of Venus.

[1] Person, *op. cit.*, p. iv.

This is not going far afield. But what we do see in Skelton is one quite distinctive kind of excellence. A variety of vernacular traditions, a vernacular kind of insight, a metre and a rhythm which had for long had contact with vernacular expression—all these are things that come together in Skelton's verse. Once again George Puttenham, cicerone of the new and more literary poetic which succeeded Skelton and put him out of favour, settles that matter for us (though he settles less than he thinks) when he ridicules

small and popular musickes song . . . upon benches and barrels heads where they have none other audience then boys or countrey fellowes that passe them in the streete, or else by blind harpers or such like taverne minstrels that give a fit of mirth for a groat, and their matters being for the most part stories of old time . . . also they be used in Carols and rounds and such light or lascivious Poemes, which are commonly more commodiously uttered by these buffons or vices in plays then by any other person. Such were the rimes of Skelton . . . in our courtly maker we banish them utterly.[1]

To accept this view of Skelton as essentially in contact with the apprehension of life of the ordinary man is not to accept what Puttenham thought it meant: that his work was crude and art-less. I hope I have shown how he drew upon, or sometimes transformed, the work of his precedessors or models. His rhythmic spontaneity and flexibility is in fact a high technical achievement, towards which we can see him working from *The Bouge of Court* on to *Speke, Parot*. But when we open our minds to what is most distinctive of the truly literary quality of his verse, what we find is amplitude, immediacy, rhythmic vitality, a sug-gestion of embodied power for growth. What Henry James called 'felt life' seems to operate in the texture of his language with a quite special freedom and directness; and when that language moves, as it often does, beyond plain speech, it moves in a different direction from that which is conspicuous in Donne, say, and the poets who followed Donne: it moves less towards wit and argumentation through figurative language, than to-wards the proverbial gnomic solemnity of the traditional and popular mind. The result is no mere mirror of life, no mere

[1] *op. cit.*, ed. Willcock and Walker, pp. 83–4.

Skeltonic realism, but something of an embodiment of life's permanent contours and essential vitality. Much may be absent from Skelton, but this, with the deep refreshment which it brings, is not absent.

When a literature—like our own—is old, and has been forming and re-forming for centuries, and has been reacting with other literatures for centuries also, there is a strong tendency for your courtly maker or his counterpart to predominate, and for writers generally to seek and expect success through naturally and studiously imitating their master Francis Petrarch or whoever may be the Francis Petrarch of the hour. We cannot but recall at this point the views of Graves and Berenson, which I quoted earlier, about multiplying tricks and devices, achieving a highly individual style, perpetually changing, displaying genius which is as frequently destructive and constructive. 'What has not been done? What is left to do?' seems more and more insistently to become the cry. Perhaps this cannot but tend to happen, as the centuries go by, and the past tends to weigh down, more and more, upon the present. But in Skelton, although he had the interests of a serious poet, and although his civilization was old rather than young, something else has happened. In his work, the dominance of artistry by reality is peculiarly thorough-going, peculiarly intimate and genuine. This may or may not be the balance which we find at the very pinnacle of artistic achievement; but I think it is one which we greatly need to contemplate, and to learn from, today.

II

DRAMATIC IRONY IN
SHAKESPEARE

I

CRITICS HAVE OFTEN FORMED too narrow an idea of irony
in drama. In the first place, it has sometimes been thought that
irony reveals the operation, behind individual character, of im-
personal force or law. E. E. Stoll adopts this view when he
writes 'in Sophocles the contrast is . . . between the *decrees of
Fate* and the "fallibility of human endeavour"—and not so
much moral as merely natural and emotional. As such it is
steeply ironical.'[1] Bradley uses the same notion: writing that
Macbeth 'uses a device which contributes to excite the vague
fear of *hidden forces* operating on minds unconscious of their influence'.[2] There is also another narrow view of dramatic irony.
This says nothing of Fate; it simply claims that irony makes the
audience envisage the tragic dénouement, vividly, before it
arrives. Professor J. A. K. Thomson thus writes of the irony
in Aeschylus's *Agamemnon* 'making us hear more and more

[1] E. E. Stoll, *Shakespeare and Other Masters* (1940), pp. 61-2. *Italics in this
and all subsequent quotations are mine.*
[2] A. C. Bradley, *Shakespearean Tragedy* (1904), p. 340. Compare R. G.
Moulton's comment on *Othello*, 'the suggestion is as if fate—or providence,
or the general course of events—was itself the spectator, holding the clue to
the issue' (*Shakespeare as a Dramatic Thinker*, 1924, p. 241).

distinctly the rumble of *approaching* doom';[1] and Quiller-Couch also, when discussing *Macbeth*, accepts this view of irony, though he distinguishes something else besides it. For although he says that the peculiar irony of *Macbeth* is 'retrospective' (reminding the audience, when tragedy has come, that it was coming all the while), what he contrasts this with, as the norm, is 'prophetic' irony which can 'prepare the spectator for what *is to come*'.[2]

It is quite unnecessary to argue here that these critics were wrong to find dramatic effects along these lines. But although these findings may not need correcting, they do need supplementing: and in one or two cases, the supplementary point is more important and central than the original one. There is not much doubt about this in principle. It takes little reflection to see that irony can contribute to drama in many ways other than those distinguished in the last paragraph. Perhaps this is seen most clearly once we recognize that, in vivid contrast to the solemn ironies of Fate and Tragedy, irony can sometimes be quite trivial, just a playwright's trick.

One example of triviality will suffice. Consider the close of Act I of Wilde's *An Ideal Husband*. Sir Robert Cheveley, the high-minded politician, is threatened with exposure. His wife is ignorant of his shady start in life, and he is sure that when she finds out their married happiness will collapse. The scene ends (with some abridgment):

Lady Chiltern: We needs must love the highest when we see it. (*Kisses him and arises and goes out. The servant enters and begins putting out the lights.*)
Sir Robert Chiltern: Put out the lights, Mason, put out the lights. (. . . *the room becomes almost dark. The only light there is comes from the great chandelier that hangs over the staircase and illuminates the tapestry of the Triumph of Love.*)

I take this feeble piece of writing deliberately, for by concentrating attention on the masterpieces of the Greek theatre we tend to overlook how irony is a device of general application in

---

[1] J. A. K. Thomson, *Irony, an Historical Introduction* (1926), p. 51.
[2] A. Quiller-Couch, *Shakespeare's Workmanship* (1931 Edition), p. 50. Compare the reference to ' "ironical", ominous lines, forecasting the future', in R. W. Chambers' discussion of *Measure for Measure* (*Man's Unconquerable Mind*, 1939, p. 285).

drama, and is therefore capable of making, with equal ease, gold or tinsel. In this scene from Wilde there is nothing of the Irony of Fate, which is something merely toyed with in the play, and thrown aside at the end. Nor does the incident prefigure any dénouement, tragic or otherwise. This is a play of intrigue: we do not know what the dénouement will be, and if we could take the tapestry as sign either of a happy or (by irony) of a tragic ending, the suspense and therefore in large part the point of this play would be lost. But Wilde's juxtaposition of shaky marriage and Triumph of Love Tapestry underlines, in its somewhat cheap way, the issues and the forces *currently* at work in his situation. It is a device for exposition, and a device for vividness. Wilde's situation was one of clash, and he sought to make the nature of the clash plain, and throw it into relief, by a readily-grasped symbolism. That the result (like the tags from *Guinevere* and *Othello*) is feeble only makes this point clearer. Wilde sought an easy significance, any more portentous one would have been an embarrassment to him.

Basically, then, irony makes for fuller and also sharper exposition, for colour and at the same time chiaroscuro. As such, its contribution may be trivial as here in Wilde, or deeply searching as we shall see in Shakespeare. To use it to stress Fate or Tragedy is no doubt specially telling and frequent, but at bottom it is simply a method of creating and controlling that richer-than-normal texture which is characteristic of literature. If so, it ought to be thought of along with other modes (with which modern criticism has been much concerned) of enriching literary texture. From ambiguity of the better-known kind it appears to differ through supplying a second sense not to supplement, but to preponderate over, and cancel, the first. Professor Cleanth Brooks has drawn attention to the place of irony in lyric poetry;[1] and sometimes admirably, sometimes excessively pursued its workings. Its greater contribution in drama (especially poetic drama) has not been fully recognized.

Identifying the work of irony in Shakespearean drama is best

[1] See his *Modern Poetry and the Tradition* (1939), and *The Well-Wrought Urn* (1947); but in this general connexion see also a remarkable essay by A. Sidgwick, 'On some Forms of Irony', *Cornhill Magazine*, 1907, an unnoticed precursor of much in modern criticism.

done not by an exhaustive study of one play, but by scrutinizing passages in several different plays where it is of special importance. This may also achieve something else. Critics have often been at work already on these passages, seeking to trace richnesses of texture in them; and it will prove to be the case that ironies can serve as a guide to literary analysis, and also (more important) as a control upon it.

Many critics (for example Bradley, Quiller-Couch, and Professor J. A. K. Thomson) have noticed that *Macbeth* is especially rich in irony. The usual attitude is Professor Thomson's: 'it employs more powerfully and overtly than any other play, the method of tragic irony, which gets its effects by working on the *foreknowledge* of the audience . . . of what is to come'.[1] Yet the irony in *Macbeth* often works very differently, sharpening the contour of what is happening, or precisely indicating its moral status.

This other, and instantaneous working of irony may be seen in a passage in *Macbeth* which has been scrutinized by Dr Leavis.[2] Lady Macbeth is welcoming King Duncan to her castle:

> All our service
> At every point twice done, and then done double,
> Were poor and single business to contend
> Against those honours deep and broad, wherewith
> Your majesty loads our house . . .
>
> (i. vi. 14–18)

Dr Leavis, with the idea of contending against the honours deep and broad chiefly in mind, suggests that part of the richness of the passage lies in the notion implicit in it of the king as the fountain of honour. I have no wish to dispute this view, although I must note in passing that the idea of the king as the fountain of honour, even if present, does not seem much to enhance the lines themselves, or illuminate the whole passage in which they come. But there is another idea implicitly present in these lines: one which is present in, or rather sustained by them from first to last, which is sustained by every important word in them, and which most sharply and emphatically does add to

[1] *Shakespeare and the Classics* (1952), p. 119.
[2] *Education and the University* (1943), pp. 122–4.

their dramatic significance and pregnancy. This is the idea, underlying what is said and contrasting with it ironically, that the Macbeths truly stand to Duncan not as hosts welcoming a guest, but as armed assailants. The idea that wounds are in a sense interchangeable with honours (which is the key to this implicit sense of the passage) comes not only at the beginning of the play, when Duncan himself says to his wounded sergeant:

> So well thy words become thee as thy *wounds*,
> They smack of honour both
>
> (I. ii. 44–5)

It comes also at the end, when Old Siward treats his son's death in battle as honourable, and a proper object for rejoicing, because he had 'his hurts before'. Moreover, there is no need for the play to establish a connexion which was a commonplace, any more than there is for a critic to stress how numerous available quotations demonstrate the frequency with which 'service' and 'business' in Shakespeare have a military sense, or how clearly, in a military context, 'single business' meant 'single combat'. 'In every point twice done' does not carry only the most obvious metaphorical sense that (by an irony, indeed, within an irony) the service that the Macbeths perform is something like putting on the king's armour. It reverberates with something just the opposite that has already been called 'this night's great business' (I. v. 67); and with Macbeth's 'We will proceed no further in this business He hath *honour'd* me of late': I. vii. 30–1 is to the point as well): the business, in one sense, is always the knifing of the king. All in all, we are obliged to conclude that the main, the essential implicit meaning of the lines is this ironical contradiction of what they overtly say. They illuminate for us what the true situation is, even through their ingenious deceit about it. Lady Macbeth's mind is so full of her plot that it leaps out at us in every word of even her most elaborate bluff. To think in a case like this that irony relates only to the future would be to reduce what is tautly exciting to mere reiterative tedium.

Indeed, the conventional view of irony exposes itself to a *reductio ad absurdum*. Irony is far too constantly present to be merely a monotonous jogging of our minds towards the future.

Only three lines before the passage which I have just examined in detail, Duncan has said:

> The love that follows us sometime is our trouble,
> Which still we thank as love.

Four lines later, he says that Macbeth's

> . . . great love (*sharp as his spur*) hath holp him
> To his home before us.

It is impossible to think that these almost uninterrupted ironies serve only to remind us of what the whole trend of the scene keeps under our eyes anyway. This irony lays bare the present: Lady Macbeth obsessed with the plot until, in effect, she cannot keep it off her tongue; Duncan all unconsciousness, gratitude, and consideration; Macbeth riding home hard, because he has seen or half-seen the chance that the event is offering him. What creates the tension is the plot that exists now, not the murder that may occur in the future.

Immediately before Lady Macbeth's speech of welcome to Duncan, there comes a passage which has been much analysed by critics. This is the brief scene where the two future victims of Macbeth's murders find his castle a place of peaceful beauty and procreativeness:

> *Duncan:* This castle hath a pleasant seat; the air
> Nimbly and sweetly recommends itself
> Unto our gentle senses.
> *Banquo:*   This guest of summer,
> The temple-haunting martlet, does approve,
> By his loved mansionry, that the heaven's breath
> Smells wooingly here: no jutty, frieze,
> Buttress, nor coign of vantage, but this bird
> Hath made his pendent bed and procreant cradle:
> Where they most breed and haunt, I have observed
> The air is delicate.   (I. vi. 1-10)

This is the subject of one of Dr Leavis's best detailed analyses, an analysis which admirably displays 'Shakespeare's marvellous power of using words to compel on the reader or listener a precise complex response'.[1] But Dr Leavis barely indicates how the complexity, still more the precision of it, comes through irony.

[1] *op. cit.*, p. 124.

Indeed, in adding 'the dramatic potency . . . is to a great extent independent of the speakers (though, of course, Banquo and Duncan bring it an intensifying irony)', he apparently suggests that it is ironical because the victims of the murders are those who have these views. Yet there would be irony in the account whoever gave it: for it is an account which is perfectly true, and yet much more significantly false. That the precision is largely an ironical precision can be seen, perhaps, if the one detail 'temple-haunting martlet' is fully understood. About this Mr Bethell says 'the martlet, we note, is "temple-haunting" as well as procreative; religion, natural abundance and the well-governed state being correlative'.[1] But could Shakespeare, at this tense juncture, have called the martlet 'temple-haunting' only so as to accord passing recognition to these worthy but general sentiments? Dr Leavis is better in saying that the word 'co-operates with "guest" and "heaven" to evoke the associations belonging to the "sanctity of hospitality" '. But these are loose and general ideas: one that is not loose and general, but completely specific and powerfully relevant, lies to hand. Macbeth's castle *is* a temple—not by reference to some idea of hospitality in general, but to the particular act of hospitality, and abuse of it, which is now to occur there. The full scope of the irony is not perhaps seen until Macduff's words announcing the murder itself are thought of in this context:

Macduff: Most *sacrilegious* murder hath broke ope
   The Lord's *anointed temple,* and stole thence
   The life o'th' *building*[2]

(I.. iii. 67–9)

Macbeth's castle is a temple, because it is to shelter the sanctified person of a king. This is the rich undertone of the passage, and it is rooted in, and demanded by, and a comment upon, the individual contour of the situation.

One other ironic sequence in *Macbeth* is of special importance, since it lies close along the vital line of the play's action, and takes up much of its dominant imagery. This is the irony which is created through three of *Macbeth*'s best-known speeches; and

[1] *The Cultural Revolution of the Seventeenth Century* (*1951*), p. 82.
[2] 'Temple' and 'building' here mean the King's body, but the essential point is unaffected.

they are speeches which insist on their continuity with each other by remarkable parallels of metaphor, rhythm, and phrase. The first is that in which Lady Macbeth gives herself up to the powers of darkness when she calls upon them to help her:

> The raven himself is hoarse
> That croaks the fatal entrance of Duncan
> Under my battlements . . . Come, you spirits
> That tend on mortal thoughts, unsex me here,
> And fill me, from the crown to the toe, top-full
> Of direst cruelty! make thick my blood,
> Stop up th' access and passage to remorse,
> That no compunctious visitings of nature
> Shake my fell purpose, nor keep peace between
> Th' effect and it! Come to my woman's breasts,
> And take my milk for gall, you murd'ring ministers,
> Wherever in your sightless substances
> You wait on nature's mischief! Come, thick night . . .
>
> (I. v. 37–49)

The second is Macbeth's brief lament, after the deed is done, that it has destroyed his peace of mind for good:

> *Macbeth:* '. . . Macbeth does murder sleep'—the innocent sleep,
> Sleep that knits up the ravelled sleave of care,
> The death of each day's life, sore labour's bath,
> Balm of hurt minds, great nature's second course,
> Chief nourisher in life's feast . . .
>
> *Lady Macbeth:* Go get some water,
> And wash this filthy witness from your hand.
>
> (II. ii. 36–47)

And the third comes when, having forgotten these sentiments, Macbeth in his turn invokes the powers of night, this time to help him murder Banquo:

> Come, seeling night,
> Scarf up the tender eye of pitiful day,
> And with thy bloody and invisible hand
> Cancel and tear to pieces that great bond
> Which keeps me pale! Light thickens, and the crow
> Makes wing to th' rooky wood:
> Good things of day begin to droop and drowse . . .
>
> (III. ii. 46–52)

One notices the recurrent invocations to night and the spirits, placed always with the same cadence; the concepts of night destroying day, and of 'great nature' (echoed in one sense of the 'great bond' of the third passage) which runs through all these; the repeated ideas of the crow or raven, and the bloody hand; and the several verbal repetitions. What follows from this? Surely, that the three speeches (though their key-words and images also spread pervasively through the play) in part stand out by themselves, moving in the play half-independently, with a logic of their own. And this has its ironical effect; for the audience, hearing the third speech, should recall not only the first but also the second. In order to call upon night as he does, there is something which Macbeth must unlearn. The irony is that he unlearns precisely what he learnt from the death of Duncan. This irony does not show how the future will belie the present; indeed, so far as the death of Banquo is concerned (which is what is in question) the future does not belie it. But it is the full nature of the present which is being explored: the compulsive monotony of what one must do when one is 'in blood stepp'd in so far' as Macbeth and his wife; and (whatever their ostensible result) the intrinsic self-frustration of such acts as his. The three speeches make a progression of which the irony epitomizes what is central to the play.

II

Simply to review a number of other Shakespearean scenes where irony proves important is perhaps somewhat sketchy, but is worth doing, because it helps to show the range of situation within which a play tends almost naturally towards irony.

Bradley, writing of *Hamlet*, Act II, Scene ii, says 'the emotion shown by the player in reciting the speech which tells of Hecuba's grief for her slaughtered husband awakes into burning life . . . Hamlet's sense of duty and shame'.[1] Is not the point rather that, in the first place, Hamlet is moved to tears by the ironic contrast between Hecuba and Gertrude?—the players, in other words, being indeed what he calls them just afterwards, 'the abstracts and brief chronicles of the time' (II. ii. 528).

---

[1] *Shakespearean Tragedy* (1912 ed.), p. 131.

Again, in Act IV, Scene vii, Claudius asks Laertes what he would undertake in order to avenge his father's death at Hamlet's hands. 'To cut his throat i' th' church,' Laertes replies; and Claudius's comment is:

> No place indeed should murder sanctuarize,
> Revenge should have no bounds.
>
> (IV. vii. 126–7)

Professor Lawlor comments: 'Claudius speaks for all avengers in the old tradition' of the Revenge Tragedy.[1] But again, we are not confronted here with a general clash of attitudes; rather, with an irony deeply rooted in the crisis of the moment. The scene reminds us not only of the murder which Claudius himself committed, but also of how Hamlet spared his life when he found him at prayers, and of why he did so—that his ultimate revenge might be indeed boundless. The incident brings before the audience all the full tensions of the situation—the character of Claudius, the snares that now beset him, and the contrast between the natures of Laertes and Hamlet.

Another scene in *Hamlet* also gains in interest if we have full regard to the ironies it contains. This is the celebrated 'to-be-or-not-to-be' soliloquy, and what follows it. Critics usually assume that the soliloquy should be taken at its face value, as having one consistent topic, and that at some point later in the scene Hamlet detects Claudius and Polonius, and begins to speak ironically. Thus two problems are created: to identify the single theme of the soliloquy, and to time the moment when Hamlet sees the eavesdroppers. But the soliloquy itself, if one remembers how it would fall on the ear of Claudius, is richly ironical. Hamlet, in cataloguing the 'oppressor's wrong', the 'pangs of disprized love', the 'law's delay' (compare his 'Sir, I lack advancement', III. ii. 34), the 'insolence of office' is cataloguing evils which with one exception are being imposed on him by Claudius himself (the exception has been brought about by Polonius). It would be only too easy for Claudius to hear, in these words, just that menace which he shows himself anxiously aware of, immediately after Hamlet leaves the stage. And the

[1] J. J. Lawler, 'The Tragic Conflict in "Hamlet"', *Review of English Studies*, 1950, p. 111.

next few lines, when Hamlet asks who would 'grunt and sweat under a weary life' if it were not for fear of retribution after death, come near the knuckle for Claudius too—which he reveals by his aside immediately before Hamlet's entry. Moreover, it is by no means an easy matter to prove (as Professor J. D. Wilson seeks to do)[1] that the soliloquy has one single and consistent theme, that of suicide; for if 'when he himself might his quietus make, With a bare bodkin' supports this interpretation more readily than any other (as perhaps it does), 'enterprises of great pith (pitch) and moment' can include suicide much less readily than revenge. When Hamlet detects the listeners (if at all) is not now in question; it is enough here to show that an awareness of *all* the ironies of the scene, not merely those plainer ones in its latter part, stresses the integration, and the comprehensiveness, of the situation as it unfolds. The tension of the scene lies less in what Hamlet means, than in what by irony, he can seem to mean.

In *Hamlet* (though less than in *Macbeth*) irony is fairly important throughout. Its relative unimportance in *Lear*, and its intermittent occurrence, begin to help in plotting its effective range. There is irony at the beginning of *Lear*, and towards the end. In the first Act, for example, there is Gloucester's outburst to Edmund against Edgar's unnaturalness as a son. Much later, the blind Gloucester gives his purse to his true son, disguised as a madman, and as he does so says all unconsciously 'That I am wretched Makes thee the happier' (IV. i. 66–7). In the same Act, Gloucester (blind) and Lear (mad) meet again: Lear, in his ignorance, recalls how Gloucester's bastard son was kinder to his father than Lear's lawful daughters were to theirs, says (when Gloucester asks if he knows him) 'I remember thine *eyes* well enough', and finally, in his madness, gives him something to read. There is nothing in all this for the future, but Edgar confirms the argument that it is the present which irony sharpens when he says:

> I would not take this from report. It is
> And my heart breaks at it.
>
> (IV. vi. 141–2)

[1] New Cambridge *Hamlet*, p. 190 (note to III. i. 56).

Through the main action of *Lear*, though, irony almost disappears. This is interesting, and helps to explain why there is so little of it in either *Antony and Cleopatra*, or *Coriolanus*, and much less towards the end of *Macbeth* than earlier on. After Regan and Goneril have shown their hand, *Lear* is a play of quite a different kind from *Macbeth* or *Hamlet*. In these, the drama proceeds because the characters are partly in ignorance about each other's actions, and therefore about their own situations: the surface of their lives conceals the dominant realities, and these do not emerge until near the end. But the central scenes of *Lear* begin, as it were, where these plays leave off. They display what happens after the usually hidden realities of life have taken control. Lear, and Gloucester, soon understand their situations only too well; the play is about how they act then. Something similar is true of *Antony and Cleopatra*, and of *Coriolanus*: in the former, Antony is conscious all the time of what he is really doing, and in the latter all the characters seem pre-occupied with assessing the actions and motives of the protagonist.[1]

On this account, one would expect *Othello*, of course, to be full of irony. Professor G. G. Sidgwick, in his *Of Irony, especially in Drama* (1933, revised version 1948) finds that this is so. Certainly his account of 'one use' of irony—'it points the significance of the situation, it brings the conflict of dramatic forces into clearer view, it heightens the sense of pity and terror',[2] leaves little to be desired. But in tracing the ironies of *Othello* itself, he seems to revert to the common notion of what irony does: saying, for example, 'we see things tending *inevitably*—so it seems to us—in one direction'.[3] If this is necessarily irony, then *Antony and Cleopatra* is full of it. But of irony in the common and proper sense there is rather less, in *Othello*, than one might expect: perhaps because the dialogue is not (as in *Macbeth* or *Hamlet*) what conceals the trap, or fills in

---

[1] See D. J. Enright, ' "Coriolanus"—Tragedy or Debate', *Essays in Criticism*, 1954.

[2] *op. cit.*, p. 63. This function of irony is also noted in S. K. Johnson's 'Some Aspects of Dramatic Irony in Sophoclean Tragedy' (*Classical Review*, 1928, pp. 209–14).

[3] *ibid.*, pp. 113–14.

the interval before it can be sprung, but is the trap itself; and is therefore too fully in use to be spared overmuch for ingenious ironies.[1]

III

One point remains to be made. If valid, it is not without importance, since its claim is to bear generally on the study of poetic texture. In the discussion so far, tracing the ironies rooted in the individual dramatic situation has several times suggested a shift in critical emphasis, and each time it has been a shift in the same direction. In examining, for example, Mr Bethell's comments on the 'temple-haunting martlet' (p. 8), or Professor Lawlor's on the speech of Claudius (pp. 10–11), what a stress on the ironies did was to put a meaning which arose directly from the given dramatic juncture, firmly before one which related (at best) quite generally to the whole situation and the framework of ideas within which it might be seen. The same consideration applied to Dr Leavis's comment on the martlet passage. It is not simply the general 'sanctity of hospitality' to which that refers, but the quite special sanctity which the irony brings out, and which exists because the guest is an anointed king.

Another similar comment of Dr Leavis's is that in which he argues that in the 'honours deep and broad' passage, quoted from *Macbeth* on page 28 above, Shakespeare is 'seizing on and realizing the conventional metaphor of the king's being the "fount of honour" '.[2] This further meaning, if present, would not be unconnected with the current situation of the play; but it cannot be felt to be connected so directly, so immediately, as the meaning suggested by the irony, and springing from the passionate resolve to kill which Lady Macbeth has expressed with such ferocity only thirty lines before. To trace the ironies appears once more to put first, in our search for deeper meanings, those which rise most directly from the concrete realities of the

[1] But, again, several ironies in *Othello* illuminate the present; for example, Desdemona's artless notion that the sun where Othello was born drew all such humours as jealousy out of him (III, iv. 31–2), whereas his birth in a hot climate was just what should have warned her. (See, e.g., Burton's *Anatomy of Melancholy*, Pt. 3, Sec. 3, Mem. 1, Subs. 2.)

[2] *Education and the University*, p. 116.

situation before us, and to put progressively more general points afterwards.

The same line of argument seems relevant to certain comments by Mr Traversi[1] on *Measure for Measure*: here, too, it looks as if ironies bring out a relatively direct enrichment of meaning. Claudio says, of his sister's chance of persuading Angelo to pardon him:

> in her youth
> There is a prone and speechless dialect,
> Such as move men: besides, she hath prosperous art
> When she will play with reason and discourse,
> And well she can persuade
>
> (I. ii. 178–182)

Here, for once, is an irony of which the *future* import is doubtless dominant: though it also fills out our sense of the present risks of the situation, and thus of Claudio's present unawareness and pre-occupation, thinking that his plan will bring safety, when it is just the plan to increase the dangers and the difficulties, Mr Traversi does not mention these plain aspects of the speech, but he does mention aspects of it that by comparison are, to speak with moderation, recondite. He refers somewhat distinctively to the prone and speechless dialect of Isabella's youth, because he calls it the 'prone and speechless *attractions* . . . of her youthful *person*'. From this, short step as some perhaps may think it, it is only another short step to Mr Traversi's next comment: 'there is even a faint suggestion of invitation and artful passivity in the adjectives'. Shakespeare's account of Isabella's prosperous art when she will play with reason and discourse is also pursued into some of its—to speak again with moderation—fainter suggestions: she can 'mould the wills of men most subtly to her purpose'. If we are happy with Mr Traversi's versions thus far, we shall perhaps be happy to accompany him a little further, when he (by now, in a sense, excusably) finds something 'equivocal' in Isabella's behaviour, or feels that her 'gift of persuasion' has 'become a little *tarnished* in Claudio's description'. Mr Traversi, to be sure, points out Isabella's complete innocence; but what he means by innocence is, in his own words, 'complete uncon-

---

[1] D. A. Traversi, 'Measure for Measure', *Scrutiny*, Vol. XI, p. 48.

sciousness of artifice'; and this presumably implies that the artifice is there.

This section began by suggesting that it might have some
general bearing on critical analysis. The fact is that once critics
begin at all thoroughly to pursue the richer meanings of poetry,
they can very easily unravel, or weave, a texture so complex
that it ceases to be a possible object of imaginative response.
Many readers are thus tempted to jettison the whole approach.
It therefore becomes of importance, first to show that some
secondary meanings are of more direct relevance than others,
and second to trace some principle which will give the critic,
pursuing this sequence of diminishing relevance, an idea of
when to stop. With the first of these problems, close attention to
irony in dramatic texture gives real help, since it indicates what
I am tempted to call *primary* secondary meanings: meanings
which are rooted firmly and immediately at the given point of
development in the work. Only when a reader is sure of these
ought he (if then) to pursue more recondite and hypothetical
associations.

III

THE ODES OF KEATS

IN H. W. GARROD'S BOOK ON KEATS there is one sentence about Keats's Odes that is a good deal more pointed and significant than its author presumably intended. Our attention is drawn in it to 'the close connexions of thought which exist between all of the . . . Odes with the exception of that *To Autumn* . . . a sequence . . . not of time but of mood'.[1] The reader's first reaction, perhaps, will be suspicion of that unremarked shift from 'thought' to 'mood'; his second, that if this is an evasion, it comes near to solving the difficulty it evades. What unites these poems is essentially a singleness in experience; and in a sense it is too elusive for the first word, but too considered, too developed, too much articulated for the second. Yet if the Odes really are a unified sequence, the best way to understand them fully is to treat them as such, and make them interpret each other. So far, this has hardly been done—in part because critics have been too ready to think (as Garrod did) that *To Autumn* stands quite by itself, and in part because they have thought *On Indolence* too bad to deserve much attention. These restrictions of interest are precipitate; and a more systematic inquiry not only offers a more sensitive, balanced, comprehensive interpretation of each poem by itself, but seems to do something in addition. It seems also to show that if we take all of them together, these poems make up a psychological document—an unexpected one

[1] H. W. Garrod, *Keats* (1926), p. 97.

40

—of unique interest. To a great extent, they are actually about that part of Keats's mental life of most significance to both him and us. They prove to be a complex and detailed poetic revelation of what Keats knew himself as the creative mood. The present study, then, has a double purpose: to add to our insight into the Odes as poems, and to indicate just how much they reveal of Keats the writer.

Let us begin with the Ode *On Indolence*, though only because its language is baldest and simplest. To trace a genuinely chronological development through the Odes, it would be necessary to show, if we took this as a starting-point, that it was written first; and this may very well not be true, though the evidence is less conclusive than Miss Lowell, for example, seemed to think.[1] But my purpose is rather to identify, as definitely as can be done, a mood which seems to underlie all the Odes, and appears in them sometimes in a more, sometimes (and *On Indolence* is an example) in a less developed form. Besides this, however, Keats's *Letters* make it clear that on March 19th, 1819 (at the beginning of the period in which all these poems were written) he was not only in the exact mood of *On Indolence*, but could almost paraphrase the poem in prose:

. . . This morning I am in a sort of temper indolent and supremely careless: I long after a stanza or two of Thompson's Castle of Indolence. My passions are all asleep from my having slumbered till nearly eleven and weakened the animal fibre all over to a delightful sensation about three degrees this side of faintness—if I had teeth of pearl and the breath of lillies I should call it langour—but as I am I must call it Laziness. In this state of effeminacy the fibres of the brain are relaxed in common with the rest of the body, and to such a happy degree that pleasure has no show of enticement and pain no unbearable frown. Neither Poetry, nor Ambition, nor Love have any alertness of countenance as they pass by me: they seem rather like three figures on a greek vase—a Man and two women whom no one but myself could distinguish in their disguisement. This is the only happiness; and it is a rare instance of advantage in the body over-powering the Mind.[2]

[1] A. Lowell: *John Keats*, II, p. 258.
[2] *Letters*, ed. M. B. Forman (2nd edition, 1935), p. 315. Miss D. Hewlett (*A Life of John Keats*, 2nd edition, p. 244) writes 'when he (Keats) wrote, or finished, the "Ode on Indolence" in May the man and two women . . .

So much for prose. The poem could scarcely do more to convey the same ideas. Keats affirms that neither Love, Ambition, nor Poetry has charm enough to tempt him from a mood of exquisite somnolence, when

> . . . ripe was the drowsy hour
> The blissful cloud of summer indolence
> Benumbed my eyes.

Both pain and pleasure seem to vanish, and they leave only a simple sensuous awareness, calm and yet somehow keen:

> The open casement pressed a new-leav'd vine
> Let in the budding warmth and throstle's lay.

This is all plain enough. Keats's mood is not subtle or complex, and it does not develop in the course of the poem. What is significant is that several turns of phrase or thought in this Ode reappear in the others; but there, they are elements of something that is more complex and that does develop. Of these, the drowsy indolence is of course one; so is the idea that Ambition is worthless because coming

> From a man's little heart's short fever-fit.

The indolent mood which is the source of the poem, and somehow mingles sleeping and waking, is not lethargy but in some sense a visionary state; not devoid of pleasure and pain, but transmuting them:

> Pain had no sting, and pleasure's wreath no flower.

Pain and pleasure have not ceased entirely, but ceased only to be disturbances, superficial additions to life. Poetry, which seems for the moment only 'my demon Poesy', the strongest of temptations,

> has not a joy
> At least for me,—so sweet as drowsy noons
> And evenings steeped in honey'd indolence.

And this indolence is a positive thing, bringing a calm pervasive happiness that—its crucial feature perhaps—seems near to a

---

became three female figures'. But while the poem is explicit that Love and Poesy are 'maidens' there is nothing to show that Keats is thinking of Ambition as female, and a little perhaps to show that he is not.

suspension of sense for some other more elusive but more illuminating kind of experience:

> O, why did ye not melt, and leave my sense
> Unhaunted quite of all but nothingness?

On Indolence seems at first to reject poetry, but it is really a poem about the mood from which Keats's poetry at that time sprang. That this was consciously in Keats's mind is to some extent confirmed by one of the sonnets *On Fame*, probably written at about this time:

> Fame like a wayward girl will still be coy
> To those who woo her with too slavish knees . . .
> Make your best bow to her and bid adieu
> Then if she likes it she will follow you.[1]

The Ode *To Psyche* clarifies the situation. Keats's mood here is much like the mood of *On Indolence*:

> Surely I dream't today, or did I see
>   The winged Psyche with awaken'd eyes?
> I wandered in a forest thoughtlessly
>   And, on the sudden, fainting with surprise
> Saw two fair creatures . . .

—here is the same inertia and oblivion and suspension between sleeping and waking. When he finds Cupid and the goddess 'in soft-handed slumber' together

> 'Mid hush'd cool-rooted flowers fragrant-eyed
>   Blue, silver-white, and budded Tyrian
> They lay calm-breathing on the bedded grass

this is almost exactly like his own condition in *On Indolence*;[2] and the interaction between Keats's own emotions, and the emotions of his subject, will prove later to be an important aspect of the *Ode to a Nightingale*. Keats has a good phrase in *To Psyche* for the central quality of his feeling: 'this wide quietness'. But as the poem proceeds, drowsy numbness is raised, as it were, to a higher power of itself:

> I see, and sing, by my own eyes inspired.

[1] *Letters*, p. 338 (April 30th, 1819).
[2] . . . Ye cannot raise
My head cool-bedded from the flowery grass.

Keats is inspired to sing through seeing the goddess (especially, one is sorry to say, through seeing her 'lucent fans'). He desires to serve the deity of a mood whose expression is more complex, more impassioned, and indeed more intellectual, than anything in *On Indolence*. His mood tends towards activity, it is a balanced tension of excitement, and here unmistakably it has something of a fuller understanding, an insight which is intellectual:

> . . . I will be thy priest, and build a fane
> In some untrodden region of my mind
> Where branched thoughts, new grown with pleasant pain
> . . . shall murmur.

> A rosy sanctuary will I dress
> With the wreath'd trellis of a working brain

> And there shall be for thee all soft delight
> That shadowy thought can win.

The stress falls largely on the melancholic aspects of Psyche the Love-goddess (she is called 'mournful Psyche' in *On Melancholy*); Keats laments that she has no

> . . . virgin-choir to make delicious moan
> Upon the midnight hours.

But the 'wide quietness' of this poem has a certain poignancy, and as the mood develops, Keats's tone becomes more complex and at the same time more incisive.

For all that, however, the genesis of the poem still lies in 'soft-handed slumber'; and that this originates the whole sequence of experience is suggested once more at the beginning of the Ode *On Melancholy*. The oblivion of Lethe is too uncompromising, wolf's-bane too powerful a narcotic, the death-moth too grim and macabre to incarnate 'mournful Psyche'. These are extreme measures that the mood cannot survive:

> . . . shade to shade will call too drowsily
> And drown the wakeful anguish of the soul.

The rejected—fortunately rejected—first version of the first stanza makes exactly the same point, perhaps more clearly:

Though you should build a bark of dead man's bones
And rear a phantom gibbet for a mast
. . .   . . .   certes you would fail
To find the Melancholy—whether she
Dreameth in any isle of Lethe dull . . .

The 'melancholy fit' falls suddenly, like an April shower 'that fosters the droop-headed flowers all'; and like the shower, Melancholy has its own reviving virtue. In this mood we are to 'glut' sorrow in the contemplation of beautiful things, 'feed, deep, deep' on them; and that experience will also be an insight.

The last stanza suggests how. 'She dwells with Beauty—' whether 'she' is the imagined mistress, or the goddess of Melancholy, or both or either, leaves the sense unaffected. The experience of Beauty is a revelation; of Beauty's meaning, and also of its transience. Melancholy is developed here to a keener, tenser equipoise of sorrow and uncertainty, and also of exaltation and elusive understanding:

> . . . Beauty that must die;
> And Joy, whose hand is ever at his lips
> Bidding adieu; and aching Pleasure nigh
> Turning to poison while the bee-mouth sips:
> Ay, in the very temple of delight
> Veil'd Melancholy has her sovran shrine
> Though seen of none save him whose strenuous tongue
> Can burst Joy's grape against his palate fine:
> His soul shall taste the sadness of her might,
> And be among her cloudy trophies hung.

This is very different from the drowsy numbness of Indolence, and its 'strenuous tongue' is like the 'working brain' of *To Psyche*. But the last two lines have a special interest: 'cloudy trophies' may hint at the elusiveness of the insight that dwells with Beauty, but the cadence of this couplet causes it, and therefore the whole stanza, to exemplify what it describes. The reader watches Joy bidding adieu, because he is taken through the experience of which the poem gives an account.

Of these three Odes, *On Indolence* in the main portrays a mood which is the embryo of the 'melancholy fit', *To Psyche* celebrates the deity of one of its forms (love-melancholy), and *On Melancholy* displays its growth and intensity and climax. The other two —perhaps the other three—Odes centre upon particular things which have evoked or represented the experience for Keats himself. To a very considerable degree they run parallel—though this has been overlooked by several critics, or expressly denied; and they have many features in common with the three Odes discussed so far. Thus in the opening lines of *To a Nightingale* the drowsy numbness is, once more, both an aching pain and a too-sharp happiness; hearing the song induces Keats to forget and also to remember what is unhappy in life—it brings oblivion that, at a deeper level, is keener knowledge. Once again the senses are stilled, but to an 'embalmed darkness' that is even so a heightened sensuous awareness divining the surrounding sensuous wealth; and when Keats thinks of 'easeful Death' it is like 'nothingness' in *On Indolence*—as the completion of this unique oblivion.

No one seems quite to have explained the imaginative movement of the poem at the point where Keats makes the nightingale immortal. Bridges regarded this passage as fanciful, and Miss Lowell as Platonic.[1] Garrod, avoiding these errors, suggests that the nightingale is immortal because Keats thinks of it as a Dryad.[2] But why is it appropriate to think the bird immortal for any reason? Why should we not suppose ourselves confronted here with irresponsible, fanciful ingenuity? The answer is, perhaps, that at the climax of his poem Keats rightly allows a new ease of movement within the set of ideas he is controlling: he uses a freedom of combination which characterizes poetry at high temperatures, as I believe it does chemistry (in both cases, oddly enough, *constitutes* is perhaps an apter word). The nightingale momentarily assumes the qualities of that ecstasy which it seems to experience, and which it induces in Keats. Within the apparently irresponsible movement of the stanza runs an exact line of what I am almost tempted to call logical development. Keats, entranced as he listens to the nightingale and responds to its apparent ecstasy, has an experience that seems to

---

[1] *John Keats, A Critical Essay* (1895), quoted in Lowell, *op. cit.*, II, p. 252 (Miss Lowell's own discussion of the poem).
[2] *op. cit.*, p. 114.

him to transcend experience; and in this stanza he claims that
the nightingale's song is unrestricted by either time or space—
which after all are pervasive features of experience. The voice of
the nightingale, we might put it, is made immune first to history, and then to geography: it can establish a *rapport* with dead
generations or with faery lands; and

> . . . the same that oft-times hath
> Charm'd magic casements, opening on the foam
> Of perilous seas, in faery lands forlorn

is not Romantic escapism or idle gesturing. Word by word, this
passage, in the free way of poetry, is indicating the definite
qualities of what was for Keats something he knew: the magic,
the 'wideness', the heightened tension, the sadness, are things
that we have by now traced elsewhere.

But like the Ode *On Melancholy*, this poem represents the experience it describes, and represents it without abridgement; it
gives not only the genesis and progress and climax, but also the
dissolution, of the mood that seems central to all the Odes. Garrod's belief[1] that at this point Keat's poem may have owed
something to Wordsworth's *Solitary Reaper* is probably correct;
but it leads him to say of

> . . . thy plaintive anthem fades

that it is 'the only false note which the Ode discovers'. Here a
too full knowledge of the psychology of composition appears to
have confused a quite separate question of criticism; reading this
poem in the light of the other *Odes* makes it clear that 'plaintive'
is here no false but the exactly right note. If it were false, so
would be 'faery lands forlorn'. Forlorn they might be, but they
would then intrude. They do not, because as ever the magic dis-
solves in its own moment of existence:

> Turning to poison while the bee-mouth sips

—and the very last words of the poem, with their uncertainty
between waking and sleeping, are not in opposition to what has
gone before, but express something that is integral to the situation, and that has appeared in every Ode so far. The poem has

[1] *op. cit.*, p. 115.

47

reverted from its climax to a calmer mood not altogether remote from the mood of its origin.

Garrod and Miss Lowell have both assumed a contrast between *To a Nightingale* and *On a Grecian Urn*.[1] Miss Lowell sees a 'direct antithesis'; Garrod describes *On a Grecian Urn* as written in 'strong revulsion' from the mood of *On Melancholy*, and of this poem as in fairly close sympathy with *To a Nightingale*. But it is rather doubtful whether the difference is more than a shift of emphasis. Miss Lowell's account, 'realization of the eternal quality of art binds and heals the bitter wounds incident upon mere living', suggests that *On a Grecian Urn* is a vicarious *exegi monumentum*. Garrod's view is not unlike this: 'the *Grecian Urn* presents . . . the world of beauty and human passions, only fixed by art'. He speaks of its 'rather formal philosophy'. 'The theme of . . . (the first four stanzas) . . . is the arrest of beauty, the fixity given by art to forms which in life are fluid and impermanent, and the appeal of art from the senses to the spirit. The theme of the final stanza is the relation of beauty to truth, to thought'.

These views distort the poem. It has no 'rather formal philosophy'. It as much expresses a mood as *To a Nightingale*; but the mood is modulated to the different object which inspires it. Between the nightingale and the urn is the difference of embalmed darkness and perpetual spring or summer; but 'Veil'd Melancholy' is never wholly absent from *On a Grecian Urn*; though too much veiled, it seems, for some critics. There is a hint of her even in the 'maidens loth' and 'struggle to escape' and the 'wild ecstasy' of the first stanza; in the second comes the eternal frustration of the dancers; their eternal freedom, in the third, perhaps makes the poet happy in sympathy, but it is happiness that trembles upon passionate regret; stanza four contrasts the eternal grace of the figures and the eternal silence and desolation of their 'little town'; and the last stanza contrasts the kindly wisdom of the urn with the waste and frustration of ordinary life.

Throughout the poem, then, this antithesis is maintained. The lovers and the musicians are protected from humanity's disillusionments only through being denied its rewards. Their triumph, so far as they have one, is in the realized perfection of

[1] Garrod, *op. cit.*, p. 104, 108; Lowell, *op. cit.*, II, p. 247.

a single poignant and yet gracious moment. This moment embraces the same fusion of quiet ('thou still unravished bride of quietness') and wild ecstasy, the same exquisite but precarious balance of grief and happiness, the same eternalization of a passing moment, that Keats himself knew in *To a Nightingale*. In *On a Grecian Urn* he is describing, as he sees it in others, what in the former poem he experienced and expressed for himself. The experience is not, of course, identical; but the type is unchanged. Keats is now the recorder, in the other poem he was the protagonist. It would simplify to say that this was a full account: the nightingale was also in ecstasy, and to some extent the loneliness of the little town and the dancer's raptures are contagious. But the urn-figures are a fuller manifestation of this rapture than the nightingale, and there is a different balance in the two poems between the poet's own mood and the object evoking it.

Garrod was critical of the words 'cold pastoral', as a departure from all that had gone before;[1] but they are, on the contrary, an exact continuation. The sculpted pipes play 'ditties of no tone' to the mind's ear only; and this coldness is not the source only in plain fact of the dancer's ecstatic permanence, for it evokes also something that is central to that ecstasy. Cleanth Brook's account, 'the scene is one of violent love-making',[2] is to say the least of it premature; it ignores the subtlety and elaboration of Keats's scene, and how carefully (even before we reach the altar and the priest) he marshalls the imaginative elements which make the whole poem, and nothing less than that, explain those so-much-discussed closing lines. He does this once again in saying that the urn can 'tease us out of thought *As doth eternity*': it leads, not to no thought, but to a unique kind of thought. And when Cleanth Brooks writes that the urn says 'imaginative insight embodies the basic and fundamental perception . . . the urn is beautiful, and yet its beauty is based . . . on an imaginative perception of essentials'[3] no doubt he is right. This does summarize, in abstract form, what Keats told his reader in the concrete form of poetry. But to gloss this with 'mere accumulations of facts . . . are meaningless' is to get away from the poem again. Keats glossed it by writing the

[1] *op. cit.*, p. 106. [2] *The Well-Wrought Urn*, p. 143.
[3] *ibid.*, p. 150.

whole Ode to convey what he thought an imaginative perception of essentials was like. A kind of peace, a kind of excitement,
a kind of regret, a kind of ecstasy, an insight that seemed central
and yet was strangely like oblivion—the list may briefly remind
the successful reader of what he found in the poem, but prose,
of course, must say obscurely what poetry says clearly.

There is one poem of Keats which throws light of particular
importance on the *Odes*. This is the sonnet 'Why did I laugh to-
night?' which we know, from the *Letters*, must have been written
shortly before March 19th, 1819, and therefore near the beginning of this creative period. It is important for three reasons: it
hints at some of the antinomies which the present inquiry has
emphasized, it declares that ecstasy is inseparable from physical
experience, which we saw Keats recognizing as the embryo of
On Indolence, and it has verbal parallels with no less than three
of the *Odes*. 'Nothing ever becomes real until it is experienced'
Keats writes, immediately before copying out this poem for
George and Georgiana Keats.[1] And then:

> Why did I laugh tonight? No voice can tell:
> No God no Deamon of severe response
> Deigns to reply from Heaven or from Hell.—
> Then to my human heart I turn at once—
> Heart! thou and I are here sad and alone;
> Say, wherefore did I laugh? O mortal pain!
> O Darkness! Darkness! ever must I moan
> To question Heaven and Hell and Heart in vain!
> Why did I laugh? I know this being's lease
> My fancy to its utmost blisses spreads:
> Yet could I on this very midnight cease
> And the world's gaudy ensigns see in shreds.
> Verse, fame and Beauty are intense indeed
> But Death intenser—Death is life's high mead.

Lines 9–10 repeat, perhaps rather obscurely, the 'advantage in
the body overpowering the mind' which Keats referred to in
describing his indolent mood of March 19th; and it has often
been noted how line 11 resembles 'to cease upon the midnight
with no pain' of *To a Nightingale*. But critics have not usually
noticed that the gaudy ensigns in shreds have clearly something

---

[1] *Letters*, p. 316.

in common with the 'cloudy trophies' of *On Melancholy* (though the two images are put almost to contrary uses in the two poems); and, more important, that the 'Verse, fame and Beauty' of line 13 are virtually the same as the Poetry, Ambition, and Love of *On Indolence*. Both by its wording and by its substance, therefore, this sonnet does something further to suggest that the Odes explore various phases of a single experience.

Any similar suggestion about *To Autumn* must be very tentative. Keats composed the other poems within a brief period in the spring and early summer of 1819, and this not until several months later. It may well have arisen from a quite independent poetic impulse. But it is not altogether fanciful, perhaps, to see it as a quiet and gentle close to the whole sequence of poems, standing to them all somewhat as the last three lines of *On a Grecian Urn* stand to that single poem. Nor would it be difficult to point out details that are reminiscent of the Odes—Autumn drowsing with the fume of poppies (drowsing, too, among the 'twined flowers', like Keats himself in *On Indolence* or the goddess in *To Psyche*), or Keats's rejection of the songs of spring, or perhaps even the mourning choirs of gnats. But however this may be, stressing the affinity serves one indisputably useful purpose: it shows that *To Autumn* is totally different from the descriptive poem of a catalogue kind. Keats has given in it a quite selective picture of autumn, and one that conveys a quite distinctive mood. How far the earlier poems have made us familiar with the analogues of this mood is perhaps an open question.

All in all, Miss Lowell was rash to say, of *On Indolence*, 'this, of course, was pure fatigue'.[1] It seems much more like an expression of the very frame of mind from which at this time, to varying degrees on various occasions, Keats found the raptures of poetic inspiration generate themselves—and do so, moreover, exactly because he was not seeking them. The other Odes document various aspects of this process of generation. Sir Maurice Bowra, writing 'the three stanzas in which Keats tells of the timeless moments depicted on the Urn arise from his own knowledge of what creation is',[2] seems to suggest this also. And there are, of course, well-known passages in Keats's *Letters* which

[1] *op. cit.*, II, p. 258.
[2] *The Romantic Imagination*, p. 142.

indicate that he regarded what might be called the embryonic condition of the mood conveyed by these poems as also the embryo of poetic inspiration. 'As to the poetical Character itself (I mean that sort of which, I if am anything, I am a Member . . .) it has no self—it is everything and nothing—it has no character—it enjoys light and shade';[1] 'if Poetry comes not as naturally as the Leaves on a tree it had better not come at all'.[2] In a word, the Odes are not only products of what Keats himself called 'Negative Capability', but taken together are a uniquely full account of what it is like and how it develops.

[1] *Letters*, p. 227 (October 27th, 1818).
[2] *ibid.*, p. 108 (February 27th, 1818).

IV

PATMORE, DONNE, AND THE 'WIT OF LOVE'

'CONTEMPORARY TASTE FINDS a more nipping and eager tang in John Donne's "sallads and onions of Mitcham", than in the "Melons and Quelquechoses" of the nineteenth century.' That is from an essay on Donne, published in 1931, by Mr George Williamson. Here is almost exactly the same idea again, but in other words: 'Who . . . would not prefer climbing, with Donne, these *crags*, where all the air is fresh and wholesome,—to gliding with Thomas Moore over *flats*, from beneath the rank verdure of which arises malaria and invisible disease?' That is from an essay on Donne which was published in 1846 by Coventry Patmore. The similarities in tone and lilt of the phrases, and almost in the metaphors themselves, make a good starting point for the present discussion; but they are not a happy accident, not a chance isolated similarity. Over and over again, we can find Patmore saying what, not long ago, we were wanting to say ourselves. In that 1846 essay, he praised Donne for 'bold instinctive perception' that goes with profundity of thought in such a way as never to sacrifice meaning to melody, and always to require the full attention of a disciplined reader.

Love for Donne, he said, was 'passionate, but voluntary (i.e., deliberate or controlled) *attention*, deriving its nourishment mainly from the intellect.' He also diagnosed what was weak in

E   53

the writing of his own time. There was Swinburne, whose metres 'satisfy the ear without any accompaniment of sound meaning, and evoke, as it were by a trick, a current of emotion that is independent of any human feeling in the poet himself'. There was Rossetti, about even whose best work was a deeply *anachronistic* quality, and a recurrent *striving* after passion which in the end left 'an impression of cold instead of warmth'. In fact, Patmore said elsewhere, the poetry of his time was too often 'artificial flowers of delicate coloured wax'. Somebody, once again, is throwing stones at the Victorians' ivory tower; but this time, from inside.

Patmore's general comments on poetry would also sometimes serve our turn today well enough. He said that art does not speak only to the emotions; that is an effeminate view; it speaks to the whole mind of man. He often used 'masculine' and 'feminine' as critical ideas, and sometimes with good effect. In masculine intellectuality he saw not only wit, but also boldness, insight, and tenacity. The feminine side included taste and moderation and tact. A true poem demanded the integrity of the writer behind it, and was an active and 'living order' reconciling a 'conflict of interests and passions' under the unit of a 'single moral idea' or 'theme'.

Thus, plainly enough, Patmore's criticism had a modern ring about it. Before turning to Patmore's poetry (which is after all the chief thing) I must emphasize that in these matters he was no isolated and eccentric figure in the mid-nineteenth century. We confuse the perspective not only of the past, but also of the present, if we do not remember that our concerns today for the intellectual, and the moral dimensions of literature, both ran strongly throughout the last century.

This is now coming to be recognized. I shall briefly illustrate it from an unexpected quarter: Charles Lamb. Lamb is often disparaged, nowadays, for just the idiosyncracy and whimsicality that was once admired in his work; but there is a forgotten side to him. It shows in his *Specimens of the English Dramatic Poets*, which he published in 1809, largely from unpublished manuscript material in the British Museum. Here his purpose, as he said in his Introduction, was to choose plays which showed the moral sense of Elizabethan and Jacobean writers: their 'greater

54

delicacy of moral perception', and their 'treatment of human life and manners'. He condemned the dramatist Fletcher, just as we might today: a 'contortion of his mind . . . craving after romantic incident, and flights of strained and improbable virtue, which I think always betrays an imperfect moral sensibility'. He hinted at a modern attitude to language, when he spoke of 'the compatibility of the serious pun with the expression of the profoundest sorrow' (for pun read ambiguity, of course). Sometimes even his illustrations are modern favourites. He admires poetry not only for its pathos, but also because it is 'earnest and weighty, rich in sense and wit'. Then he quotes the opening lines of Donne's sixteenth Elegy:

> By our first strange and fatal interview . . .

Patmore also picked out Donne's Elegies (including the *First* and *Second Anniversary*) for special praise, and several times quoted a passage which is often quoted today:

> Her pure and eloquent blood
> Spoke in her cheeks, and so distinctly wrought,
> That one might almost say, her body thought.

Lamb, praising one of Webster's lyrics, spoke of 'that intensity of feeling which seems *to resolve itself into the elements which it contemplates*'; Patmore's version of the idea was: 'the song which *is* the thing it says'. What idea in current criticism could be more familiar than that?

Later critics have no doubt strengthened and deepened these ideas, and made them more orderly; and there is no simple continuity between Lamb and Patmore and the critics of the present day. Nor is there any simple link between what is distinctive in Patmore's poetry and any tradition of Roman Catholicism. He wrote his best verse after his conversion, and his essay on Donne, together with his most conspicuously 'metaphysical' work, a long time before it. What we need to take out of the historical complexities is the fact that modern attitudes to poetry, and even to the link between poetry and wit, are not ingenious recent inventions, but run back right through the nineteenth century.

A reader who shared these attitudes will immediately see the triviality of certain criticisms made against Patmore. Take his earliest important work, that picture of Victorian domesticity and of so much else as well, *The Angel in the House* (an unfortunate title perhaps: at all events, the 'angel' is far from a merely sweet Victorian bride). Some of the unambitious, everyday touches in this were found ridiculous by earlier readers. Such judgements spring from a narrow idea of what can get into a poem. Within limits, modern readers will admire the neatness and humour and dramatic detachment of parts of the poem; and sometimes, Patmore deserves admiration for the dexterity, and the intrinsic rightness and truthfulness, with which he made these down-to-earth incidents grow into powerful and disturbing realities. Here is an example: the bridegroom is driving off with his bride as dusk falls on their wedding day; realistically enough, he can't make conversation; but (and this too is convincing) the bride can:

> 'Look, is this not a pretty shawl?
> > Aunt's parting gift.' 'She's always kind.'
> 'The new wing spoils Sir John's old Hall:
> > You'll see it, if you pull the blind.'
> I drew the silk: in heaven the night
> > Was dawning; lovely Venus shone
> In languishment of tearful light,
> > Swathed by the red breath of the sun.

'Night was dawning': this 'wit which is more than wittiness' is frequent in Patmore. Often it is much more like Donne than it is here: often enough Patmore displays a good deal of Donne's exploring subtlety, his close yet unforced argumentation, and even his fondness for recondite yet telling astronomical metaphors. Patmore's two lovers dancing, full of desire yet decorously keeping their distance, are like twin circling stars whose attraction *is* in their separateness. The departed lover (this is from *The Victories of Love*, sequel to *The Angel*) is like a comet:

> . . . the strange waif that comes to run
> A few days flaming near the sun,
> > And carries back, through boundless night,
> > Its lessening memory of light.

But also like Donne, Patmore could explore his subject, and subtly, through the metaphor which is not recondite at all, save in the sense that it is disconcertingly humdrum:

> Have you not seen shop-painters paste
> Their gold in sheets, then rub to waste
> Full half: and lo, you read the name?
> Well, Time, my dear, does much the same
> With this unmeaning glare of love.

It is clear that Patmore was not only a deeply thinking poet, seeking sexual love, in its fulness, as a paradigm of man's essential quality and his characteristic relation with God; but also a poet whose thought regularly entered the fibre of his language, and grew into a concrete embodiment of itself. I must now say something in disparagement of Patmore, and I hope this praise of him will not be obscured by it. Acquaintance with his work is enough in itself to put an end to the worn-out myth of Victorian poetry as just a dream world.

To do that is very salutary; but something else is salutary too. This is to bear in mind that Patmore and Donne, besides being somewhat alike, are also profoundly different; and that the difference between them is that one is an interesting, reputable, and important poet, and the other is a great poet. Open the works of one, and then the other, at random; read a few lines of each; and three times out of four this fact strikes like a blow between the eyes. Some recent writers on Patmore seem never to have felt that blow: like the one who said he was actually the greatest of the metaphysicals, because he had all Donne's learning, and also perfect taste.[1] Another recent writer, Professor J. C. Reid, has certainly felt it—unless I invert his meaning when he writes 'the two poets can hardly be compared with respect to tension and profundity of effect'.[2] He does not, however, go far towards locating just where this difference in greatness, this crucial difference, actually resides.

This line of inquiry has real importance; for in the end it throws a strong and revealing light on one aspect of Donne's own greatness. Only, to be sure, one aspect; but that one is truly

[1] Frederick Page, *Coventry Patmore* (1933), p. 174.
[2] J. C. Reid, *The Mind and Art of Coventry Patmore* (1957), p. 252.

central and vital. In recent years, the usual thing has been to approach Donne, and also related poets like, say, Marvell, by way of a contrast between these writers on the one hand, and writers like Tennyson or Shelley or William Morris, on the other. (There is Milton as well, but this time he doesn't affect the discussion.) Mr Eliot, in fact, considered Metaphysical poetry along just these lines.[1]

If we approach Donne this way, then undoubtedly what will seem distinctive in him will be what Mr Eliot said, sensuous apprehension of thought, or tough reasonableness and wit. And it is easy to go further still along something like this line, which Mr Eliot also did in parts of his essay of 1931, saying that Donne was a greater *poet* than Herbert or Vaughan *in that* he was a greater 'master of language' than them; and that his 'merit' was to have achieved 'a natural conversational diction instead of a conventional one'.[2]

Patmore may be a better poet than Morris; but Donne's real greatness stands out, and with about equal clearness, whether we compare him with one of these poets, or with the other. Yet if we compare Donne and Patmore, it isn't any longer Donne's power to make 'feeling and thought interpenetrate' which is distinctive of him—in fact, the very phrase is Patmore's own. Nor is it his wit. I should be sorry to say more than I mean. Certainly, Donne's wit, and Patmore's wit, turn out on really close examination to be not the same. So do the respective ways in which the two poets fuse their thoughts and feelings. A really complete account would no doubt take this in. The point, though, is that when Donne is set up against Morris, these are the qualities that leap to the eyes, that seem as sharp as the difference in real merit, that naturally move to the centre of the discussion. Set Donne up against Patmore, that is no longer so. To put it loosely, they *both* seem witty, argumentative poets; they both seem to fuse thought and feeling; they both make a contrast with what Patmore called the rank verdure, or the delicately coloured wax flowers, of Romanticism in decline.

Is there a difference between Donne and Patmore clear enough to leap off the pages sometimes, in the way that a differ-

[1] Essay on *Andrew Marvell*.
[2] In *A Garland for John Donne*.

ence in wit, in the fusion of sense with intelligence, did when
Donne is compared with Morris? Yes. The difference is, that
Donne's verse is almost always creating in his reader's mind a
profound impression that behind it there is a rich and wide and
sensitive contact with reality. This is what, in the end, the wit
and argument and hyperbole serve; and what makes them matter. I do not of course mean attested bits of Donne's biography:
but the realities of what life is, and how it is lived, as these are
envisaged within the poem. In Patmore, that is only present
from time to time; and too often, the opposite is there: too often,
the verse seems to *congeal* between the reader and the realities,
and obscures those realities from him.

First, consider Donne's poem, *The Extasy*: the two lovers
whose souls seem to be in communion together,

> And whil'st our souls negotiate there
> We like sepulchral statues lay;
> All day, the same our postures were,
> And we said nothing, all the day . . .

if we recall the grave, controlling rhythms of this poem, and the
extraordinary, the in fact *ecstatic* tranquillity with which it proceeds from this spiritual love, into physical love, it seems fair to
compare it with nothing less than Patmore's vision of Adam and
Eve making love before the Fall of Man:

> 'And are you happy, O, my Hero and Lord,
> And is your joy complete?'
> 'Yea, with my joyful heart my body rocks,
> And joy comes down from Heaven in floods and shocks,
> As from Mount Abora comes the avalanche.'
> 'My Law, my Light!
> Then I am yours as your high mind may list.
> No wile shall lure you, none can I resist!'

Admittedly, this is the worst passage in Patmore that I know.
But it comes from *The Unknown Eros*, which is agreed to contain
his best work; and it is catastrophic. It is nothing but a series of
gestures at what it is supposed to dramatize, and what wit there
is in it seems only to make it triter and shoddier than it would be
otherwise.

The point may be clinched by another comparison, where Patmore is much nearer to Donne in style. In Donne's *The Canonization*, crowded hyperboles and ingenuities do not come alone, but with them and in them comes a deep and significant human experience envisaged through the poem:

> You whom reverend love
> Made one another's hermitage;
> You, to whom love was peace, that now is rage

—this, in fact, is from the grammarian's point of view, a mere subordinate clause (a neat and witty one, notice) in the prologue to an invocation. But it focuses, for a moment, something that the turn of a phrase or a rhythm indicate in this poem, underneath the neat argument and controlled wit, all the time; and this something is, a rich and living awareness of what men and women are, and what love between them can be like. It is fair to set this beside a passage from Patmore which opens with something very like the opening idea of Donne's poem: 'for Godsake hold your tongue and let me love', and which is also a neat and witty argument explored through a metaphor:

> Leave us alone! After a while,
>   This pool of private charity
> Shall make its continent an isle,
>   And roll, a world-embracing sea;
> This foolish zeal of lip for lip,
>   This fond, self-sanctioned, wilful zest,
> Is that elect relationship
>   Which forms, and sanctions, all the rest.

The continent of the outside world that at first surrounds their private love, but in the end will be wholly encompassed by that love, is really very neat and apt indeed. Yet: 'The more serious and subtle music of life which he had not in his heart he could not put into his rhythms', said Patmore of Shelley. Nor, in the hasty ideas of these tripping lines, could Patmore; and these very lines give a hint, perhaps, of what is near the centre of Patmore's relative weakness. They do so in their use of the prophetic future: the pool of private love that *shall* make the ocean of a universal charity. Patmore undoubtedly had considered (and very interesting) views about the nature of love between men and women and the place of that love in the whole scheme of things. In a sense, he was a much more philosophical and meta-physical poet than Donne. Perhaps that is the trouble. Where in Donne the poem is as it were filled with a great volume of genuine experience, in Patmore there is often instead a kind of stridency, the stridency of one self-preoccupied through the pre-occupation of his own ideas; and with this, as is usually the case, a kind of hastiness, sketchiness, in the realities, about which the ideas *are* ideas. This is what was wrong with the lines about Adam and Eve: 'My Hero and Lord' . . . 'as your high mind may list' . . . 'My Law, My Light'. What is wrong is not that we might reject this as the proper relation between a man and a woman; but that phrases like these are daubs in the general direction of what experience is, even when men and women relate themselves in just this way. If one doubts that, one can turn for illumination to the *Spiritual Canticle* of Saint John of the Cross; which is exactly to the point. This poem necessarily re-lates its two lovers as sovereign and subject, because the bride is the poet and the bridegroom is God. But then, the poem is rich, open-eyed, many-sided, lively, even something like playful. It encounters and reveals and explores all the things about such a relation that Patmore's lines do not merely ignore, but actively hush up.

One truly vital contrast between Donne and Patmore (once we turn from merit itself, to what merit *lies* in) is therefore the different degree to which their work embodies a broad and rich and sensitive responsiveness to experience. And it is this which is surely the right starting point for an account of how and why Donne himself was great: not the claim that he was a great re-former of language—the point on which Mr Eliot laid his chief stress, in his essay of 1931. Admittedly, this is the starting point, not the whole story; and to go beyond that proper starting point, and write the whole story, is to have to include an ex-amination of how that awareness transpires through the details of language and sequence in individual poems. One further concession: probably, by a kind of *tour de force*, we could actually put this basic point, though really one about experience, contact with life, as if it were a point about use of language. That is in principle true, because every contact with life that a poem gives its readers is given to them by means of language and through language. But what a roundabout perverse, paradoxical way of doing things this would really be! And we have lived with that paradox long enough.

V

EARLY EPIC AND
MODERN POETRY

THIS BRIEF ESSAY EXAMINES not the cause, but the result, of a remarkable literary fact: that since Keats hardly one English poet has made his reputation with a long poem, especially a narrative one. At first, this was not for want of trying; in spite of Edgar Allan Poe's pronouncement in 1847 that a long poem was a contradiction in terms (poetry's essential task being to excite by elevating, and this being something that could not go on for long). But later, when Poe's influence came back into English poetry through French poetry, it was, on the whole, for want of trying. Modern poets would not give Poe's reason against long poems. They want poetry to excite not so much by elevating as by concentrating, and a long poem would simply engulf the subtle and precise structures of argument, ambiguity, or image they have usually aimed at. But the effect is the same. And, of course, the usual defence of this by now familiar kind of complex literature is that which Mr Eliot gave in his essay on 'The Metaphysical Poets': modern civilization is complex, so, naturally, it constrains the artist to create a complex modern art.

Without in any way attacking this principle, still less the art it leads to, perhaps one can point out that complex modern life might make us want not complex but outstandingly simple poetry—on the ground that the complexities were, after all, of superficial importance, and that a major poet would be able to take his readers through them, to the massive simplicities beyond. This is just what Matthew Arnold said, almost exactly a hundred years ago, in the celebrated *Preface* that he wrote for his own poems. Arnold's contemporaries—is this like modern critics?—admired Shakespeare for ingenuity and richness of imagery. Arnold said that, *as influences*, these were just the worst parts of his work; and he called on writers not to succumb to the complexities of modern life, but to see through them to life's basic, simple realities.

I do not know even what kind of evidence would prove one of these two critics right as against the other; and, in fact, as so often with poet-critics, both were writing the criticism which would justify what they were going to write as poets. Arnold as poet was turning at the very same time to the *Prose Edda*, to Persian history, and to Celtic legend, for situations which had the simple but abiding significance he admired; and in style he was trying to reproduce in English what he found in Homer. Once, in *Sohrab and Rustum*, he came within sight of success. But he was striving against the main trend not only of his time but of his own temperament, too; and in some cases there is less difference than there might be between Arnold's narrative poems and those he reacted against. I say 'reacted against' because he was not alone in turning to early epic and saga; and, indeed, some contemporaries and followers of Arnold turned to these things for reasons rather like Arnold's reasons.

Tennyson, for example, transformed the *Idylls of the King* until, at least in intention, they portrayed those basic human forces which keep society going, or break it up. William Morris went to Icelandic literature for a simpler and therefore truer picture of human passions and of what was at the root of human virtue and heroism. Later on, C. M. Doughty wrote his long epic, *The Dawn in Britain*, with an idea of heroic action which he found conspicuously absent in contemporary public life but present in Anglo-Saxon poetry. And both Morris and Doughty believed that this more primitive literature had not only a more significant concept of human excellence, but also a concreteness and directness of diction which excelled later literature. This care for the technical resources of poetry actually links them with other Victorian writers; for the Victorian period was not, as is sometimes thought, a time of derivativeness and complacency about the language and techniques of verse, but one of anxiety and widespread experiment. Doughty's admiration for early English is a link with, of all people, Hopkins. 'I am now learning Anglo-Saxon, and it is a vastly superior thing to what we have now', Hopkins once wrote—though of course his idea of setting modern English to rights was utterly different from Doughty's. And there were many other experiments and speculations about a language for poetry: the metrical experiments of Tennyson or William Barnes, for example, or the combined experiment and discussion of Patmore or Hopkins himself, or the use of common and colloquial speech by all of these and also, perhaps, by Christina Rossetti and the Brownings. Yet, even so, much of the poetry of this period—much even of the colloquial poetry of Browning—seems to us now to have been written in a diction; in a language that had not fully maintained its contact with the language used in life's ordinary important affairs.

Some reasons why this happened are not specially important now. We have come to recognize them clearly, they cannot impair our present practice. For example, Morris's sense of the grandeur of primitive heroism went only skin deep: constantly (in translation as well as in original poems) he changes a plain heroic incident into one where the chief quality is some subtlety of literary medieval atmosphere, or some elusive colouring of pathos. Similarly, when Tennyson retells from Malory how Lancelot is caught with Guinevere, he simply *removes* the disquieting realities that Malory knew all about; he makes the whole thing trite and prim, and he tries to conceal this by a borrowed literary eloquence.[1] There are sharp limits to the range of experience that the Victorians could come smoothly to terms with—but we know all about this now, and even, I hope, know that somewhere we must have such limits ourselves. Another thing is that some of these writers were not, perhaps, clear whether they aimed at recapturing the fundamental mode of treatment of the early epic, or wanted the quite different and much more sophisticated pleasure of partaking in some literary

---

[1] Tennyson, *Idylls of the King: Guinevere*, ll. 98–130; Malory, *Le Morte d'Arthur*, Book xx, Chapters 3, 4.

tradition of narrative ritual—whether vaguely medieval, or classical. Arnold makes Rustum's horse weep at the death of Sohrab—a deliberate Homeric echo, ingeniously modified and skilfully worked into the story; but it has independent life only as a scholarly diversion. And this failure to distinguish between two quite different motives for turning back to primitive models may underlie much of the derived, literary diction that intermittently blurs the verse of Tennyson or Morris.

But there is another reason why the Victorians fell into this diction: and it is a reason which is still important, for it comes from an attitude to writing which (despite all our reaction from them) we and the Victorians have in common. This is the belief that literature should explore what might be called the fine grain of experience, should parade an especially sharp, subtle, manifold awareness, and should display to the reader what is so elusive, or minute, or half-conscious, or fleeting, or involved, that without this help from the artist he would miss it. In this, oddly enough, writers of the nineteenth and of the twentieth century are one. Of course, the particular details that interest them are different. The Victorians strove for vivid but minute sensuous details, or for an elusive, subtle shade of atmosphere or sentiment. Modern poets (and also, perhaps, Coventry Patmore and Browning—here is the point where these categories begin to fail) have pursued what is multiple, paradoxical, or half-conscious in experience, or some complex structure of many different kinds of idea and feeling. And perhaps they pursue the vivid sensuous detail, too. But the basic likeness within this unlikeness is surely beyond dispute. One fact may bring this out with unexpected clearness: the astonishing and, I think, rarely noticed identity between Virginia Woolf's famous essay on 'Modern Fiction'—so expressive of the modern view of literature and of experience—and the first two volumes of Ruskin's *Modern Painters*; for both of these writers say the same thing: that the world is richer than the artist can ever portray, and that its richness consists in what is elusive and complex and ever-changing.

This view may be admirable: but I want to ask what happens when poets take it and let it govern their work. It demands of them all the time what is vivid, unexpected, subtle; and very few writers of any kind can keep this up. The result is an un-remitting quest for rich and new forms of expression, for in-genious novelties or unprecedented luxuriances of language; and the result of this is a constant wearing out of every new dic-tion as it is introduced. Why does this come about? Because modern poetry's basic mode of writing constantly tempts the writer, when his own vision falls short of that unremitting origi-nality which it demands, to rely on being tided over by the latest rich poetic diction—which his contemporaries are busy accumu-lating all the time. And a poetic diction which is full of expres-sions and techniques invented to be vivid, searching, or spec-tacular, is not only a standing temptation to the minor or fitful artist: it is also exactly what will be most likely by its very bril-liance and difficulty to bluff readers for a time, even when there is nothing in it. So we get the present situation, with a radically new kind of poetic expression being invented every decade, and likely, just because of its richness, to be mechanically exploited almost from the start. This is not, needless to say, an attack on modern poetry; but an attempt to indicate what endemic ten-dency to bad it is, which lies hidden in its particular kind of goodness.

We now almost take it for granted that literature should have this special kind of originality, should pursue subtlety and com-plexity, and should strike out in unexplored areas of the fine grain of experience. Yet it is hard to believe that, after several thousand years, men have only just discovered the true nature of poetry; so perhaps our eager acceptance of this critical ideal is because it is related with special closeness to our own life—our mainly urban society, with its extraordinary degree of leisure, non-violence, sophistication, and comfort. This is not at all to say that the modern standard is a false one, but only that our circumstances have helped us to see one way of producing major art, and see it with exceptional clarity. But to recognize that our kind of life has helped us to this insight is to recognize that another kind of life might lead men to other insights, and indicate quite other modes of creating literature.

The Homeric literature which Arnold was trying to learn from, and the early Icelandic literature that Morris admired, show another mode of writing. Their method is not, as Arnold seems to have supposed, simply that of selecting a great central theme. It penetrates much more intimately into the detail of the narration, and what it is at heart is this: that the author does not pursue the subtleties and complexities of experience, but just the contrary. From the modern point of view, he persistently under-tells the story. He avoids really individualized descriptions of scenes and places, or accounts of the stream of a man's con-sciousness, or multiplicities of image or thought or elusive feel-ing. When Odysseus reaches Ithaca at last, he simply does not recognize it, and grumbles because it is such a barren place. His wife, as mistress of the house, receives him while he is disguised as a travelling beggar: Homer makes the occasion significant not by pursuing the half-thoughts and fantasies that might per-haps have floated through her mind—which could have been the modern way—but by showing ironically how she remained in simple ignorance all the time. When Priam comes in unex-pectedly to Achilles to beg for his son's body, and kneels down to him with his hands on Achilles' knees, Homer merely says that everyone stared one at another in amazement, as if he were a fugitive from justice.[1]

At the climax of the *Song of Roland*, when both the heroes are at the point of death, and Oliver strikes Roland because his wound has made him blind, the poet recounts every step in the incident as though it were perfectly simple and almost trivial. In the Anglo-Saxon *Fight at Finnsburgh*, the crucial words of one hero to another, before they fight and one of them is killed, are simply, 'It is laid down for you already which of two things you are going to get from me here'. Or take a prose example: at the end of the Icelandic *Njal's Saga*, one of the only two survivors from the long and bloody and bitter feud is shipwrecked, and comes as a castaway to claim the hospitality of the other; and *he* simply springs up and gives him the welcome of lasting friend-ship, as if this were a matter of course, or something he had been waiting to do for a long time—which is true. There is no com-ment, no elaboration at all.[2]

This kind of writing is not to be found throughout early epic

[1] *Iliad*, XXIV, ll. 480–4.
[2] *Chanson de Roland*, l. 1995; *The Fight at Finnsburgh*, l. 27; *Burnt Njal*, Ch. 158.

literature; and, if anything, the most striking examples of it often occur when epic is on the point of changing from the oral to the written form, and the specialists feel it is losing its earliest qualities. Again, it occurs outside epic—occasionally in Malory, for example. But early epic is the central place to find it; and it is a kind of writing which poets forget, and cease to be able to use, at their peril. For its simplicity and understatement put the minimum strain on language. They cannot create a rich diction which may trick both writer and reader into mistaking what is empty and secondhand for what is alive and new. They leave language purposely bare; and require the reader to grasp for himself (almost in spite of how the tale is told) a deep significance in what the casual eye finds plain or formal. To emphasize that this style is important is in no way to suggest that poets should try, now, to write epic poems about either ancient or modern battles. Indeed, it has no necessary bearing on the writing of any kind of epic today. The most famous epics of later times, once the written form of literature is established and dominant, have usually tried to do something much more ambitious and comprehensive than earlier epics—to write, as it were, the document by which a whole society or tradition of culture could stand or fall: its final statement, its justification, in fact its myth. And these later epics depart in one way or another from the direct style that grew out of oral conditions. They are brilliantly elaborate or they exploit subtleties of sound, or rhythm, or literary association—think of Tasso or Virgil or Spenser. No doubt, too, our modern society, with its strange amalgam of sophistication and bewilderment, its strangely complex yet fragmentary nature, would direct anyone who did try to write its epic into a peculiar complexity and variety of style and also substance. I think Pound's *Cantos* illustrate this. Moreover, to issue a call for the authentic modern epic would very likely be a waste of time: for by contrast with the profusion of good primitive epic, the good literary epic is very rare—so rare, in fact, that it seems as if few societies or cultures produce more than one masterpiece in this kind. If so, that masterpiece perhaps comes at some distinctive point in a society's history—perhaps at the climax of its achievement, or perhaps just after this; and these are views into which Virgil and Camoëns and Milton, for example, can be fitted with varying degrees of ease. And it would be a doubly bold man who not only settled when this opportune moment was, but also claimed that our own society has reached it.

I am in no way arguing that poets should now try to write epic; only that there is a certain mode of writing which is common in early epic, and which any society at any stage of development needs to remain sensitive to, and able to use, if its general capacity for literature is to remain robust and healthy. This mode of writing is like a line that we cannot allow to vanish from the literary spectrum. Its value is not simply that it brings pleasure; more than this, it brings renewed stimulus and discipline and power.

I foresee two objections to this train of thought, and I mention them because, in each case, showing where they are wrong enables me to take the train of thought further. The first can be put in the categories of modern literary criticism by saying that to call for writing where the author gains his effect just by starting off the imagination and knowledge of the reader is to call for a literature of the 'stock response'. Wanderer returns home; father risks life for son; enemies are reconciled; warrior makes desperate stand: these, it might be said, are now conventional situations where a writer can grasp a success he does not really earn. In part, of course, this is a straight error of fact. The epic poet adds to his plainly narrated incident by where he sets it in his whole poem, and by many things elsewhere in that poem which accumulate a charge for the crucial event. The meeting between Achilles and Priam is recounted plainly, but it has a significance which Homer took twenty-three and a half books to build up. In the Babylonian epic *Gilgamish* the hero, Gilgamish himself, has the plant of eternal life stolen from him while he is bathing in a little stream of fresh water. It is stolen by a snake who is attracted by the smell of the plant, and carries it off in his mouth, cursing Gilgamish as he goes. By itself, the incident is slight and almost grotesque. But it is this very grotesqueness that gives it pathos, coming as Gilgamish's last failure in all his sufferings and heroic deeds in search of the secret of eternal life.

But there is also something more to say: it is that the whole idea that stock responses in literature are necessarily bad is again something that springs from the peculiar conditions of modern life, and has point largely because of those conditions: for it assumes that an experience will mean much to us only if we are shown more in it than we have seen before, or can see for ourselves. It may be true that—save for elusive subtleties which only the artist can reveal—the ordinary person's life now is indeed uneventful and trivial; but this, if true, only shows how far our recent past has been a historical oddity. We need, in fact, to distinguish sharply between the response which a reader can bring to a poem, because that poem makes a call upon what has been potent and moving in his experience; and one which a reader brings to one poem out of relics and residual traces left in his mind by others. This second kind of response, though, is barely relevant to early epic, with its simple mode of narration, its constant under-statement. Its relevance is to later literary epic which often tries to work in a sophisticated tradition, and an artistic, elevated language. There has been quite enough discussion of it in recent years, and I can leave it entirely aside here.

I mentioned two objections to the train of thought I have put forward: the second is that modern literature cannot learn from early epic, because modern life is utterly different from the life which that epic describes. At bottom, this argument can only live at all if we blur the distinction between subject-matter and mode of composition, which I tried to draw earlier on. But if this distinction is ignored, the argument might go like this: primary epic draws on deep and poignant emotions such as those that invest the permanent separation of parents and children, or husbands and wives; it deals with slavery and torture and extermination, whether of a family or of a whole city; and it records hatreds intense enough to bring about massacres or treachery on a grand scale. And because the creators of epic knew that life could contain these things, and yet could contain heroic actions, too, they rested their poems on certain basic convictions—that man's environment is hard and stern, and that good men as well as bad suffer ignominy and pain; yet that, even so, men can have physical or moral powers so great that they almost surpass belief. But, the argument would run, the evils of those primitive times have quite disappeared in our modern progress and enlightenment and rationality; and so of course the basic notions then have no point for us now.

You may wonder why I have troubled with this objection; it must sound ludicrous at the present time, or at any time in recent years. So many of the evils of primitive times have come back into our life. But I do so in order to stress how the security, and the non-violence, and even the comfort which have created our modern critical attitudes, have all stopped. And this early epic poetry has now acquired a relevance not only for its technique, but also for its underlying convictions and principles—its basic attitudes which have an almost dramatic aptness for our own time and for our own predicaments.

PART TWO

VI

AN ANALYSIS OF SWIFT'S
SATIRE

I

SATIRE COMES FROM THE LATIN, and originally meant 'a mixed dish offered to the Gods'. This is very apt. Dedication to the powers of righteousness points to the serious ethical function of satire; and the medley, the rich variety, points to a complexity in technique which often baffles the literary critic, presenting him with a hard resistant nucleus that he has to skirt. Swift has suffered much from this. We have been told too often of his simplicity, and of his conciseness. Such praise positively conceals his best qualities—his subtlety, ingenuity, wealth of content, and fineness of balance. The rich medley remains unscrutinized. The dish is passed to the gods before one learns the recipe.

To suspend praise for Swift's simplicity, and unravel a little of his complexity, does not conflict with his own view of what he wrote: but conforms to it. He praised a simple style himself:[1] but it was *simplex munditiis*, a phrase which was used by Horace of dressing hair, and which points to the final result of thought and skill, when every hair is in its place. In one of his essays (*The Importance of the Guardian Considered*), Swift even begins a list of some satirical techniques: 'We have several ways here of abusing

[1] *Tatler*, No. 230.

75

one another, without incurring the danger of the law', he writes; and mentions particularly 'insinuation', which will prove to be a key term. What Swift protests against, on the other hand, is never richness and pregnancy of meaning, but 'enthusiastic' jargon, solecisms, cant, and affectation. Even so, there is profit only in examining one part of his richness. Men write satire, he says, for two reasons:[1] first, to 'laugh with a few friends in a corner'; second (of which laughter is perhaps the principal *method*) 'to mend the World', to expose and attack what is ridiculous or vicious. Few people have ever got far with inquiring where a joke comes from. This present discussion, therefore, examines only the second function which Swift allots to satire. It asks how he organizes his work so that its satirical indictment is created; and how much, in this or that given case, the indictment contains.

This question, one might think, could be answered by tracing Swift's use of rhetoric:[2] rhetoric, in its traditional form as we find it, say, in a book like Puttenham's *Arte of English Poesie*. Puttenham, certainly, is aware that satire is complex: 'Ye speake in derision or mockerie, & that may be many waies', he writes. Then he lists these ways, giving their traditional names, and also entertaining new English ones that he has made up: *Ironia* or the 'Drie Mocke', *Asteismus* or the 'Mery Scoffe', *Hiperbole* or the 'Loud Lyer', and so on. But analysis in these terms would do nothing to show how satire is actually generated. The rhetorical classification is quite mechanical, and merely recognizes the presence of satire or of some sub-species of it. The same is true even of the more technical categories of rhetoric, like catachresis (using words beyond their established senses), litotes (understatement for praise), or meiosis (understatement for blame). To recognize these figures is not to understand how they create satire, and it is to ignore how the details they classify do not function alone, but catch fire in their contexts. The texture of satire at its keenest is truly organic; its part inter-relate; sometimes it approaches the richness and integration of a poem.

One thing in satire is unique: the gap that it creates between

---

[1] *A Vindication of Mr Gay and the Beggars' Opera*.
[2] Something of this sort has recently been done in Professor John M. Bullitt's able *Jonathan Swift and the Anatomy of Satire* (1953).

substance and tone, between what is said and how it is said. There is no simple explanation of why, in satire, this gap can become lethal: but it can. This, though, is a point about satirical method. There is also something fundamental about what might be called the satirical situation, that in which satire can arise. It is the same situation as that in which invective can arise; for both of these (in Swift's own phrase) seek to mend the world: and this is to attack not Nature (a futile game) but people. Satire is an indictment by one man of others. It is bi-polar. Perhaps we could call the two poles the quarry, and the hunter. In Swift a type-figure of the hunter comes again and again: the plain honest man, good-hearted and common-sensical—someone like the Drapier of the *Drapier's Letters*, or the ostensible author of the *Letter of Advice to a Young Poet*. More strictly, the hunter in Swift is the joint personality which emerges from this picture and from that behind it of Swift himself, seeing its foibles and sensing (because creating) it honesty and strength.[1]

II

How is this complex personality made vivid for the reader? Largely—as with poetic complexity—by figurative language, which can create a sense of the satirist's personality because it so much controls the *tone* of his writing; and therefore our whole sense of his mind, and of how it approaches its task as writer. Other things, of course, can do this too: an autobiographical detail (the ostensible author of the *Letter of Advice to a Young Poet* was always being beaten at school for verses with false quanti-

[1] Since this essay was completed, Mr W. B. Ewald Jr. has published a valuable study (*The Masks of Jonathan Swift*, Harvard) of how Swift created not merely one, but several forms of 'ostensible author' or *persona* in the course of his literary life. Much of what follows in the next two pages of this article receives support and important amplification from his book. This also shows how the *personae* belong closely to their historical context, their 'foibles' often satirizing what Swift saw in his antagonists. It does not, however, always bring out how much the good qualities of the *persona* may contribute to the whole structure of the satire: this is noticeable, I think, in the discussion of the *Drapier's Letters*.

In what follows I have, like Mr Ewald, written of the *Letter to a Young Poet* as by Swift, though the possibility that it was written by someone closely imitating him cannot be dismissed (see *The Works of Jonathan Swift*, ed. H. Davis, Vol. IX, pp. xxiv–vii).

ties), or a distinctive kind of authority for what in fact needs none, like 'I am assured *by our Merchants*, that a Boy or Girl before twelve years Old, is no saleable Commodity' (*A Modest Proposal*). Comparisons can be largely implicit: '*I have known a Factor* deal in as good Ware . . . as the Merchant himself that employs him', Swift writes, pointing out that actors can sometimes converse as well as gentlemen. This is from the *Letter of Advice to a Young Poet*. In the same essay the same kind of language, this time overtly figurative, helps create a picture of Swift's principal victims:

Maggots being what you look for, as Monkeys do for Vermin in their Keeper's Heads . . .

Your cunningest *Thieves* [plagiarists] . . . use to cut off the Portmanteau from behind [use only the Index of a book] without staying to dive into the Pockets of the owner.

(he) bakes it with Poetic Fire, after which it will *ring like any Pancrock*.

Little by little, comparisons like these divide the reader's world into two, with the honest author on one side, and his odious or ludicrous victims on the other.

The method of depicting these two sides is, so far, not wholly parallel. We come to see the author because he *draws* analogies with the merchant and the pan-crock: we see his victims because they are *described* as monkeys or thieves, or their labours as vermin or crockery. The complete parallel would be easy to find, but it is relevant at a later stage. For the moment what is important is that these descriptive metaphors may be of two kinds. They can be (like those just quoted) quite general and vague as description, though potently scornful; or on the other hand their descriptive force can sometimes be much more precise. A good example of this is Swift's 'Verse without Rhime is a Bell without a Clapper' (*Letter of Advice to a Young Poet*). This is not an attack on blank verse: it attacks degenerate rhyming (such as the bad poet might become proficient in, Swift says, by assiduous attendance at parlour-games like *crambo*). Yet the metaphor does not assume that a bell without a clapper is bad, and leave the matter there. It indicates why. Its point is that bad rhyming verse clangs and booms with the futile monotony of a senseless bell. This comparison is not unexplained abuse: but condemns what it attacks, and also describes it.

Another example is Swift's attack on index-scholars: in *The Tale of a Tub* he calls their way of going to work:

the choicer, the profounder, and politer Method . . . by which the whole Book is governed and turned, *like Fishes by the Tail*.

The first words of this make it plain that the comparison is with eating, not cooking; and the *statement* insinuated about these pseudo-scholars is that they treat the books of their betters with the casual thoughtlessness of the diner. Swift uses the technique again at the end of the *Letter of Advice to a Young Poet*, when he suggests that perhaps every rich man ought to have a tame versifier on the domestic staff:

for, perhaps, a Rhimer is as necessary amongst Servants of a House, as a Dobben with his Bells, at the Head of a Team.

A Dobben is a leading draught horse, and not disagreeable in itself, like thieves or vermin. The comparison disparages by *describing* the bad poet, as he plods along mechanically like a horse, and produces nothing but the inane jingle of the horse's bells. In all these cases, the metaphor conveys not mere scorn, but a specific fact, a real piece of information, which justifies scorn.

III

Working on a larger scale, Swift can sometimes write a whole essay around a single complex analogy. The best example is the difficult *Discourse Concerning the Mechanical Operation of the Spirit*. Here Swift's purpose is to attack fanaticism in religion, and his method is to create an overwhelmingly strong idea, from a multitude of converging details, of fanaticism or enthusiasm as a mere bodily excretion, which produces troublesome physical disorder unless it is evacuated like the other excretions. Throughout the essay, three comparisons help to bring this about: the product of the enthusiast's brain is likened to that of the nose (Analogy 1); the anus (Analogy 2); and the genital organs (Analogy 3).

These, says Swift, are not mere random likenesses. They are

there because of a real organic continuity. He can argue legitimately for this:

Besides, the Spinal Marrow, being nothing else but a Continuation of the Brain, musts needs create a very free Communication between the Superior Faculties and those below.

But even here, a careful choice of words has interlocked a real connexion and a fortuitous likeness. 'Spinal marrow' brings out not only a significant physiological linkage, but also a chance physical resemblance, for Swift has already been telling his readers a humorous fable about the brain:

It is the Opinion of Choice Virtuosi, that the Brain is only a Crowd of little Animals . . . like the Picture of Hobbes' Leviathan . . . their Food is the Air we attract, and their Excrement *Phlegm*.

Both the first two analogies are here.[1] But Swift goes further: colds and rheums are merely an 'epidemical *looseness*' of the little animals of the brain; and he has not yet finished with the phlegm analogy. Among the fanatic preachers:

A Master Workman shall *blow his Nose* so powerfully as to pierce the Hearts of his People . . .

and quite unscrupulous pus draw the link tighter still:

It is frequent for a single *Vowel* to draw Sighs from a Multitude, and for a whole *As*sembly of Saints to sob to the Musick of one solitary *Liquid*.

Plainly the liquid, besides being a consonant and an excretion, can also be alcohol. But although Swift elaborates this joke for a while, he in the end retracts it. Enthusiasm 'cannot be imputed to intoxication by wine, but must needs have a deeper foundation'.[2]

[1] It must be left to the reader to decide whether Analogy 2 is also present at the beginning of this piece, where Swift likens the enthusiastic audience to Mahomet 'borne to heaven upon nothing but his *Ass*'; an idea resumed later when the Puritan preacher is likened to Darius's horse, which came to neigh through covering a mare (Analogy 3). Swift, in this second passage, avoids the word 'horse', using 'animal' or 'beast' throughout instead.

[2] Swift also adds the analogy with belching at this point, and in the parallel passage in the *Tale of a Tub* reminds his reader that the Latin word (*eructatio*) also meant to deliver an oracle (1720 edition).

So far as he himself is concerned, though, 'deeper' here no has laudatory meaning; it simply means 'lower down the body than the mouth or even stomach'. Swift is introducing Analogy 3 into his scheme, and has another tale to tell; this time, why the Puritans preach through their noses. They do so, he gravely recounts, in imitation of the 'Banbury saint' whose inspiration, when it had no oratorical outlet, drove him along less reputable channels, and made him catch syphilis. The surgeon cured the parts primarily affected; but the disease then retreated to the original seat of disturbance, and passing by the nose on the way, 'broke down the bridge and retired to headquarters'. Other metaphors, throughout the essay, sustain this ingenious myth. When the body troubles the mind, it is with 'huge Rippon *Spurs*', with a '*Thorn* in the Flesh' that is a 'Spur to the Spirit'; and 'the *seed* or principle which has ever put men upon visions in things invisible is of a corporeal nature', Swift adds. Finally, he links Analogies 1 and 3 by linking the preacher and the wooer:

If we inspect into the usual Process of modern Courtship, we shall find it to consist in . . . an artificial Form of Canting and Whining by rote, every Interval, for want of other Matter, made up with a Shrug, or a Hum, a Sigh or a Groan.

Thus, all in all, the whole essay is made up of one complex analogy: and this is developed through a medley of devices—plain statement, pun, exaggeration, fable, individual metaphor—which can only be unravelled by methods not unlike those of poetical analysis.

IV

Satire is an attack by ridicule upon evil. If the author reveals this evil too blatantly, or stresses it too much, it will be hard for him to maintain the suave tone which ridicule requires. But satire will have a clear superiority over invective only if, besides its own achievement, it can also do all that invective does. Veiled or not, the brutal facts must in the end transpire. *Insinuation* (Swift's own word) brings this about: the brutal fact is a wolf in sheep's clothing, slipped in under the fact which is, or seems, innocent.

An Analysis of Swift's Satire

Insinuation is largely what creates the effectiveness of *A Modest Proposal for Preventing the Children of Ireland from being a Burden to their Parents*. The central idea of this essay is well known; but beneath the single vivid and hideous image, there is a richness of concealed meaning which even Swift himself seldom rivals. In ten short pages, while the reader's attention seems to be occupied primarily with his horrifying fantasy of turning all the babies into meat, he marks out just what Ireland was like at the time, and just who made it so. The record is complete: yet Swift seems never to have had to begin it. Below, in diagram form for clarity, are a few of the 'sheep-statements', as one might call them, with some indication each time of the concealed wolf:

Text	*Insinuation*
. . which would move Tears and Pity in the most Savage and inhuman breast.	But doesn't in human ones, they are harder still.
From (200,000) I subtract thirty thousand Couples, who are able to maintain their own children.	85% are starving.
I have been assured by a very knowing American[1] of my acquaintance in London, that a young healthy Child . . . is at a year Old a most delicious wholesome Food.	London is the place to meet those who treat humans as animals.
Those who are more thrifty . . . may flay the Carcass . . .	And people would.
. . . the Skins of which . . . will make admirable Gloves for Ladies, and Summer Boots for fine Gentlemen.	While some starve, some live in trashy luxury.
The poorer Tenants will have something valuable of their own which . . . may . . . help to pay their Landlord's Rent.	And the landlords would take it.

Many of these are obvious enough: though fresh barbs protrude at each reading. But the crucial point is this: for all that it is a satire, *The Modest Proposal* manages to insinuate facts, and in a way which is detailed, comprehensive, and damning.

[1] The point of this is simply that the American has had a chance to learn from 'savages', whom Swift mentions a few lines later.

Another important device in Swift for insinuation is the catalogue. Professor Bullitt has discussed this in his book, and written of the 'witty juxtaposition and, by inference, equation' of the supposedly virtuous and admittedly vicious in lists like 'Beaux, Fidlers, Poets and Politicians', 'Parliament-, Coffee-, Play-, and Bawdy-Houses'. This 'uneasy quality' he regards as a form of 'diminution' (what I have called disparagement), and he says that it helps Swift to amuse as well as abuse. But this amusement, this wit, appears on his analysis to draw the sting from Swift's attack, and to do so by design: 'we are continually *surprised out of anger* by the wit of the juxtapositions . . . the element of witty surprise is strong enough to *startle the mind from* the sense of total contempt'. Surely this is to overlook what the catalogue is: not an arbitrary juxtaposition, but a juxtaposition which through its quality of paradox is a challenge to the reader to recall the facts which remove the paradox: which make the catalogue plainly a valid one. It is a challenge, that is, to find the hidden insinuations.

In the list above, for example, 'Beau' is a term which we know must point to bad qualities. But once we recall this, do we and must we not trace the same qualities in a Fiddler? even a poet? why, even a politician? We reflect; the insinuations come out; and the catalogue turns into a condemnation because of what it precisely, though covertly, states. Similarly with a list like 'turn our Courts, Exchanges, and Shops into Desarts' (*Argument against Abolishing Christianity*). This is no joke. The likeness is real, and the list a challenge to detect it. Another barbed list comes not much later:

If the Physicians would forbid us to pronounce the Words Pox, Gout, Rheumatism, and Stone, would that . . . destroy the Diseases?

Simply by picking on these diseases and not others, Swift implies they are the chief ones. Then he so arranges them as to imply that they come from vice and excess. This we take for granted of pox. But gout, the reader begins to recall, can come from vice too:

> O may I live exempted (while I live
> Guiltless of *pamper'd appetite obscene*)
> From pangs arthritic that infest the toe
> Of libertine excess.

83

is Cowper's charming periphrases in *The Task*.[1] By now the challenge to detect Swift's implication is created; and we come to realize that all four diseases can come from the same kinds of excess. What brings us to our end, Swift is saying, is above all our vice.

V

Satire is not paradoxical only in its catalogues: it tends towards an unobtrusive kind of paradox in all that it says. But the paradoxical assertions of satire are not left to hit or miss the mark simply as chance directs. They are constantly being, as it were, 'justified'; and this is what creates the double sense that irony requires. The unjustified paradox comes as a witty surprise, and so far we merely watch the writer conducting a poised, delicate verbal game. Then the second, serious meaning emerges, the truth shows behind the extravagance, and the writer has begun to mend the world. This almost continuous texture of paradox is maintained by utilizing—through seeming defiance—the over-riding control which words exercise upon their own context. Often enough, one part of a sentence virtually dictates what can come in another part; or at least, dictates the sense which the other words must have, if the whole sentence is to mean anything at all. Swift knows how to exploit this linguistic compulsion. Often he writes so that his words display a centrifugal force: they seem to refuse contact with each other, like similar magnetic poles. This is the challenge to the reader, who is driven to find senses for the words which force them into contact; and it is in the search for these second senses that the ironical second meaning—the true meaning—of the whole sentence emerges, and the jabbing point of the irony goes home.

The first sentence of the *Argument against Abolishing Christianity* shows this clearly. Here it is, with two vital words left out:

I am very sensible what a Weakness and Presumption it is, to [   ] against the general [   ] and Disposition of the World.

In the first space, the words 'Weakness and Presumption' plainly make the reader expect a disparaging word like 'rail' or 'cavil',

[1] *The Sofa*, II. 103–6.

or at least a neutral one like 'argue'. In the second, 'general . . . Disposition of the world' makes him expect an approving or at least neutral word, like 'wisdom' or 'outlook'. Instead, Swift chooses words which, if taken at their face value, would disintegrate his sentence:

I am very sensible what a Weakness and Presumption it is, to *reason* against the general *Humour* and Disposition of the World.

There is the paradox: Weakness and Presumption are rational, and the World is not. The two intruding words force us to reinterpret the whole sentence; and this only settles into sense again, when we have seen that its writer's presumption lies not in thinking to correct the world's wisdom, but in hoping to put right its irredeemable folly.

In Swift's text, another example follows almost at once:

This may perhaps appear too great a Paradox even for our wise and paradoxical Age to endure; therefore I shall handle it with all Tenderness, and with the utmost Deference to that great and profound Majority which is of another *Sentiment*.

Why does the heavily ironical last word threaten to disintegrate the whole sentence? Because for Swift it was nonsense that something rational like an opinion should defer to something irrational like a sentiment; and it is a sharp let-down, that the great and profound majority have nothing better than this for the individual to defer to. But even as this centrifugal force develops in our minds, the words develop senses which counter it. After all, 'great and profound' may mean only 'large and abysmal'. 'Paradoxical' may be not a word of praise ('paradox-understanding') or a neutral word ('paradox-loving'), but merely an ironical synonym for *ir*rational, incomprehensible—in fact, *mad* (a point for later in this discussion). Thus, little by little, the sentence prescribes what meaning it must have, if it is not to be nonsense. The ironical implications emerge. 'Insinuation' begins.

The word 'Wit' is especially useful to Swift in manoeuvres like these, because the distinction between true and false wit was a commonplace:[1]

[1] See Addison, *Spectator*, No. 62.

two young Gentlemen of real Hopes, bright Wit, and profound Judgement, who, upon a thorough Examination of Causes and Effects, and by the mere Force of natural Abilities, without the least Tincture of Learning, having made a Discovery . . . (*Argument against Abolishing Christianity.*)

In this passage, 'wit' is clearly driven into meaning 'false wit'. First, a 'bright' wit sounds suspiciously like a small one, and true wit is never without learning. The sentence can accommodate these facts only when we recollect that 'real hopes' might mean only keen ones; that we have seen a pun in 'profound' before; that the 'mere' force of natural abilities is more disparagement than praise; and that when right and wrong are in question, causes and effects may be a ludicrous irrelevance. Resolving the paradox transforms seeming praise into final condemnation.

The sequel to this passage brings out how Swift could also shape his metaphors so as to confirm the senses which he allots to his words. 'Tho' a Wit need not have Religion,' he writes, 're-ligion is necessary to a Wit, as an Instrument is to the Hand that plays upon it': the Beau–Fidler–Poet parallel once again. The next metaphor is a perfect emblem: '. . . and for this the Moderns plead the Example of their great Idol Lucretius, who had not been by half so eminent a Poet (as he truly was) but that he stood tip-toe on Religion, *Religio pedibus subjecta*'. Swift ingeniously saves Lucretius by the parenthesis; but the 'tip-toe' (which is quite arbitrary) settles once for all whether the victim is wit or religion.

This contrast between the two kinds of wit shows the ambiguity between the good variety of something, and its bad variety, which is basic to satire. Swift can make very slight touches indicate that he means the bad variety of what he refers to: 'You may in a short time arrive at the Accomplishments of a Poet, and shine in that Character', he writes: or, 'our prettiest Performers that way' (*Advice to a Young Poet*). In each case a concealed metaphor of the Beau or fiddler or player prescribes the spurious sense for 'Poet'. 'I could produce many more shining passages out of our principal poets of both sexes' (*A Collection of Genteel and Ingenious Conversation*) does the same: for Swift, principal women poets simply do not make up a class. Similarly, 'monstrous Wits in the Poetic Way' are not great but deformed ones; and 'those whose Genius, *by continual Practice*, hath been wholly turn'd upon Raillery and Invectives against Religion' prescribes the spurious sense for 'genius': the true kind is unaffected by practice, however assiduous.

VI

This points to one further technique of satire. To identify the spurious sense of a word is to indicate the fools or rogues who give it that sense:

There are, by computation, in this Kingdom, above ten thousand Parsons, whose Revenues, added to those of my Lords the Bishops, would suffice to maintain at least two hundred Young Gentlemen of Wit and Pleasure, and Free-thinking Enemies to Priest-craft, narrow Principles, Pedantry and Prejudices, who might be an Ornament to the Court and Town. (*Argument against Abolishing Christianity.*)

These Young Gentlemen are branded, in the first place, by the insinuation that they are so expensive they must be extravagant, and (through the metaphor 'ornament') that they are a little too much like porcelain. But the insinuations affect the rest of the passage. To begin with, we detect the less obvious meaning of 'narrow Principles': the contrast is not with humane Principles, but with broad *licence*. But in this bad sense, 'narrow Principles' is a phrase which the passage forces upon the young gentlemen. It means, 'what *they* call narrow principles', it is imputed to them. If so, however, it means 'true principles'. But 'Priest-craft . . . Pedantry, and Prejudices' can in that case also be imputed, and they come to mean true religion, learning, and sound opinion. Only then, with the spurious senses firmly allotted to the victims of the satire, does the passage settle down to its ironical sense.

This trick can also be played with a metaphor:

To what Purpose shou'd we go thither for Coals or Poetry, when we have a Vein within ourselves equally Good and more Convenient? (*Advice to a Young Poet.*)

is an example, and another is

the Quarrel is not against any particular Points of hard Digestion in the Christian System, but against Religion in general. (*Argument against Abolishing Christianity.*)

Coals and poetry, spiritual food and physical, are not of course indistinguishable to Swift himself. They are jumbled together by the ostensible author, the Drapier-figure, because Swift is treating him like a ventriloquist's doll: and this doll is using the comparison which (Swift implies) would seem cogent to the victims of the satire. These are imputed metaphors, foisted by the hunter on to his quarry. Similarly, when Swift speaks (in the *Modest Proposal*) of a new-born child as 'just dropped from its Dam', he is using the language of those whom he is attacking, those who treat parents and children too as they would treat animals, and 'as they have already devoured most of the Parents seem to have the best title to the children'. And when he writes:

The number of Souls in this Kingdom being usually reckoned to one Million and a half, Of these I calculate there may be about two hundred thousand Couple whose Wives are Breeders

'Couple' and 'Breeder' are words for animals, but the metaphor would come quite naturally to his opponents. He has slipped his own literal word in at the beginning, it is the word 'soul'.

VII

I have been arguing so far that criticism of Swift as a writer has in part been hamstrung, because critics have scarcely had such instruments for scrutinizing his satire as could make that scrutiny sharp and full. For this, one must develop at least the rudiments of a theory of satire. Not to recognize that satire is likely to create a sense of its author's personality and mood, to impute its meanings and metaphors, to suggest (through paradox) one meaning, then eradicate it and employ another, is like not recognizing that poetry can work through rhythm or imagery or choice of diction. But once the instruments of scrutiny have been distinguished, they can help not only with Swift's general quality as a satirist, but also with what is most distinctive of him.

This most distinctive quality establishes a profound difference between Swift and his contemporaries. It is something which makes us see him, in our final assessment, either as a monster, or as rising head and shoulders above the others, a larger, wiser, and in a true sense profoundly humaner figure. It shows clearly, against the contrast of what Pope has to say in his *Epilogue to the Satires*. In these two Dialogues, Pope sets out the reasons why he has persisted in satire, and puts objections to it into the mouth of a friend. But one feels as one reads that, brilliant though Pope may be, fine as is the stand he takes, searching as is his regard, there is at bottom something shallow in his thought—that there is, in fact, only a thoughtlessness which his high-minded stridency manages to betray. It seems that (as Bagehot said of a man who had not read Homer or seen the sea) 'there is a great object of which he has no idea'. There is a reason against satire enormously more cogent than any he allows to his poor interlocutor: one which might be put in Swift's last known spoken words, 'they had much better leave it alone'. For the weakness of moral satire, satire that aims at mending the world, is that unless men really can be laughed or mocked *out* of folly and vice, these attacks on young gentlemen of wit and pleasure come much too near the knuckle. If men are irredeemable, then the satirist who laughs in a corner with a few friends is merely one more of the ingenious 'projectors', the fiddling buffoons, whom he attacks with such laboured but misplaced high-mindedness. Second time round (to revert to an analogy used before) the wise man is the fool, the hunter finds that his first quarry is himself.

From the beginning, Swift knew he might prove to be this fool. This is what drives him to begin all afresh, midway through the famous 'Digression concerning Madness' in the *Tale of a Tub*: that he does so is a point which has not, I believe, been properly noticed. The first half is a conventional Swiftian attack on that 'Enthusiasm' which is the origin of all 'schemes' in philosophy and all great empires and conquerors in history. Here, Swift's account of this condition is that of the *Mechanical Operation of the*

Spirit: 'vapours ascending from the lower faculties to over-shadow the brain'. Half way through the piece, he is still condemning enthusiasm and all that it creates:

the Brain, in its natural Position and State of Serenity, disposeth its Owner to pass his Life in the common Forms, without any Thought of subduing Multitudes to his Power, his Reasons, or his Visions . . . but when a Man's Fancy gets astride on his Reason . . . and common Understanding, as well as common Sense, is Kicked out of Doors; the first Proselyte he makes is Himself, and when that is once compass'd, the Difficulty is not so great in bringing over others . . . for, Cant and Vision are to the Ear and the Eye, the same that Tickling is to the Touch.

So far, his course is the plain one. But then, suddenly in the middle of a paragraph, the passage modulates until it somersaults. The second, deeper level of Swift's mind comes to the surface. The argument turns more and more into an admission that in a mad world (which is what this world is), wisdom and reason cannot possibly bring happiness: so perhaps, after all, folly and blindness make a kind of wisdom of their own. Swift never quite gives in. Partly he evades the disastrous admission: it is 'what is generally *called* happiness' that is 'a perpetual possession of being well deceived'. But in a passage like the following, one can see that what Swift mocks at a level of witty frivolity also attracts him powerfully at a deeper level of truth:

How fading and insipid do all Objects accost us that are not convey'd in the Vehicle of Delusion! how shrunk is every Thing as it appears in the Glass of Nature! So, that if it were not for the Assistance of Artificial Mediums, false Lights, refracted Angles, Varnish and Tinsel, there would be a mighty Level in the Felicity and Enjoyments of Mortal Men. If this were seriously considered by the World, as I have a certain Reason to suspect it hardly will; Men would no longer reckon among their high Points of Wisdom, the Art of exposing weak Sides and publishing Infirmities.

The attack on folly never quite disappears, but the second half of this whole digression turns into a full-scale *Eloge de la Folie*: 'a Man, truly wise, creams off Nature, leaving the Sour and the

Dregs for Philosophy and Reason'; and it culminates in Swift's admitting (or is it boasting?) that he, the author of these momentous truths, is mad himself.[1]

In Book IV of *Gulliver's Travels*, Swift is of course known to treat human beings as utterly depraved. The grey horse whom he refers to always as 'my master' found us a 'sort of animals to whose share some small pittance of reason had fallen, whereof we made no other use than by its assistance to aggravate our natural corruptions'. But Swift's virtual despair over mankind did not need always to be stated outright. It weaves into the texture of his irony: the implication that removing one abuse will only highlight others is constant. Perhaps the most striking thing about the *Argument against Abolishing Christianity* is how it insinuates that although free-thinkers are corrupt, they are little worse than anything else which is not a mere dream, but a reality. It is no good to abolish the Christian faith, Swift says, in an effort to reduce political strife. 'There is one darling Inclination of Mankind . . . the Spirit of Opposition': prevent men from quarrelling about one thing, they will ferret out another. Nor can we hope that if religion is abolished, education will no longer inculcate 'grievous Prejudices'[2] like virtue, conscience, and the rest: those all stopped long ago. England's 'Christian' neighbours take a pride in the *name* of Christian, but the Turks are more shocked at Infidelity than they are. Even the ministers of religion are no more than 'ten thousand Parsons reduced, by the wise regulations of Henry the Eighth, to the Necessity of a low Diet, and Moderate exercise, who are the great Restorers of our Breed'. Insinuation here is powerfully compressed: 'wise' (unless imputed) means shrewdly lucrative;[3] the parsons live

---

[1] F. R. Leavis, in his essay on *The Irony of Swift*, notices this: 'It is as if one found Swift in the place—at the point of view—where one expected to find his butt.' He considers, though, that the ambiguity disappears, and concludes that Swift 'never found anything better to contend for than a skin, a surface, an outward show'. It is very hard to agree with this. Professor R. Quintana, in his excellent new survey, *Swift, an Introduction* (Oxford), notes the 'dramatic change of tone' at this point, and says that 'irony is complex' (p. 65), but does not pursue the matter.

[2] 'Grievous' here reminding us of the strength of our depravity as well as of the strength of conscience.

[3] Swift's hostility to Henry VIII is clear from his *Preface to the Bishop of Sarum's Introduction* (1713).

temperately because they are obliged to (otherwise they might ruin the Breed as effectively as the rest do); and the moderate exercise is not walking instead of running, but half-hearted fulfilment of duty. Hint by hint, the essay grows into a condemnation of the whole existing basis of civil life. As it proceeds, we come to see why Swift has said that, 'whether from the Affectation of Singularity or *the perverseness of Human Nature*', he could not share the majority view: the perverseness is not his own private eccentricity, but the general way of life.

This comes again in a poignant twist at the end of the *Modest Proposal*, where Swift says how relieved he was to think at last of a simple and attractive idea like cooking all the babies, after he had been 'wearied out for many Years with offering vain, idle, visionary Thoughts, and at length utterly despairing of Success'. The passage uses the very word 'projector' (which means Inventor, Planner in the bad modern sense) that Swift had used ironically of himself at the start of the essay. But there it casts a satirical light on the Proposal; here the vain and visionary schemes are the common-sense projects of an economic kind that he had put forward all to no purpose. But 'let no Man talk to me of these and the like Expedients, till he hath at least some Glimpse of Hope'. He himself has none any more.

The same despair shows in Swift's very last work: the three dialogues (fruit of a wonderfully sharp but seethingly exasperated perception) which make up the *Collection of Genteel and Ingenious Conversation*. Here in the Introduction Swift satirically claims that this work ought to bring him immortality: and says why. By means of these dialogues, just everyone can master the art of polite conversation, and shine in society: and were there not ancient heroes who even attained divine honours, merely 'upon the merit of having civilized a fierce and barbarous people'? At bottom, this is what Swift believed that he confronted himself: not flaws in a good society, but a fierce and barbarous people, a world of latent Yahoos.

In fact, this last work is symbolic. By now Swift's attack is only an oblique one; he has, in the main, replaced his attacks on folly by the infinitely patient cataloguing of folly. His other very late work, the *Directions to Servants*, is much the same, although he ironically called it 'very useful as well as humorous'. There is no missionary faith now, only a hopeless, amused, slightly incredulous record of limitless fatuity. 'It is today as entertaining and amusing, as it was in its own time. Indeed, in many respects it is as true of today,' writes Swift's editor, with unconscious irony. It was only a laugh in a corner for a few friends—indeed, by this time Swift was short even of them.

VII

HARDY'S MAJOR FICTION

I

THE GROWING PESSIMISM of Hardy's later novels has been stressed often enough in the past, and has usually been located in two particular aspects of his work. These are, first, his 'philosophical' asides ('the President of the Immortals, in Aeschylean phrase, had finished his sport with Tess' is enough in illustration of this familiar story: the phrase itself will need re-examination later); and second, his apparently growing pre-occupation with problems of marriage. To see this second issue simply as the product of difficulties in Hardy's own married life is very uninformative: more to the point are the divorce cases (the Parnell case being the best known) which became national sensations in the later 1880s and early 1890s; and also, at least for *Jude the Obscure*, the important influence of Ibsen.

Recent criticism of Hardy has also emphasized something else: a special aspect of his connexion with the south-west of England. An earlier generation of writers on Hardy have somewhat misrepresented it. Amiably if innocently equipped with haversack and large-scale map, they cycled over Wessex and noted Hardy's accurate geography or his intimate and affectionate knowledge of rural occupations and customs. More recently, though, Hardy has been seen as one who registered the impact upon rural England of a great historical change, one which went to the very roots of life. One cause of this change

94

was the swift and decisive decline in British agriculture which followed almost instantaneously on the completion of the railroad links to the American Middle West in about 1870. The other, less spectacular but in the long run much more far-reaching, was the industrial revolution in agriculture, which was progressing steadily in the later years of the century, and which has even now far from completed its radical transforming work. As symbol of this second force, one might take a pair of incidents from Hardy's own work. In *The Mayor of Casterbridge* (1886) the new mechanical seed-drill which is to replace the methods in use since the time of the Anglo-Saxons is for sale in the marketplace. Someone has still to buy and use it. In *Tess of the D'Urbervilles*, only five years later, the mechanical harvester dominates and controls the whole scene of the corn-stacking (Chapter 48) and reduces the tired, dazed human beings who serve it to automatons.

Modern criticism of fiction often seems at its weakest when it tries (or fails) to consider the pervasive drives in a book which unify it sequentially through from beginning to end. This weakness is perhaps the result of a certain uneasiness which (for reasons obvious enough) often shows itself when the critic turns his attention to plot. Yet such attention is necessary if the pervasive unifying drives of the work are to be located; and certainly the full seriousness and import of Hardy's major novels will be concealed from the reader who fails to apprehend their plots: plots, that is, not as mere summarizable sequences of events, but as the central force which gives the book its unity and which is intrinsic to its meaning.

The first step is not difficult. It is simply to combine the two more or less familiar points from which this discussion started; to see Hardy's deepening and harshening gloom as not a mere self-ingraining philosophical bias, but rather as something in most intimate relation to his vision of the passing of the old rhythmic order of rural England. Once the novels are seen from this point of view, they suggest a surprising development in Hardy's thought. They suggest not just a growing pre-occupation with the rural problem, nor even a growing sense that the earlier way of life was inevitably vanishing. They suggest something more disquieting: a gathering realization that that earlier way did not possess the inner resources upon which to fight for its existence. The old order was not just a less powerful mode of life than the new, but ultimately helpless before it through inner defect.

II

In arguing that a thought or an attitude comes increasingly into focus in a writer's work, it is always easy to claim too much and hide too much. Yet in the present case the change looks convincingly steady. *The Return of the Native* (1878) has a half-tragic ending in its present form; and Hardy's original intention seems to have been to make it more tragic rather than less so. Yet throughout the book, the stress falls on the revitalizing power of rural life, and on how its vitality is intrinsically greater than that of modernity. Eustacia and Wildeve, and at first Clym too, are alienated from it: indeed, this very alienation is behind their ostensible successes (the marriages, for example). But because of the alienation, the successes are ill-placed and precarious, they are the successes of those who have lost the soundness, the inner strength, the power to choose and to achieve wisely, which belongs to men whose life is in harmony with their world. By contrast, Venn the reddleman suffers reverses, but they do not impair his integrity; his vitality runs submerged, but it runs with the tide of life. The gambling scene on the heath is fantastic enough, but it tellingly conveys this. Moreover, the whole rural ambience can ultimately assert a greater vitality than the city life from which Clym has come. As he gives himself to that ambience, he is regenerated from a basic source. By the end, Egdon triumphs, even if on its own stern terms. The renegades have been destroyed or won over. Even if Venn had never married Thomasin, the faithful would have been in possession. The novel resolves in an assertion of the old order, its regenerative austerity, its rewarding unrewardingness.

The next novel is very different. Henchard is the only major figure in *The Mayor of Casterbridge* (1886) who stands integrally for the traditional qualities. Farfrae is an agriculturalist, but of the new kind: he prospers by chemistry, machinery, book-keeping, elementary economics. His traditional songs are partly a social accomplishment, neither sincere nor insincere. His kindliness and even his amorousness are conventional. Henchard's daughter Elizabeth-Jane is turning into a cultivated young lady (I would sooner over-rate than under-rate Hardy's own educatedness, but I cannot help seeing something of importance in his seeming assurance here that education could without loss be self-education). Lucetta is entirely *déraciné*. On these premises, contrast with *The Return of the Native* is vivid. From beginning to end Henchard's course is downward. Whenever his older way of life meets the new, it is defeated. Step by step, he comes to work for the man whom he once employed, and in the end he feels himself driven away to his death; while those who were once his labourers work the new, harder (and easier) way, for a shilling a week less than they had had from him.

Yet although this relentless decline of Henchard's is (as we take its meaning) what unifies the book, Henchard still stands above the others in psychic virtue. In the conventional sense, he is both less moral than them and more so. He is violent and a liar and in one sense intensely selfish, but his generosity is true magnanimity, and he has reserves of affection and humility that they quite lack. The essential is something else, though: that his whole nature, good or bad, is centred upon a deep source of vital energy. The rich stream of life still issues from life's traditional order. It does not bring success, but even so, it brings greatness and in a sense goodness. Farfrae prospers through *skill* which the new mode of life has impersonally taught him, Henchard is able to struggle on, though defeated, because not of what he has learnt but of what he *is*. He blocks out something like the full contour of the human being.

That Henchard should stand out as a human rather than a man was surely part of Hardy's intention. His lack of interest in 'womankind' is stressed more than once, and we are reminded of how Marty South is also in a sense made sexless at the end of *The Woodlanders* (1887). But to turn to *The Woodlanders* not for an incidental parallel but in general, is to find that Hardy has now moved further still. Marty South and Giles Winterbourne do not display (like Henchard) a defeated strength, but strength all the same. On the contrary, the impression they leave is of debility. So far as goodness itself goes, they are to be sure alone in having contact with it: 'you was a good man, and did good things'. But the springs of goodness are now no longer the springs of strength. Rather the opposite. Such vitality as there is lies on the other side, in the self-assurance and plausible fluency of Fitzpiers, in the passionate sensuousness of Felice. Grace Melbury has a thwarted contact, anyhow, with the traditional order: but what it does for her is to make her impassive and acceptant.

In *Tess of the D'Urbervilles* (1891), Hardy moves further. Tess is 'a pure woman', admittedly; but this is not the feminine counterpart to Henchard's 'A Man of Character'. It is not Tess's sexual misadventures which impugn her as a woman of character; and Hardy is indeed at pains to show, in the later part of the book when she resists the now twice-reprobate Alec, that she is comparatively faithful and steadfast. But she has a weakness nearer her centre: alienation and dreaminess which Hardy depicts unsuccessfully in the ride at night when she tells her young brother that we live on a blighted planet (and becomes so engrossed that she causes a fatal injury to the horse), and which he depicts again, this time with brilliant achievement, at Talbothay's dairy when she tells Dairyman Crick how 'our souls can be made to go outside our bodies when we are alive'. Again, this incident is nodal in the book, and I must return to it. For the present it is enough to say that its nodality is stressed by Hardy, in that he makes this the very moment when Angel Clare first gives Tess any special attention.

This dreamy unreality in Tess is no personal quirk. It results from her heredity, and is reflected in her parents. Moreover, Hardy is at pains to stress that among country folk, degeneration of an old stock is common enough. The race is in decline. It seems a positive disparagement of the old order. The contrast with Henchard is revealing. Quietly but clearly, Hardy indicates that in Tess there is something self-destroying. So there was, in a sense, in Henchard. Yet how differently does the stress fall, provided that the reader follows only the contours created by the author!

Tess of the D'Urbervilles also dwells, quite for the first time, upon another unattractive side of rural life. This is what appears in the barrenness and crippling toil of life on the upland farm of Flintcomb-Ash. Hardy links his picture to contemporary agricultural realities (the farm belongs to an absentee landlord) but the essential things which make life hard on it are those which have made rural life hard since the beginning: stony soil, cold wind, rain, snow, callous masters—things that can be found in the Wakefield *Second Shepherd's Play* as easily as in this novel. Should that be in doubt, it may be confirmed from *Jude the Obscure* (1896). In fact, there is something like a parallel here to the double indictment of *Tess*. Jude Fawley is 'crazy for books . . . it runs in our family'. Later, when the now adult Jude sees a stonemason's yard and glimpses for a moment that happiness for him lay only in a life like that, Hardy passes decisive judgement upon bookish tastes in labourers' families. A still clearer parallel with *Tess*, however, is Hardy's insistence in this novel upon the essential harshness of rural life. 'How ugly it is here', thinks Jude, as he drives off the rooks from the brown featureless arable of the upland. This is in part an ironical judgement upon Jude. Hardy is at pains to stress the rich human associations of the scene. Yet some of these associations are themselves associations of human unhappiness; and the whole chapter goes far to endorse Jude's revulsion from the drab landscape and the inevitable greed and callousness of the farmer. Nor are this revulsion, and the inescapable grounds tending to justify it, incidentals. They initiate the whole train of events. Jude's quest for learning is to escape a life of grinding toil that he could not but wish to escape. And what are now the compensations of rurality? Only Arabella, whose work is to wash the innards of the newly slaughtered pig, and whose attractions take their force from brutal humour, coarse sensuality, and a rooted tradition of deceit.

III

This discussion of the later novels has not, of course, said all that there is to say about them. It has virtually ignored Hardy's rich, intimate contact with the rural tradition in every book before *Jude*, and also his profound dependence upon, and loyalty to, its characteristic virtues. These matters have often been discussed elsewhere. It remains true that in these later works the essence of plot, the distinctive trajectory of the narrative, is the steadily developed decline of a protagonist who incarnates the older order, and whose decline is linked, more and more clearly, with an inner misdirection, an inner weakness.

Two of the novels invite a closer examination, if we wish to see how this movement of decline lies at the centre of unity and meaning: these are *The Mayor of Casterbridge* and *Tess of the D'Urbervilles. Jude the Obscure* clearly has another kind of concern; and *The Woodlanders*, surprisingly enough, proves largely to have it as well. Indeed, there is a sense in which this novel has a much looser organization than the other late ones. Deep and powerful as its awareness of rural life undoubtedly is (one cannot keep from mind, for example, the picture of Giles at the cider-press spattered all over with his apples and their juice), yet much at the centre of this work pursues another concern. Grace's response to Fitzpiers' infidelity, and the gradual rebirth of her affection for him, are not Wessex products. The novel resolves itself by amiably decanting these two characters into the middle-class urban life of the Midlands. The psychological change that we see in Grace is barely connected with Hardy's rural interests; and that, I think, is why the whole episode of their reconciliation is treated with a lightness and even something of a gentle half-ironical detachment, that distinguishes the book clearly from *Tess*. At one point Hardy brings the difference out starkly through a metaphor. This is when Grace, running swiftly through the wood to meet Fitzpiers, just misses the man-trap (which is in itself, by the way, another scrap of evidence for the view that Hardy was beginning to dwell on the harsher side of country life). Her destiny is to evade, though barely, the issues of life in their brutal sharpness. All the man-trap does is whisk her skirt off: in Hardy's making this the occasion of her being reconciled to Fitzpiers we are to see, I think, that the whole sequence is meant to have something slight about it. Tess turns back to Angel, as she labours at the rushes in the snow-laden barn; as she comes to grasp her case, and Angel's, in terms of the plainest, the essential relations between women and men as human animals. We are in a different world, a world that has not skipped over the man-trap. It is *The Mayor of Casterbridge* and *Tess* that warrant further questioning.

IV

The word 'theme', now the most hackneyed of clichés in criticism, is also one of its bugbears. An essay, a philosophical discourse, even a collection of different pieces, or a mixture of short stories and essays, all these may equally well have a single theme. The word has no necessary connexion even with imaginative literature, let alone with the narrative forms of it; and is therefore a standing temptation to the critic to overlook the whole narrative dimension of what he studies. But it is usually this narrative trajectory which makes a novel a novel and which makes any particular novel the novel which it is. Only within the context of this central and determining force can the real significance of detail (incident, imagery, metaphor, local contrast) be grasped at all. To connect, say, Giles Winterbourne's meeting with Grace while he holds up his apple tree in the market-place merely with 'the theme of rural fertility', or Marty South's selling her hair with 'the commercial theme', would be grotesquely uninformative. The significance of both these incidents, prominently placed at the outset of the narrative, is that the two characters are made to carry out, at the start, ritual gestures by which they formally (though unwittingly) surrender their essential strength. The reader has it pointed out to him, through a symbol, that he is to watch what overtakes characters who put off their birthright. The fatal act (symbolically) would be meaningless if it did not come first: and its nemesis follows in orderly sequence.

A tree embodies not only Giles' essential strength, but also that of Marty's father. In an aberration from his proper rural life, he wants it cut down. When this is done, he dies. As for Marty's hair, Hardy invests this with almost talismanic virtue. While Felice wears it as her own, her luck prospers. Towards the end of the book, her secret comes out. At once she loses her power over Fitzpiers, and almost immediately after she meets her death. Similarly with the contrast between how Grace meets Winterbourne (under his flowering apple tree—but he hands it to someone else, and walks away with her—) and how she first meets Fitzpiers (he has bought the right to dissect her old nurse's body after she is dead, and Grace goes to buy it back). These meetings are no mere specimens of a theme, but exact pointers to a narrative movement; they come at the start of a relationship, show what its significance is, show what it will bring if it is pursued. For Grace to progress with one is to pursue the forces of life, with the other to pursue those of death. Similarly with the incident where Marty helps Giles to plant the young trees (Chapter 8). This does not merely take up the theme of rural order. It exactly indicates how Marty is Giles' proper strength and counterpart. His trees will flourish if he chooses her to help. Its point is driven fully home only by what follows it: that the very next thing he does is to give up the tree-planting with her (but she finishes alone) and turn for his help elsewhere. These details have significance within a frame created by the basic narrative movement of the book; and as this basic movement takes its shape out of them, it reciprocally determines what meaning they shall have.

'From beginning to end, Henchard's course is downward—whenever his older way of life meets the new, it is defeated.' This narrative movement is what embodies Hardy's deepest interests, and the essence of his moral insight, in *The Mayor of Casterbridge*. But there is more to be said about the exact nature of the struggle, and the downward movement, as he envisages it; and it is at this point that such matters as incident and imagery can take their proper and proportionate place in our awareness of the whole work. For it seems that Hardy has employed a single basic metaphor through which to embody the war between Farfrae and Henchard. Local incidents and metaphors have their allotted place within it; and in spite of the recurrent suggestion that Henchard (like Old Hamlet) is 'a *man*, take him for all in all', the basic metaphor through which Hardy sees the struggle between Farfrae and him, is that of a struggle between a man and an animal. This begins with the animal in possession of its territory. Henchard arrived on the scene during, as it were, the pre-history of the book. Now he is in occupation at Casterbridge. Farfrae is passing through on his way to emigrate. But as the novel pursues its course, Farfrae takes possession of the terrain. It is now his rival who thinks to emigrate. Instead he is persuaded to live in his own old home, now occupied by Farfrae; and like an animal, he becomes domesticated. 'Henchard had become in a measure *broken in*, he came to work daily on the home premises like the rest.' Later he is likened to a 'netted lion', or to a lion whose fangs have been drawn. When he describes how Farfrae (now mayor, as he himself once was) forced him away during the royal visit, he says 'How angry he looked. He drove me back *as if I were a bull breaking fence . . .*'

Several other incidents in the book sustain this metaphor. Henchard and Farfrae fighting in the corn store is, in a sense, animal against man: it is poignantly like the earlier fight in the barn between Henchard and the bull. The parallel extends even to Farfrae's wrenching Henchard's arm 'causing him sharp pain, as could be seen from the twitching of his face', and Henchard when he 'wrenched the animal's head as if he would snap it off . . . the premeditated human contrivance of the nose-ring was too cunning for impulsive brute force, and the creature flinched'. Finally Henchard crawls away like a wounded beast to die in an empty hovel that is more like an animal's lair than a place for a man. His final instructions for how he is to be buried are not appropriate for *felo-de-se*: they are appropriate for the burial of an animal.

Henchard's character, moreover, is that of a beast; in the true, not the townee, sense of that word. His immense natural energy, his simplicity, his having no skill of any kind save that of hay-cutting, and his liability to enslavement above all through a disabling, yearning, dog-like need for human affection, all these features of his nature are tellingly relevant. Henchard is not, of course, *simply* an animal. Far from it. At no point does metaphor become literal truth. But it is through this metaphor that we must see the struggle which constitutes the narrative and the unity of the book, and which predominantly defines its significance. Indeed, only awareness of this metaphor will bring out all the full issue between old and new, or the full, the frightening length to which Hardy pursues it. 'My furniture too! Surely he'll buy my body and soul likewise!' Henchard says at one point (one cannot but—though it is an unhappy touch—see the caged singing-bird which Henchard brings Elizabeth-Jane at the end as a wedding present, and which he leaves behind when he goes away to die, as linking with this idea of his giving up 'body and soul' together). Yet even this is insufficient to bring out the lengths to which Hardy pursues his central conflict. Henchard is more than enslaved, he is *tamed*. That is something more thorough-going. It is the measure of what Hardy sees as at issue. The work of his novel, focused in the metaphor of man and beast, is to depict and narrate the conquest and domestication of one way of life (the traditional way) by another.

V

Tess of the D'Urbervilles also has unity through a total movement, and the nature of this movement also may be grasped through a single metaphor. It is not the taming of an animal. Rather (at least at the start) it is the hunting of one. Several remarks and incidents in the book make this explicit, notably Tess's letter to her absent husband when he has deserted her ('I must cry to you in my trouble—I have no one else. If I break down by falling into some dreadful *snare*, my last error will be worse than my first.') So does the night she spends in the wood with the wounded pheasants: which of course brings powerfully back to the reader that earlier night in a wood, when she fell into the snare set for her by Alec. Throughout, Tess is harried from place to place at what seems like gradually increasing speed. Even the very start of her relation with Alec is relevant: 'the handsome, horsey young buck' drove up early in the morning in his gig to fetch her. At the end, it is especially clear. When the hunt is over, Tess is captured on the sacrificial stone at Stonehenge, the stone where once, like the hart at bay, the victim's throat was slit with the knife. With these things in mind, Hardy's much abused quotation from Aeschylus ('in Aeschylean phrase, the President of the Immortals had finished his *sport* with Tess') takes on a new meaning and aptness.

Yet Tess's career represents more than a hunt. What this is, can again be summed up in a metaphor; to which one is almost inadvertently led, if one attempts to summarize. That Hardy should have divided his book into 'phases' is itself, perhaps, an indication of the field in which his mind was partly working: the word was good nineteenth-century currency in history and natural history. 'Phase Three' is entitled 'The Rally'. Tess (after the death of her child) strikes out for new country. She leaves the snug and familiar environment of the 'Vale of the Little Dairies'; surmounts the challenge of barren Egdon Heath which lies across her path; and enters a new territory, the 'Vale of the Great Dairies', where life runs upon a basically different pattern. To this she almost completely adapts herself: so much so, that she finds a mate in Angel Clare, and almost succeeds in —there is only one word to use—in germinating. This word is less odd than it seems at first. Hardy lays great stress on the rich blossoming fertility of Tess's environment during this period, and also stresses, discreetly but with great force, her own richly sensuous nubility, her genuine bond, in the truest sense, with the milch cows and with the lush blossoms where the fruit is setting.

The rally fails. Tess has to abandon her favourable environment, and is forced on to a harsh upland soil where existence is more difficult. She now struggles not at the level of reproduction, but for mere survival. But, resistant, for a long time she does survive. Her strength is shaken when the Durbeyfield family is finally driven off the soil; and in the end, what Darwin called sexual selection begins to work against natural selection. Tess gives up the struggle. She is driven out of her natural habitat altogether, and goes to live, kept like a pet, with Alec in Saltbourne.

Here is the second, bigger metaphor, embracing the first, through which Hardy embodies his central fictional movement. The central train of events demands description in Darwinian terms: organism, environment, struggle, resistant adaptation, fertility, survival—and one more: Hardy has envisaged an individual life at the depth of, and to the length of, the ultimates for a species: establishment at one end, and at the other, extinction.

Many of the incidents in the book bring this total movement into focus. For example, Hardy provides the reader with an index to it by two scenes, one at the beginning and one at the end; one at Tess's highest point, one at her lowest. In the first, Angel looks back down the road and sees the village girls in white, dancing in springtime on the green: Tess, still almost totally united with them, stands by the hedge. In the other, he looks back, after what he thinks is their final parting, over bare open countryside and an empty road: 'and as he gazed a moving spot intruded on the white vacuity of his vision. It was a human figure running.' It is Tess, at the end of the change she has suffered, now totally alienated and isolated. Tess and her family take refuge in the family vault (Chapter 52). In terms of the hunt metaphor, they have been run to earth, and this parallels the sleep-walking scene (Chapter 37) when Angel lays Tess in the open tomb: within the larger movement there is a recurrent smaller sequence. Tess at the dairy says that 'our souls can go outside our bodies' if we 'lie on the grass at night and look straight up at some big bright star'. It is exactly what she does at the end of the book, on her fatal last night on Salisbury Plain. Meanwhile, Dairyman Crick was balancing his knife and fork together 'like the beginning of a gallows'. Most striking of all, Hardy re-invites us to register the total movement of Tess's career, in all its integration, by an ingenious and vivid résumé of it at the close of the story. He does this through the days that Tess and Angel spend together after Alec's death—partly a psychological fugue, partly a kind of total recall, partly both. Leaving Alec and sin behind her for a second time, she rejoins Angel, and the rich woodland of their first two days together is a match with the rich vale of the dairies. The empty manor house they sleep in matches the ancient house where their marriage was so nearly consummated before. Barren Salisbury Plain matches the uplands of Flintcomb-Ash. The scene at Stonehenge corresponds both to Tess in the vault, and to the moment when she hung on the wayside cross to rest, and looked like a sacrificial victim. Her whole tragic life is mirrored in little at its close. Everything possible has been done to make the reader conscious of that unified total movement in which meaning chiefly lies.

To notice things of this order is to realize, in effect, that Hardy's novels (like many others) need a special mode of reading. The incidents in them which strike us as improbable or strained or grotesque invite (this is not to say that they always deserve) the kind of response that we are accustomed to give, say, to the Dover Cliff scene in *Lear*. Admittedly, Hardy has local failures; but incidents like the Stonehenge one are intrinsically at one remove from the probable and the realistic. Almost, it is necessary for them to be unrealistic, in order that their other dimension of meaning, their relevance to the larger rhythms of the work, shall transpire. Again and again, it is those larger rhythms (as they form from local detail, and in doing so prescribe the meaning of that detail) which finally expand into the total movement of the novel; transmitting the author's sense of life, the forces that operate through it, the values that chart it out and make it what it is.

From what has so far been said, a new reason may perhaps be advanced as to why Hardy gave up fiction. It is both the strength (because of the integrity that it brought) and the limit of his achievement, to have seen the source of life-creating strength for human beings as connected always with a certain limited context, the traditional rural order. As time passed, he lost confidence in the strength of this order to resist and survive; and in part, even seems more and more to have regarded the element of drabness and harshness in rural life as not a product of change and modernity, but as something in that life which was ineradicably evil. This being so, he had no position to which to retreat. He does not seem ever to have viewed human nature as itself possessing an inexhaustible vitality and innate power to transform, from its own resources, its waste land into a fertile one. To say this is to notice a limitation in Hardy's power to offer inspiration; whether it is also to notice a limitation in his sense of truth is an open question. It is hard to be sure that the human species is unlike most others in that it does not wilt, out of its natural habitat and communal order. However that may be, by the middle 1890s, Hardy's course in fiction seems to have become one that he could neither retrace, nor pursue.

VIII

'TESS OF THE D'URBERVILLES'
AND
'THE AWKWARD AGE'

WHEN THESE TWO NOVELS are studied in conjunction, they cast light on each other; and when they have done this, the results cast light generally. That they have something in common is obvious. In his Preface, James wrote that *The Awkward Age* dealt with 'the account to be taken, in a free circle, of a new and innocent presence'. Hardy's sub-title runs, *A Pure Woman*. I am not, however, examining them together merely for this general similarity of theme. It is not as if I had chosen as theme, 'the Good Wife', and illustrated it by *To the Lighthouse* and Homer's *Odyssey*. *Tess* was published in 1891, *The Awkward Age* in 1899, and between them they document a whole period of English life.

James's 'free circle' of aristocratic finer essences, devoted, in 'an age of transition' to 'real' talk, and the 'play of mind', has strong roots in the upper-class life of the time. The upper class of this novel is metropolitan and cosmopolitan. There is a Duchess, but an Italian one. There is Mr Vanderbank, who works hard at his office all day (he is Deputy Chairman of something called the 'General Audit') and by this means is able to keep up his position in society. There is Lady Fanny, who is always on the point of 'bolting' with one of her lovers to 'one of the smaller Italian towns'. Finally there is Mr Mitchett, who is exceedingly rich, 'the son of a shoemaker and superlatively hideous'. There is no true aristocracy, but a plutocracy. The 'Awkward Age' is not just the time of life when a girl is more than a child and less than a woman. It is awkward for society as a whole. James is responding to his time, as we see it also, say, in Wilde's *An Ideal Husband*: paradoxically, the society of the notorious divorce cases of the late 1880s and the '90s, and of the Empire, Leicester Square. *Fin-de-siecle*, Edwardian plutocratic prosperity: its counterpart being Cecil Rhodes (the Jameson raid into the Transvaal occurred exactly mid-way between the publication of my two books), and the writings of Kipling. The Empire, Leicester Square was made possible by the Empire which is portrayed in *Kim*: this was published in 1901, when James was writing *The Wings of the Dove*, his next work after *The Awkward Age*.

If *Kim* represents one of the nether worlds beneath the glittering façade of *The Awkward Age*, *Tess of the D'Urbervilles* represents another: it is a picture of English rural life at a certain definite time, the great late-nineteenth-century rural depression which took two million acres out of cultivation, drove a million people from the farms to the towns, and went on until the war of 1939. Hardy's novel, that is, also grasps a whole society in a definite stage of its development. Indeed, the link between Hardy and James is closer still. American wealth was sending Americans (including James) across the Atlantic to avail themselves of European culture, just as it was sending American corn across the Atlantic to occupy the European markets; and it was just the arrival of the first cargoes of middle western corn, along the new railroad from the prairies to the Great Lakes, which brought about the English agricultural depression. The opening of that vital railway link, in fact, and the instantaneous slump in English farming which followed it, almost coincide with the first of Hardy's novels.

James and Hardy, then, are drawing upon and representing whole societies: one the city plutocracy, the other the impoverished countryside hidden behind it. But neither has presented his reader with a mere neutral slice of life; rather an interaction between the society he has chosen, and a certain distinctive human quality: the Pure Woman for Hardy, Innocence for James. One might try to express this by saying that the novels are concerned with what was 'representatively human'. But that word representative is dangerous. It certainly means nothing like 'average' or 'typical'. Admittedly, what James himself said might make one think it did. 'Half the attraction was in the current actuality of the thing; repeatedly, right and left, as I have said, one had seen such a drama', a drama that makes us ask, he adds, 'those questions that are of the essence of drama:—what will happen, who suffer, who not suffer? . . .'

This is from James's Preface. Yet he goes on there to say that the novel studies how this general situation of innocence intruding in the circle of free talk 'came *in a particular instance* to be dealt with'; and it is only when we come to see just how particular the particular instance *is*—how highly exceptional, in fact—that we fully locate what James has to say about innocence and the free circle. James takes his characters through a very special sequence of events.

The picture of the stylish, raffish circle that centres upon Mrs Brookenham and Vanderbank is not, to begin with, a quite neutral one. We see it, from the start, as it is scrutinized and silently deplored by someone from an earlier and more genuinely distinguished age: Mr Longdon. Next, we do not see the heroine, Mrs Brookenham's daughter Nanda, simply as an innocent girl about to be exposed to a world of decorous roués. The essential point is always sustained: it is, how astonishingly she resembles her grandmother, the supreme product of that earlier and better age; with whom, as a young man, Mr Longdon was vainly in love. The initial situation is odd enough in itself; and clearly it has remarkable potentialities.

They are remarkably developed. Young ladies often fail to marry the men they are very much in love with; but it is not often that, like Nanda, they try hard to avoid doing so, in order to leave these young men to their mothers. Again, Mr Longdon offers to make Vanderbank rich, if he will propose to Nanda. Vanderbank refuses: not because he has no love for Nanda, not because he has designs upon Mrs Brookenham. The explanation lies in the complete reversal of things, as between the beginning of the book and the end. Vanderbank at first seemed to comprehend the defects of his time; the upshot is that he cannot comprehend at all. It is he who is old-fashioned, out-of-date. He refuses Nanda because he sees her as simply one of his elegant but shabby set. So in one sense she is. She understands everything, however shabby it may be. What Vanderbank fails to see is that even so she is in essence still perfectly good and innocent, and that this kind of innocence is in his time the only possible kind. Nanda sees her mother's situation (the brilliant, gay, neglected wife in the last years of a wonderful prolonged youthfulness), she sees Vanderbank's too, and she takes a truly extraordinary course, so as not to hold them apart. What she does is to establish herself for good with the elderly Mr Longdon: her own grandmother's erstwhile suitor. Partly, what we see here is how a deep affinity of spirit can bring two people together even in a most extreme case. But we are meant to see also that Nanda's goodness and comprehension operating together are so great that she will accept a role which leads in the end to a full-scale tragedy. Earlier critics have already pointed this out.

The radical affinity between two very different kinds of innocence is very prominent at the end of *The Awkward Age*; but not at the end only. It comes all the way through: when, for example, Mr Longdon first invites Nanda to his country house— a place to which the febrile London world of the novel is quite alien; and when Nanda herself says midway through the book:

'I'm little by little changing him—gradually showing him that, as I couldn't possibly have been different . . . the only way is for him not to mind and to take me as I am.'

Mr Longdon's pursuit is not only of the face he remembers from his youth, but of an essential integrity which is shop-soiled only in appearance. That is confirmed finally on the last page; where James emphatically relates the particular story again to the whole society within which it has occurred:

She continued to explain; '. . . We can't help it . . . There's so much else that's *extraordinary* that if we're in it all so much *we* must naturally be . . .' She might have been, as she wound up, a very much *older* person than her friend. 'Everything's different from what it used to be.'

'Yes, everything,' he returned with an air of final indoctrination. 'That's what *he* ought to have recognized.'

'As *you* have?' . . . 'Oh, he's more old-fashioned than you.'

'Much more,' said Mr Longdon with a queer face.

Another transformation is 'little Aggie', the counterpart of Nanda. She is brought up in perfect innocence on what looks like the old pattern. James tips the reader off about her early on, but it is the whole movement of the narrative which makes it clear that her kind of innocence, what Milton called a barren excremental whiteness, is one of the dangerous, not one of the safe ways to grow up. All these things, by the way, are specimens of what critics sometimes call 'the theme of appearance and reality'; but this theme is treated in every narrative work where the end is substantially different from the beginning.

James was proud of the 'doing', as he called it, the sheer achievement of presentation, displayed in *The Awkward Age*. Certainly, several of the outstanding scenes move to their climax and resolution with the ordered inevitability of a ballet. In this connexion, perhaps the most interesting character is Vanderbank. He is unlike Nanda or Aggie or Mr Longdon in that while they really *change*, what we see in him is a kind of progressive *unfolding* of what has been there all the time. This is common in the serious novel, though I am not sure that critics have explicitly distinguished it. Vanderbank's true quality is more and more clearly revealed. At the start, he has the marks, admittedly, of the easy world to which he belongs. His speech is full of informalities, and his mind shows something that a strict judge could call vulgar. But he is so quick to detect his own faults, that we are almost persuaded he is sound. Then, bit by bit, he is exposed. At the end, in the section where he goes to tea with Nanda at last, he reaches almost the bottom of James's scale. He has casually neglected Nanda for months, but now at last he comes again, and is as adroit as ever. James's deep moral revulsion emerges in the intensity of the irony at this crowning phase of the book (the italics are mine):

Vanderbank had not been in the room ten seconds before he showed that he had arrived to be *kind*. 'I think it was most particularly nice of you' [to have sent the invitation]. 'The only thing that upset me a *little*,' he went on, 'was your saying that, before writing it, you had so hesitated and waited. I hope very much, you know, that you'll never do anything of that kind again. If you've ever the *slightest* desire to see me—for no matter what reason: if there's ever the *smallest* thing I can do for you, I promise you I shan't easily forgive you if you stand on ceremony.'

—What is this but the unkindest of all ways to talk to a girl who is in love with you? Then he notices that the old-fashioned Mr Longdon has sent Nanda the British Poets—in twenty-four volumes: not, for all that can be said in their favour, what she is most in want of. He says, 'Are you doing much in the British Poets? But where the deuce, you wonderful being, do you find *time* to read? *I* don't find any—it's too hideous—one relapses, in London, into illiteracy and barbarism. I have to keep a false glitter to hide . . . my rapidly increasing ignorance.' Those words barbarism, false glitter, ignorance, have (to speak with restraint) more than their face value.

Only once in their conversation did the reality emerge: a single 'speaking look' passes between them. The climax is Van's offer of a bargain: 'Show Mr Longdon, somehow or other, that I'm not a brute . . . In short,' the young man said, *quite flushed with the intensity of his thought*, 'let us have it that you may quite trust *me*, if you'll let me a little—just for my character as a gentleman—trust *you*.' Now at last the situation is clear: Van will be obliging enough to make love (or thereabouts) to Nanda's mother. The condition is that Nanda will square his reputation. As Mr Mitchett quietly but eloquently says, when his turn comes for tea, 'I look all round and see everyone squared and everyone but one or two suited'. Nanda's final burst of tears, 'a passion as sharp and brief as the flurry of a wild thing uncaged', is ferociously justified by the suppressed intensities of the scene.

Thus the narrative of *The Awkward Age* takes the characters to extremities; it shows human beings at a high tension of challenge and response and moral choice: grandeur, heroism, passion, even depravity, are words which have here a plain use. This narrative development, to a point of intense focus, is what organizes the human insight and the moral discrimination of the book, and is that through which alone James's ideals transpire.

Much else transpires also, of course: James's insight here was not merely into value alone, it was also into fact, into what men and women have it in them to do. It was human insight, in a wide sense, into the fabric of life; into how the high challenges and the high responses can evolve from the daily fabric, into the ruthless logic and integration which may show in that evolving. Into, in short, the potentialities of life itself, as these might be displayed with singular completeness in a single remarkable event.

Now turn to *Tess*. Once again: Hardy's moral interests in purity and in its opposites are embodied in his narrative, and embodied in it over its whole course. We simply do not see what discriminations he is making, unless for example we see the moral reserves on which Tess can draw, when once adversity settles on her; or how Angel's mother can begin by saying 'there are few things purer in nature than an unsullied country maid'; but at the end will say 'Don't, Angel, be so anxious about a mere child of the soil'. Nor does what is wrong with Alec D'Urberville come plainly out until he has developed from a rake, on through a hedge-preacher, back to a new kind of rake.

In fact, he ruins Tess because his is a nature for which the word 'steadfast' has lost its meaning, and everything in life is a scheme, an enterprise, a fad. But how this is so, and why it is so, are things mediated by nothing less than the whole narrative, which begins with Alec in his smart pillar-box of a nouveau-riche mansion, and ends with him in his smart disreputable sea-side lodging.

We are not, though, concerned with moral discriminations by themselves—rather with something which takes these in: with the book's whole grasp of life and of its potentialities. To see its full meaning from this point of view, we must again respond to the total curve of the narrative. Not at the level of a skilfully organized intrigue (here Hardy can be sadly deficient): but as registering a sequence which explores life to one of life's extremes; and which indicates, therefore, part of the limits within which life is lived.

The essential development of the book is easy to locate: Tess is at first deeply and fully set in the traditional and organic life of her rural society, and as the novel proceeds she is steadily driven out of it, until by the end of the work she is a complete outcast. In the essay on 'Hardy's Major Fiction' I argued this out in some detail, and suggested that Hardy's use of symbol and incident in *Tess* was such as to emphasize this movement both by sign-posting it and, as it were, by summing it up. Both *Tess* and *The Awkward Age* prove on examination to be works which have a closely organized narrative movement that is rich with meaning and strong for unity; and in each, the narrative develops an initial situation to a very extreme and special condition. The stress differs, certainly. In *Tess*, it is less on a moral extreme than on what I might call a human and emotional one. In *The Awkward Age*, there is still development to an extreme condition, but it is a moral extreme. Vanderbank turns out to be a genuinely depraved character, Nanda a truly heroic one, in spite of the almost unbrokenly decorous surface of their lives.

Fiction does not only take a narrative to great lengths. It also depicts in depth. Here, Hardy's novel seems to me much the greater. Tess the individual human, Tess as part of a social texture, Tess as ultimately an animal with an animal's task of maintaining life—Hardy sees all of these, they all enter into his account; but *The Awkward Age* constantly seems to invite awareness of what it then passes over in silence, or even positively excludes. It seems to give with one hand and deny with the other. For example, we read that Vanderbank gives out 'the sacred terror', a wonderful personal magnetism. So he must, if a girl like the heroine is to be in love with him; but we never see it. We are given to understand that his society is a plutocracy, its male characters have to engage in affairs, and to make money, and this is partly what coarsens them. Mr Brookenham is notoriously efficient, loves to talk about his job. We never see this either. And what *is* his job? 'Oh, Rivers and Lakes—an awfully good thing. He got it last year.' It's worth 'twelve hundred—and lots of allowances and boats and things. To do the work'. These are mere gestures, they will not do what James needs for his picture of a money society. Again, the scheme of values in the book depends upon our seeing the second heroine of it, little Aggie, as a specimen of foolishly naïve innocence at the start. This is how she shows it:

'O Nanda, she's my best friend after three or four others'.—'After so many?' Mr Longdon laughed. 'Don't you think that's rather a back seat as they say, for one's best?'—'A back seat?'—she wondered with a purity. 'If you don't understand,' said her companion, 'it serves me right, as your aunt didn't leave me with you to teach you the slang of the day.'

—'The slang?'—she again spotlessly speculated.

Little Aggie spotlessly speculates a third time: but there is no need to quote any further. This is good fun, but it is not 'felt life', in James's own wistful phrase. It is a gesture at life; a mere minimum preliminary to a moral discrimination. Take another case: Mrs Brookenham says that she was in love with Vanderbank, and obviously, her love is not like the love that her daughter has for this much-loved young man. What *is* it like then? We need vitally to apprehend it, because it is the kind of love, something sensuous and amorous, which runs through all the intrigues and liaisons of the world the novel depicts. Yet, here is James describing one of Mrs Brookenham's beautiful promiscuous cronies in her evening gown:

Tishy's figure showed the confidence of objects consecrated to publicity: bodily speaking a beautiful plant, it might have taken the last November gale to account for the completeness with which, in some quarters, she had shed her leaves. Her companions could only emphasize by the direction of their eyes the nature of the responsibility with which a spectator might have seen them saddled.

Turn back to Hardy. 'Having been asleep in her clothes, Tess was as warm as a sunned cat.' This physical side of Tess we have got to have, it is a real and significant part of the book, and Hardy gives it us here in a phrase. Mrs Grendon, no doubt, was not like a sunned cat. What was she like? Was she really like a tree in winter? Morally, perhaps. But physically? No. James's moral insight is communicated at the price of no communication over what the moral insight was insight into; and through a good deal of this novel, he seems to have too full a sense of the issues, the necessary moral discriminations; and too thin a sense of the life, the realities, between which those issues must lie.

In the last few paragraphs I have reached the details of James's book; and such things are not to be reached and assessed effectively, save through the major contour of a novel: where it starts the reader, where it takes him. The human significance of a fictional work is commonly based upon an exploration of life to one of life's extremes, and on the completeness of this exploration in its length and in its depth. This 'trajectory' of a narrative work is not merely relevant as plot, intrigue, entertainment: it is central to imaginative order. Any criticism which neglects it suffers from a major defect.

IX

WYNDHAM LEWIS
The Massacre and the Innocents

————————

I

'MODERN LITERATURE', as that expression is still often understood in Britain, may be a very fine thing, but about most of it
there is a radical disadvantage: it does not belong to ourselves,
it belongs to our fathers. The most remarkable work of Yeats,
Lawrence, Joyce, Pound, and (the *Quartets* aside) T. S. Eliot all
appeared within the space of little more than a decade, and we
are still, in a literary sense, reeling from it. Our whole critical
method and discipline is under its deep influence, for one thing:
for another, most people still think that it is these writers who are
modern literature. Yet this, by now, is out of the question. If no one
else can claim modernity instead, there is no such thing.

Critics have recently, and rightly, been stressing how rich and
contemporary a grasp D. H. Lawrence had upon the England
that he knew; but to read the much-praised Chapter XII of his
last novel, *Lady Chatterly's Lover* (1930), is to see that the answer
to his satirical 'England, my England! But which is *my* England?', is that it is an England of the past. Its rhubarb and lemon
in the greengrocers', its new big Primitive chapel, its criss-cross
of gentlemen's parks and railway sidings, horse carts and lorries,
new semi-detached villas and the occupants of them who poach
the rabbits, may still exist (so do the Roman earthworks): but

they belong to history. In fact, behind the total contrast in *attitude*, and behind some real differences of detail, there is a deep similarity between the Midland world of Lawrence and that landscape of factories, mineowners' residences, and artisans' dwellings which was enthused over by Disraeli. Here Joyce and Lawrence know similar worlds. In both there is a muddle in the drabness, the squalor is in decay, it is socially recessive, the author's world retains a certain shabby patina. It can accommodate, for example, the Christmas tree scene at the beginning of *Aaron's Rod*.

What distinguishes the mid-twentieth century is something with less patina and far less accommodatingness.

I am far from claiming that Wyndham Lewis does everything for 1957 that Lawrence could do, say, for 1927: but his is a case which makes one wish to apply to the *writer* something which Arnold said of the *critic*.

Judging is often spoken of as the critic's one business, and so in some sense it is; but the judgment which almost insensibly forms itself in a fair and clear mind, *along with fresh knowledge*, is the valuable one; and thus knowledge, and ever fresh knowledge, must be the critic's great concern for himself. And it is by communicating fresh knowledge, and letting his own judgment pass along with it—but insensibly, and in the second place, not the first . . . that the critic will generally do most good to his readers.

The basic value that novelist offers reader is fresh knowledge in the sense of massive or violent insight into a reality which is normally the reality of his time. Moral discriminations will no doubt be integral to this, but they will also be consequential, and often be subordinate.

Joyce, Lewis, Lawrence, and Eliot (and, I would add, Edwin Muir) were almost exact contemporaries; but, of the four, two died in middle age, and Lewis's work was crowned by decisive achievement, and settled into a crystallizing comprehensiveness, only late in his life. This is why it makes sense to see him as writing of our world, of the world a generation later than (save for Muir) the others. Even from the start he was the most clearly a man of this century, the most clearly unthinkable in any previous one. Why? Because for him alone the 1914–18 war, best symbol and also plain start for our time, proved a decisively fructifying experience. 'With me,' Lewis writes awkwardly but validly, in his autobiography *Blasting and Bombardiering* (1937), 'war and art have been mixed up from the start. It is still.' At the very beginning of that book, he speaks of the war as of people crossing a bridge.

The bridge is red, the people are red, the sky is red . . . upon one side of this bridge is quite a different landscape to what meets the eye upon the other side, as if the stream crossed by the bridge separated a tropic from a polar landscape.

A significant image: the red, and the polar landscapes recur in Lewis's mid-century cosmos. *Blasting and Bombardiering*, with the grim humour of its inhuman bombardments, and its lumbering chaos of mud, is incidentally one of the finest of British war books. Its author's response to the war, and the intensity of that response, show also in his painting: the devastated landscapes with their stern aimless gunners, the frozen frenzied violence of *Battery Position in a Wood* or *A Battery Shelled*, for example; or *War Scene No. 1*, with its forbidding city towers, another significant symbol, in the distance; or *The No. 2*, an ambitious water-colour dominated by a great arc of flaring yellow and the stooping demon-like figure of the gunner. Recently, these works were shown in a general exhibition of Lewis's art. Their seminal significance for his later painting, and his books, was inescapable.

Several of them appeared, with other works, in his first one-man show: *Guns*, 1919. The little-known catalogue to that exhibition deserves attention. Its twin points of reference are Van Gogh's terrifying picture of the prison yard—which Lewis saw as basically adequate to the experience of war—and Uccello's famous perspective battle-piece. But the latter 'does not borrow from the *fact* of war any emotion, any disturbing or dislocating violence, terror or compassion—any of the psychology that is proper to the events of war.' Lewis did. 'It is certain that the philosophy of the war, all the serious interpretation of it, has yet to be done.' One thing above all that he got from the war years shows up in *The Art of Being Ruled* (1926): 'I found myself in the blood bath of the Great War, and in that situation *reflected on the vanity of violence . . . that side of Sorel seems to me too literary*' (my italics). With that quiet, final judgement upon the extremism of the man of books, the key word comes out. *Violence*. The three dimensions within which Lewis has constructed his vision of contemporary life could be given, perhaps, three titles: *violence*, the *machine*, the *megapolis*.

<h1 style="text-align:center">II</h1>

These three things are the bases of Lewis's order; but how does he see them? Violence comes in Lawrence, sometimes with a powerful and occasionally even with a disquieting charge of sexuality; it is not, though, among his decisive insights. When it comes in Hemingway, it is with heroic overtones that the author does not so much diagnose in the contemporary fabric, as desiderate. No one thinks that the violence in Lewis's pages, often sickeningly emphatic and detailed, has anything heroic about it; but the relation he sees between violence and sex is worth scrutiny. There is a beating-up, for example, in *The Revenge for Love* (Lewis's novel of leftism and the Spanish War in the 1930s) which would hit a biassed critic as clearly sexual: Jolly Jack Cruze, the fascistic blond dapper satyr, turns up on the scene just as the Stalinist Percy Hardcaster and Jill the upper-class join-the-masses Communist (Jolly Jack has his eye on her) have had a squabble. Jack capitalizes the occasion with vicious thoroughness. At first, the sex link is clear: 'Old Jack's fighting glands were all in good order, thank you . . . chance had delivered his worst sex-foe into his clutches. The interest of all his glands was engaged in this transaction.' And when the first blow falls, ' "Well done!" called out Gillian . . . "He's got what was coming to him." ' But as Jack's brutality swiftly mounts, the experience somersaults. Violence *expels* sex. The scene is one of fright, disgust, embarrassment, and routine hospital squalor. ' "Here, fetch a taxi—don't stand there picking your teeth" ', is Jill's (and Jack's) response to the scene: its end is a trolley disappearing into an operating theatre.

Take with it the scene in Lewis's first important work, *Tarr* (1917): Kreisler rapes Bertha Lunken, and Lewis unobtrusively but clearly indicates that (as the plot requires) the rape is complete. Once again, there is the sudden eruption of the kind of violence we so unjustly call 'brutal'; but once again, violence makes short work of sex. To the reader it is as if a surgical operation were being forcibly performed—with a mechanical insistence related to the relative powers of muscular contraction and the physiological functions of the protagonists. To say that nothing could be less erotic is an under-statement: few things could be more anti-erotic. A drawing of 1912 satirically entitled *Courtship* (Victoria and Albert Museum, London) snaps up the same point: brutal suddenness, greed, machine-like energy. A detached contemplation, focused upon suddenness and ferocity quite at the expense of eroticism, is clear also in the account of the woman thrown to demons in *Malign Fiesta* (1955); but I am coming back to this.

Lewis is interested in violence for its suddenness, unpredictability, thoroughness, and squalor: the meaningless twist of events in 'The Bishop's Fool' (a short story in *Rotting Hill*, 1951) that in a few seconds has a country parson scuffling on the ground and ignominiously kicked in the genitals; the lethal fight in *The Red Priest* (1956). Clearest of all is the fight in the Canadian hotel lounge which is fulcrum in *Self Condemned* (1951) and which breaks up the 'private world of joy' that two wartime English expatriates had been creating for themselves.

'We have had our baptism of fire, have we not, in the violent life of this hotel? It is an astonishingly violent place, but *no more violent than the world* of which it is so perfect a microcosm.'

That italicized phrase locates the target: violence is no meaningless device for enlivening a story, but a permanent, imminent and deeply significant hazard of life. There is no element of relish. Even a phrase like 'horrified fascination' would be misleading. What violence evokes in Lewis is the horror it justifies in the timid man (the urbanized intellectual whose very existence it unremittingly threatens); and at the same time the cold, intent, and comprehensive regard of the courageous man. For those who can sense the controlled fury with which Lewis writes of Kreisler or Cruze, or the compassionate but decisive judgement passed on the Red Priest by the novel of that name taken in its entirety, this cannot be in doubt.

The reaction seems to me to be validly and valuably of our

time: most of us being in fact urbanized intellectuals who live nevertheless in (to use Plato's phrase) a city where any thing can happen to any man. Once or twice, Lewis seems to me to pay a price for this contemporaneity: the price of turning his record from literature into journalism, of seeing his material as a mere discrete fact about a certain few years, rather than as one focusable form of enduring human reality. This is true of the juvenile gang warfare at the beginning of *The Red Priest*; but it is exceptional. Normally violence undergoes a deep integration into his total awareness of life. One way of seeing that for Lewis it is usually more than a mere post-war freak is to notice the potentiality, the atmosphere of violence—the brutality, massiveness, intense emotion, callousness—throughout those fine early stories, *The Wild Body*. These appeared in 1927, but seem to derive from Lewis's experiences abroad during the 1900s. They are set in traditional rural France and Spain; they show *homo ferox* in a world whose survival into the twentieth century is a mere accident. 'A world of sodden mammoths', Lewis called it at one point. The same awareness, deep and general, shows in Lewis's pre-war art: *Figure Composition* (1912–14), for example, with its burly nudes in their greedy dance, or *Man and Woman* or *Kermesse*, with their stocky aggressive dwarfs. The experience of the war was a focus rather than a true genesis for him.

III

Lewis sees violence as a result of the mechanical in life. Kreisler not only rapes Bertha; he pursues the prim little Russian refugee Soltyk from café to café, slapping his face as publicly as he can each time, in order to provoke a duel; he conducts the duel (or rather caricature of a duel) with the obsessed rancour of a malignant puppet; finally he departs upon a motiveless and suicidal fugue, drawn as if by gravitation to the homeland that has repudiated him. Lewis's comment much later (*Rude Assignment*, the second autobiography, 1950) was, 'Kreisler is a *machine*, aloof and violent'. So, too, the boxing-champion draft-dodger who beats up René in *Self Condemned*: 'a crouched, medium-sized figure was dancing in front of him. There was no angry face—there was hardly any face at all. *It was an engine rather than a man.*' Man is *homo ferox* because he is *l'homme machine*, and (if one may somersault one's metaphors) the hand of the machine may be traced in all he does.

Does this sense of the mechanical in life go back to what is as boring as any other extreme, some kind of old-fashioned materialism? Not as Lewis employs it: the analogy is too free-hand and flexible to invoke that desiccating affinity. The link (and this is a mark of his modernity) is rather with a mathematician like Norbert Wiener, who traces servo-mechanisms in the human body, but as counterpart to this, analyses mechanical processes by mathematics that make them seem half human. Two widely separated quotations, taken as pointers merely, may clinch the matter. One is from *The Caliph's Design*, an important early pamphlet on art and especially architecture which calls upon artists to seek a genuine mastery of 'the machine as a new mode of being'. The relevant passage runs:

Life, simply, however vivid and tangible, is far too material to be anything but a mechanism, and the seagull is not far removed from the hydroplane . . . every living form is a *miraculous mechanism*. [My italics.]

The other passage is from *The Art of Being Ruled*: it must be read in the light of this remark about the seagull:

Men are tigers, wasps and wolves, or parrots, sheep, geese and asses, or the humdrum monkey, rather than men.

The mechanical may be the modern, but it is also the animal; and it is also the primitive. This is where Lewis's opposition in *Paleface* to Lawrence's primitivism has its place. To take the Indian as ideal is not simply to prefer intuition to intelligence; it is to find a deceptively self-concealing outlet for a distinctive and wide-spread modern weakness. Lawrence's devotion to the peons is '. . . really an expression of the worst side of the Machine Age . . . Machine Age Man is effusive about them *because they are machines* like himself; and Mr L, at least, makes no pretence of admiring his savages because they are free . . . I would rather have the least man that *thinks*, than the average man that squats and drums and drums, with "sightless, soulless" eyes.' This distorts Lawrence, but for the moment that is not the issue: which is the range of reference that Lewis gives the mechanical. The breadth of that range shows again when, later in the book, he says that primitive and non-European art was dominated by mechanism, but then moves straight on to the rest of nature: 'the insect and plant worlds, much more than the animal world, have always carried their structure outside . . . and thrust it upon the eye. The insect world could be truly said to be a Machine world.' Finally, perhaps the fullest statement of all: an essay entitled 'Inferior Religions', an explanatory appendix to the short stories in *The Wild Body*:

The fascinating imbecility of the creaking men machines that some little restaurant or fishing boat works, was the original subject of these stories . . . The boat's tackle and dirty shell, or the hotel and its technique of hospitality, keeping the limbs of the men and women involved in a monotonous rhythm from morning till night . . . in case of a hotel or fishing boat, for instance, the complexity of the rhythmic scheme is so great that it passes as open and untrammelled life. *This subtle and wider mechanism merges, for the spectator, in the general variety of nature. Yet we have in most lives the spectacle of a pattern as circumscribed and complete as a theorem in Euclid.* [My italics.]

It is in this book too that Lewis writes of laughter as distinctively the human acting as machine. All in all, Lewis makes the central contemporary invention enlighten the whole range of life.

IV

This rich insight has, admittedly, its trivial manifestations: loathesome Melanie wooing loathesome Dannie in *The Apes of God*, 'the burglar of his electricity meantime got shocks from the handle of the machine'. It shows most significantly at the other extreme, though; when it does this, it can govern the path of a book from its beginning through to its end. But first, Lewis's apprehension of Megapolis. Here the reader encounters his modernity and contemporaneity in its starkest form.

What Lewis said about Kreisler bridged violence and mechanism. One of his most ambitious paintings, *The Surrender of Barcelona* (1936), now in the Tate Gallery in London, bridges both of these and Megapolis. What it shows is the ritual moment of entry into the surrendered town. There is no violence, save by implication: the shrivelled figure dangling from the gibbet bang in the centre of the canvas. But the burly, armoured warriors are automata, robots: when their visors are up, they have either no face at all, or a mere machine-like disc. Yet on the whole, humanity (or inhumanity) is subordinate to architecture; and this (save for one building in the extreme corner, which is faintly reminiscent of the Baptistery at Pisa) belongs to no medieval city. Its vast flat windowless walls, round towers, simple inhuman masses, smoke stacks (as they seem), and grim gaping casemates cannot be in anything but reinforced concrete. It is a Barcelona of the Maginot, the Siegfried line; insofar as it is a city, it is the megapolis of twentieth century war.

Megapolis shows early in Lewis's art (*New York*, 1914, for example; or his largest oil painting, *Revolution, c.* 1915—this was probably known also as *The Crowd*). Moreover, his fiction has always been essentially urban. But his later works deal not with urbanity, but monstrosity. 'This bush metropolis had the appearance of an English midland city, which had gone in for skyscrapers' (Momaco in Canada, *Self Condemned*). We know it only in its hotel corridors, in the noises that come through the wall, the hostile anonymity of the 'Beverage Room', the trivial vice of aimless nomads, the rooms and streets lit by artificial light (the exclusion of daylight in this part of the book is remarkably thorough); above all, in the unspeakable spiritual incarceration of the individual. One comparison will clinch the point. René's wife Hester commits suicide, she throws herself under a truck; it is in much the same way and even for something of the same reasons as Anna Karenina. Tolstoi recorded his scene directly, and his context for it was a lively railway platform, with children, cheerful young men, a rosy-faced coachman, lace on Anna's costume, a sinister little *peasant* working on the rails. In *Self Condemned*, René hears of his wife's suicide by a telephone call at a dinner party: there is a taxi caught in the street; a police officer at his table in a bare room; a bell and a glass of water to stop René vomiting; and the mortuary slab with its concentration camp *graffito* described with one touch of pity, and otherwise complete painterly exactitude.

Easily Lewis's most powerful account of the megalopolitan is in *The Childermass* (the massacre of the innocents), and its sequels making up *The Human Age*.[1] These books are not set in London or New York, but in the afterlife and the underworld. They take their reader into Limbo and Purgatory and on into Hades. Lewis was presumably unable to complete the final volume before he died: even so, the work constitutes his most ambitious and impressive record of the megalopolitan. But if it does so, it is by what is almost a poetic method: Lewis selects certain features of the real world, and intensifies them until they interlock with the compelling force of a trauma. In *The Childermass*, the megapolis of 'Third City' is always in view, but it is across the river. The quality of its life is only reflected in the interminable preliminaries to reaching it, the barren and forbidding fog-swept landscape with its gangs of (in effect) convicts who are violent if they can be; and above all in the central figure of the book, the Bailiff who is the Charon of this Lewisian Styx, and who switches to and fro between inexhaustible vulgar loquacity, uncompromising self-advertisement, and ruthless, aimless, Punch-and-Judy brutality. The work as a whole looks as if it owes a good deal to *The Castle* and to *Ulysses*; it is certainly too diffuse and sometimes too heavily gesticulated; but it displays an astonishing richness and fertility, and for 1927 (when it was published) a remarkable prescience.

It is important to notice the *depth* at which the essential impression in *The Human Age* is created. Angeltown, a kind of Frank Lloyd Wright garden city, appears briefly at the end of volume three, but in the present context it has little importance. Third City itself is a place of luxury hotels and service suites, banks and limitless credit, cafés and vast piazzas, aimless crowds in flashy ties or immaculate city suiting, public orators, crowds massacred by armed police, occasional attacks from outside with (seemingly) atomic weapons, and behind it all an interminable bureaucracy which becomes more and more suave and uncomprehending as the narrative penetrates closer and closer to its core. Matapolis in Hades has fewer windows and more patina, but in reality it is a concentration-camp city, full of police

---

[1] Volumes two and three of *The Human Age*, *Monstre Gai* and *Malign Fiesta*, were published in England by Methuen in 1955, and in the U.S. by Farrar, Straus and Cudahy in 1957. The final volume, *The Trial of Man*, was presumably unfinished at the time of Lewis's death.

guards and punishment cells and amiable inhabitants for whom the word 'humanity' is meaningless, save as reminder of the queer ease with which humans die under torture. But it is not the *properties*, as one might call them, of these cities which mainly create their significant record. Rather it is the way in which the narrative as a whole conveys the tone and rhythm of the megalopolitan world. Through the whole book move the two figures from earth, representing the two basic human types as Lewis sees them (in *The Art of Being Ruled* he borrowed Goethe's distinction between 'puppets' and 'natures' for this distinction, and it is one of each we see here). They move through the two cities at the aimless, decorous, dusty pace of modern leisure. They seek to comprehend, they seek a job which (until almost the very end) neither finds. It is through this pattern of interminable appointments and interviews and targetless disquiet, that Lewis essentially re-creates the mid-twentieth century world. As perhaps always when it is significant, insight is carried by the total narrative.

V

There is a counterpart in Lewis's work to this vision of the modern megapolis. This is the picture of a drab, denuded, under-cultivated countryside in, say, 'The Bishop's Fool': a story which in spite of its touches of polemic and journalism, develops a quite remarkable power. Needless to say, it offers an incomplete version of the contemporary reality in Britain, and in some ways it even fits the 1930s better than the present time. An early counterpart of it is the 'time-hallucination' scene in *The Childermass*, when a mirage of the faded cosiness of rural England, ploughman and rook and horse and hedge all harmlessly devoid of life, turns up as a momentary pocket in the red landscape of the Bailiff's Limbo. It is proper equivalent to the nightmare of the Big City.

Lewis, though, was no mere Jeremiah futilely declaiming against decay. He knew that decay means transmutation; and perhaps the most admirable thing about his whole achievement as a man was the seemingly intense effort of concentration which he brought to apprehend and register this transmutation; even to accept it, to adapt himself to it, in spite of clear and profound revulsion. What emerges above all from *The Art of Being Ruled* is the conviction of an imminent planetary change in human life so profound as essentially to be a transmutation in the biological sense. This is just what Lewis states of the central figure in *The Red Priest*: 'He is the last of a species (to which we all belong) and in him in travail—and there are none of us do not experience the travail too—is another species.' The source of the transformation is indicated as early as *The Caliph's Design*:—'the machine as a new mode of being'. *Paleface* clarifies the point, and performs the important service of clarifying how certain of Lewis's particular aversions seem to him (arbitrarily, I would for the most part concede) to be applications of the one general principle. 'As the White spirit shrinks, oppressed under its burden of war, business insecurity, blood-tax . . .' and whatever else results from the machine world which once annihilated the red man, but now is rounding upon its presumptuous white employer,—as that spirit shrinks, it regresses along certain lines of thought and attitude which simplify for it a cosmos too tense and complex to be received whole any longer. Back to nature (Lawrence's cult of the red man), back to childhood, back to female intuition. Two more of Lewis's bugbears, homosexuality and lesbianism, fit the same scheme: the machine-dominated personality turns to these, as it would turn to anything, in its galvanic search for what will sustain the sexual engine. *Time and Western Man* threads another strand into the total fabric. The modern preoccupation in writing with process, becoming, the stream of consciousness (Joyce and Gertrude Stein) was mistaken by its originators for a cult of the alive and organic: yet what it ultimately offered the reader was not the living movement of the rational consciousness, but a mind turned mechanical and automatic. All these exemplify modern man's 'will to live as a machine'. 'Our epoch finds its highest expression in dynamical puppets,' Lewis writes in *The Vulgar Streak*.

The discursive, polemical books are scrappy, prolix, tangential to their main arguments or even centrifugal from them, and, above all, written with a kind of smudging, fudging abundance of style which exhausts and bewilders and exasperates. But we must recognize the kind of problem and the kind of mind they present. What these books present is something like a metaphysical system: one compares Hegel, Kierkegaard, Bergson. All the many aspects of experience are made to turn one way, are made to reverberate to the one note which sounds throughout them. Often enough, no doubt, the assimilations are arbitrary; subject them to close scrutiny, they collapse. But the total vision has a power and an integration and above all a *relevance* which make it survive local fissures. In Lewis the links are not metaphysical, not created by logic; they are loosely empirical, itself a symptom of our time. Yet so far as total apprehension goes, the quality of system is there all the same. Negative, on the whole, in the earlier books ('Human nature has brought us to Ice Age conditions' in *Blasting and Bombardiering*), in the latest ones it constitutes the fullest confrontation of our own time and future which is known to me. 'We have been forcibly, violently reborn' (*Rotting Hill*). Particularly important in this connexion is the chapter called 'In Praise of Rootlessness' in *America and Cosmic Man* (1948):

. . . occasionally in the air [of America] one thinks that one detects something so far not met with; the electric intoxication of the air breathed by prisoners set free. The American air is conditioned by these immigrant multitudes, hollow with the great *ouf* with which they have turned their back upon the European world . . . *I ought perhaps to say that our America, at the opening of what has been called the 'atomic age' is not any longer across the seas. Instead, it is a time, not a place; namely, the cosmic era which lies beyond the ruin and disintegration of atomic war.* [My italics.]

Someone has really looked into the future, tried to catch its very feel, and come back to tell.

VI

The discursive works are often thought-provoking, it is true; yet one turns back with relief to the novels. Admittedly, they have their wooden patches; on the other hand, from time to time they are superbly taut and vivid and incisive. But the remarkable fact about Lewis's work is his capacity for what Arnold called *architectonic*. The insight drives deeper and deeper through the movement of a book's narrative. This power of Lewis's fiction to establish itself dynamically, as the total unity takes shape in sequence under the reader's eye, is strong enough to override the sometimes ill-digested discursive digressions, or the clumsy turns of dialogue. In his best novels—*The Revenge for Love, Self Condemned, The Human Age*—the distinctive sequential integrity of fiction is achieved, and local flaws barely impair the considered record that it conveys.

This movement is visible in *Tarr*, although that book is not, I think, truly successful. One by one the characters drop into the ritual act by which they assume their role and betray their essential puppetry. ('Tarr had witnessed, not himself at all, but another man snatched into his role.') Bertha poses for Kreisler, Kreisler strikes Soltyk, Tarr marries his discarded mistress because she is pregnant with Kreisler's child. In *Snooty Baronet* (a minor though remarkably clear and unified novel), the affairs of Kell-Imrie, the detached and superior *libertin* who tells the story and depicts himself as the only man with a rational intelligence, are taken just to the point where he is seen to have been the puppet of puppets: public opinion, he writes at the end, has it that 'I have become *unhinged* (that is the expression, as if I were a door)'. Vincent Penhale (*The Vulgar Streak*), seeming at first to be the gifted poor boy making good, the intelligence shrewdly at work among a set of mediocrities, emerges finally as having lived in a kind of automatic and disastrous somnambulism, blind to the humanity that uninsistently surrounded him. (Mr Hugh Kenner, by the way, has little ground for seeing Penhale as a part-portrait of the author.) *The Revenge for Love* and *Self Condemned* raise another important matter to be touched on in a moment. *The Human Age* cannot now be decisively assessed: but one may hazard a guess that the whole work would have recounted, in symbolic rather than allegoric form, Lewis's idea of the planetary transition from boom megapolis through nuclear cataclysm into 'my America, my new-found land', the era (if any) after the fusion.

Now for the total movement of narrative in *The Red Priest*. I should be extremely surprised if Lewis himself looked on this work as a trivial interim piece, which is what most of his English reviewers suggested. If he did, I should venture to think him mistaken. The novel makes it clear that the Red Priest himself, though his parish is in the West End and his wife from the English upper classes, is 'a man from one of the backward epochs of humanity', a 'Cromagnon'. Given the depth of the fissure over which Lewis sees humanity now poised, however, he is not so very backward. Even his name, 'Augustine Card', may point to his meaning: he gropes (I would claim no more than this) towards representing the whole phase of history between that Doctor who founded an era of Western Culture, and the precarious house of Cards which it now is. And surely, with his yearning to fuse Christianity and Communism, his intellectual curiosity that only leads on to disaster, his immense physical power that he cannot keep from senseless violence, his greed and love of display, his incapacity not to draw on capital and devour his inheritance,[1] his desire to justify himself and be a scapegoat all at once, surely with all these things he is a representative figure for the 'backward epoch' in which we ourselves have all been living. If so, what happens to him in the course of the story is what completes the meaning: of his own accord he destroys his London environment, plunges back into the frozen primitivism of the Canadian North-West, and meets his death in an obscure scuffle in an igloo. 'Human nature has brought us to ice-age conditions.' To complete the allegory, Augustine's posthumous son is born on the shores of a lake in Africa. Lewis does not commit himself. The son's name is Zero.

VII

Only now, I believe, is it time to revert to the passage from Arnold, and consider what Lewis offers as 'the judgment which almost insensibly forms itself . . . along with fresh knowledge'. In large part, Lewis's judgement upon modernity has emerged already, carried by the insight into our world which is the fresh knowledge his work offers. To diagnose his diagnosis is to reveal what he has taken his stand against. Yet something must be said about the positive values which transpire from his work. Too often, Lewis is taken simply as a champion of the intellect. That this attitude is present in his discursive writings is clear enough. But Lewis's fiction draws on more of his mind than his polemics;

[1] It is borrowed, in fact, from his wife; and is ultimately a windfall from Africa.

and it tells a different story. An early work like *Tarr* may not do so; and indeed, the picture in that book of the heroine's talent for discussing art in the intervals of showing off her legs, and the way in which she is offered as a womanly ideal, are radical failures. Lewis has gone a long way since then, though. *The Human Age* is perhaps a test case. Here Pullman, the central mortal character, is superbly subtle and intelligent; it is he, in fact, who repeatedly breaks through to a comprehension of the environment, and his human shrewdness stands in contrast to the rigid simplicity, the almost silly innocence, of the angelic nature. Yet as the narrative advances, we find more and more that this intelligence is what transpires in Pullman as damnable. Ultimately he out-devils the devil, becomes his Chief of Staff, teaches him how to corrupt even the fallen angels a little further. Yet there is a redeeming side to Pullman; and it is nothing other than his obscure but growing awareness of the evil of his intelligence, and growing desire to abandon its pretensions and ask simply for forgiveness.

To clinch this, one might take a scene in the book which seems to clinch the opposite. Driving with Pullman through the savage landscape of Hell, Satan throws a promiscuous French woman to be raped and then eaten alive by wild-animal devils. The seeming venom against sexuality might be taken as confirming Lewis's misogyny, his loathing of physical love. It confirms nothing of the kind:

> Pullman was trembling . . . the woman's denunciation of Sammael immediately before the climax had affected him in a way he had to be very careful not to reveal. His sympathy for the woman grew and subterraneously developed; . . . he started trembling as in response to horror, because of the violent conflict in his psyche. He was on the verge of an outburst. The woman, praying and crossing herself, was doing what he ought to have done.

What she had said to Satan, as she did this, was 'You believe you are a handsome man . . . Yours is a beast's head, and not a man's. You are an animal—not one of the high animals . . .' Pullman, on the other hand, seeking to extenuate a momentary touch of concern on his part, tells Satan that he has acquired the habits of the unintelligent, *though himself of the small intelligent minority.* It is this intelligence, the whole scene conveys, which brings it about that he can steel himself against the atrocity, and continue his drive as the devil's smooth and favoured visitor.

Self Condemned also springs its surprise. In the first third of the book, René poses as the superior man, the intelligence in a world of nitwits, and his wife seems silly, sexy, and slightly nasty. By the beginning of the Canadian section, one notices that Hester's frilly charm is less in evidence than her preventing care: it is she who refuses to be nostalgic or to give way. As time passes, it is she who sees that René is making the adaptation to New World life at the price of himself, and who remains a thin though authentic source of human feeling and spontaneity. Canada may be something she cannot adapt herself to ('I am much too old to change my way of thinking and feeling'). It may in the end crush her out in suicide. But she is the one who retains her integrity. René gets his established place in a New World university. What is he then? 'Only a half-crazed replica of his former self . . . a gutted shell or . . . an empty hangover of himself . . . a glacial shell of a man.' He, in fact, settles for a living death. Hester lives with a true if modest life. It is this same quality of gentleness and patience and simple true affection which emerges in Margot's feeling for Victor Stamp, the one valid attitude throughout the whole world of mechanical self-importance and rancour and greed of *The Revenge for Love*. What this superb novel seems to me to do is gradually to focus out, and then (in final tragic assertion) to *crush* out the one human attitude which the author can endorse with his whole mind. Here is his endorsement, and savage irony against the opposite, in the closing paragraph of the book:

But meanwhile a strained and hollow voice, part of a sham culture outfit, but tender and halting, as if dismayed at the sound of its own bitter words, was talking in his ears, in a reproachful singsong. It was denouncing him out of the past, where alone now it was able to articulate; it was singling him out as a man who led people into mortal danger, people who were dear beyond expression to the possessor of the passionate, the artificial, the unreal, yet penetrating, voice, and crying to him now to give back, she implored him, the young man, Absolom, whose life he had had in his keeping, and who had somehow, unaccountably, been lost, out of the world and out of Time! He saw a precipice. And the eyes in the mask of THE INJURED PARTY dilated in a spasm of astonished self-pity. And down the front of the mask rolled a sudden tear, which fell upon the dirty floor of the prison.

There is the same endorsement, at another level of achievement, in the tradition-rooted dignity and patience and unobtrusive affection represented by Victor's wife in *The Vulgar Streak*, or by Augustine's in *The Red Priest*. Perhaps also there is something similar in René's Canadian friends McKenzie and Trevelyan.

This side of Lewis is vitally relevant: it shows a compassion, even an affection, for humanity taken at its most simple and spontaneous and unassuming. It redeems his work from aridity and severity, and confirms it as an affirmation of mankind, even if (and is there no cogency in this?) a limited and chastened and saddened one. Some of Lewis's paintings (the lyrical portrait of Mrs Honeyman, for instance; and above all, several portraits, named or otherwise, of the artist's wife) go further; they convey a real sense of exhilaration, of beauty, of delight in the things of the world. But in his writing he lacks access to a rich fount of joyful awareness, of the raw material of regeneration, such as was in the main open to Lawrence. Yet this, precious though it is, cannot be thought essential to a writer. What is essential is what will sustain in the reader, in spite of satire or pessimism, a conviction that the work has grown from judgement and control, nor from total repudiation and blind rancour. Neither Lawrence nor Lewis succeeds here unfailingly: but both do so in the main; and while it is true that Lawrence can show an awareness of human potentiality far greater than Lewis's, it is also true that his repudiation of the contemporary scene can be more sweeping and exasperated. Besides this, he did not, I think, make the basic adjustment of which there are signs in some of Lewis's latest works. These, notably *America and Cosmic Man*, reveal a gusto,[1] a zeal for life, which drive Lewis towards seeing

[1] A little-known passage from the early *Caliph's Design* is relevant: 'simply for human life at all— . . . to increase gusto and the belief in that life—it is of the first importance that the senses should be directed into such channels, appealed to in such ways, that this state of mind of relish, fulness and exultation should obtain. . . . It is life at which you must aim . . . life, full life, is lived through the fancy, the senses, consciousness.' The general context, of course, is that of the visual arts.

the present as bringing a future which, though radically new, may yet bring its radical good.

I should be sorry to close this essay on Lewis by speaking only of the values to which his work testifies. Most important of all in his life's whole work is his insight into the case of twentieth century man; his unique vision of the watershed, or the abyss, of the present. Most important in his fiction is his capacity to transmit and to intensify both his insight and the judgement that passes insensibly with it, through the total unifying movement of narrative. His ideas were always developing, and his work always had to be exploratory of them. He strained his powers to the uttermost or beyond. He probably wrote too much too carelessly. There are enough bad patches and loose ends, it may be said, to prevent any of his books from being unreservedly a masterpiece. Yet there is no real doubt by now that Wyndham Lewis established himself as among the great writers of the century, and among (though not equal to) Yeats, Lawrence, Eliot, and the other geniuses born in the astonishing decade of the 1880s.

X

'TANK IN THE STALLS'
Notes on the 'School of Anger'

ANYONE IN BRITAIN who has anything to say about Angry Young Men had better say it quickly: the field is now trampled over so often, it is rapidly becoming contaminated. I must therefore snap up a passing reference in the London Letter of the current *Manchester Guardian Weekly* (July 4th, 1957), since this may be my last reputable chance. No one, by now, need be surprised to find passing references in the weeklies. The surprise would be not to. The trend seems to have begun with John Wain's *Hurry on Down* (1953); although the name is taken from an in essence quite irrelevant context, Leslie Paul's *Angry Young Man* (1951) which is about angry youth in politics, left-wingism, and unemployment during the 1930s. It is just accident that this originally political label is attached to the string now so often wrapped around Kingsley Amis's *Lucky Jim*, John Osborne's *Look Back in Anger*, George Scott's part-autobiography *Time and Place*, and the rest. Although the chief danger may be facile generalization, it is a nominal risk to say that these take less of a political stand than a stand against having any political stand. This, indeed, is explicitly the gist of Mr Amis's recent Fabian pamphlet. I hope in a moment to offer a hint as to why this attitude should have developed. The first thing to notice is how frequently these books and their authors are now made into a shuttle-cock by the press and the weeklies and in conversation. (The latest is a strip cartoon in the *Daily Mirror*.) The second, to trace if one can the curious way in which this interest in them has been limited.

'A new kind of "hero" ': (quotation marks multiply as mark of one's embarrassment). This is what one is now so often told has arrived. Since every event has a cause, it must be proper to ask what has brought him. K. W. Grandsen (*Twentieth Century*, March 1957) hints that he is the product of a generation of writers who are having it both ways, or nearly: trying to run with the establishment and hunt with the 'creative opposition' —enjoying both the sweets and the bitters of success. Geoffrey Gorer (*New Statesman*, May 4th) offers sociology: young men who pass through the present educational system of state school and grant-aided university (more like the sweeping steps of the British Museum than an educational 'ladder': and so it should be), marry into a higher class than they come from—'male hypergamy'—and get adopted into it. The price they pay is psychological strain which they or their representatives then put into plays or novels. Hence 'the new hero': tough, rude, clumsy, ill-dressed, ill-washed, an enemy of phoney 'culture' and phoney everything—and successful with that unexplained but decisive success which usually belongs to *Zeitgeist* figures.

I have not forgotten the *Manchester Guardian Weekly*; but why it justified re-opening this question must wait for a moment. There is no 'new kind of hero' at all. No one kind. This becomes clear as soon as the investigation turns to cases. There may be a simplification or a generalization to be made: this isn't it. The hero of *Lucky Jim* may be rude and ill-dressed; but all in all he is human and considerate in a world mainly of paper cut-outs, he gets the livelier job and the superior girl, and his clumsiness is the formidable kind: it is a true driving force, it arrives. Charles Lumley (*Hurry on Down*) ends with more money, but by chance, not by drive; at the end of the book 'he valued his niche simply because it gave him the means, through his new wealth, to put himself beyond the struggle'. The social aim is 'neutrality', opting out from a social war: 'his demands on life had grown smaller and smaller'. Jimmy Porter of *Look Back in Anger* ('Lucky Jimmy Porter' I have heard him called: there are no on-the-spot fines in Britain, but we need them for such bad and misleading jokes as that) isn't successful at all, doesn't want success, and couldn't but destroy it if he got it. No one, on the other hand, could be less of a rubber-boat-always-knocked-about-but-always-comes-up figure. Joe Lampton (in John Braine's *Room at the Top*) is remarkably competent and remarkably successful: but finds (or so we are told, for the end of the story is thin) that success, wealth, marriage up the ladder, prove a sham. Thomas Hinde's *Happy as Larry* seems relevant here. Larry Vincent too is just as much a hypergamist as Jimmy Porter. He and his wife also live in an attic flat. He too is always out of a job and into a pub. But he is totally ineffective instead of successful, a feeble-minded trouble-making intolerable saint instead of an over-bearing bully, and a Londoner instead of a Midlander or a Northerner. Kingsley Amis's second novel (*That Uncertain Feeling*) is perhaps a minor document in the case. Lewis, its hero, is somewhere between Jim Dixon and Joe Lampton. John Wain's *Living in the Present* seems not to be in the genre at all.

This is the merest sketch: but clearly, the differences between these characters are as clear as the similarities or clearer. Of course these books reflect contemporary social pressures and tensions. Of course one can see in them some of the social and psychological difficulties which confront successful risers in the educational system (and these were by no means many until the very recent past); or the spread of south-of-England subtopian amenities or pseudo-amenities to the industrial north (this I suspect to be one of our most important recent changes); or the garish drabness, rootlessness, and money-making cynicism which have been common (and their opposites have been common too) in post-war England. What does all this amount to? It amounts to a very simple fact, the simplicity of which we seem rather to have forgotten: various aspects of the total social spectrum have been turning up in novels. New ones have to turn up for the first time.

The *Manchester Guardian Weekly* was simply reporting that Siegfried Sassoon had been awarded the 1957 Queen's Medal for Poetry: 'today's angry young man is notoriously tomorrow's recipient of honours', it said. The completely casual reference is index of how familiar the idea has grown. 'Today' and

'tomorrow' were being used somewhat freely, since the reference
back was to Sassoon's savagely ironical war poems, the jolly
general who fraternized with the troops and 'did for them all
with his plan of campaign', or the silly audiences at shows:

> I'd like to see a tank come down the stalls
> Lurching to ragtime tunes, or 'Home Sweet Home',
> And there'd be no more jokes in music-halls
> To mock the riddled corpses round Bapaume.

The anger of Sassoon's war poems was not, of course, the kind
with which this note is concerned. Were there no earlier analogy
whatever to the situations and attitudes of Amis, Wain, Osborne, etc., then the problem might be other than it is and
harder than it is. By good luck, however, that earlier analogy is
ready to hand:

> Acting on Chitterlow's advice to have a bit of a freshener before
> returning to the Emporium, K— walked some way along the Leas
> and back, and then went down to a shop near the Harbour to get a
> cup of coffee. He found that extremely invigorating, and he went on
> up the High Street to face the inevitable terrors of the office. . . .
> After all, it was not an unmanly headache; he had been out all night,
> and he had been drinking, and his physical disorder was there to
> witness the fact . . . he pulled his spirits together, put his hat back
> from his pallid brow, thrust his hands into his trousers pockets, and
> adopted an altogether dissipated carriage . . . Just for a moment he
> was glad that his patch at the knee was, after all, visible, and that
> some, at least, of the mud on his clothes had refused to move at
> Chitterlow's brushing. What wouldn't they think he'd been up to?
> He passed them without speaking.

'K—' is not Kafka, it is *Kipps*. H. G. Wells in 1905 was already
busy with such topics as rising in the world, the petty Jack-in-
Office, phoney middle-class culture—Miss Walshingham and
her wood-carving class. *Mr Polly* (1910) had less education than
Jimmy Porter got from his white-tile university or Joe Lampton
from a correspondence course in a PW camp; but he still had
some. There are other resemblances. 'At first there were attempts
to bully him (Polly) on account of his refusal to consider face-
washing a diurnal duty, but two fights with the apprentices

next above him established a useful reputation for choler, and the presence of girl apprentices in the shop somehow raised his standard of cleanliness to a more acceptable level.' The futile, angry scene with which the book opens does not occur until Polly is thirty-seven; but it is like the opening scene of *Look Back in Anger* in that it too displays a cosmic disgust which is focused upon the speaker's squalid home life, and which is provoked by what, in 1905, was no bad shot at a psychological malaise:

> He suffered from *indigestion* now nearly every afternoon in his life, but as he lacked introspection he projected the associated discomfort upon the world.

Wells' dialogue dates, of course. 'Hole! . . . 'Ole! . . . Oh! *Beastly* silly Wheeze of a hole!' is not mid-century conversation and is not mid-century humour. What Jimmy Porter says is 'Let's pretend that we're human beings, that we're actually alive' (which is not mid-century humour either). Wells may be different (in ways not relevant at present, he is profoundly so), but Wells is what, in anger or oblivion doesn't matter, John Osborne is looking back to.

Nor Wells only. Given that we are concerned not with one unique thing, but with a related variety of things which have been getting into English novels in recent years; and given also that to trace a partial resemblance is not to claim a total identity, the parallels go further. *Jude the Obscure* is one:

> 'If that can be done,' said Jude, 'at college gates in the most religious and educational city in the world, what shall we say as to how far we've got?'
> 'Order,' said one of the policemen, who had been engaged with a comrade in opening the huge doors opposite the college. 'Keep yer tongue quiet, my man, while the procession passes.'
> . . . 'Well. *I'm an outsider* to the end of my days' (Jude) sighed after a while.

—or Bob Sawyer, sixty years earlier still, giving a party which included a young gentleman 'in a shirt emblazoned with pink anchors': certainly no happier than Larry about his landladies, and clearly looking in anger at them:

'That's her malevolence, that's her malevolence,' returned Mr Bob Sawyer, vehemently. 'She says that if I can afford to give a party I ought to be able to pay her counfounded "little bill".'

Perhaps there is no need to go back along this tightrope any further. The shifts and differences are of course great. The 1950s have their distinctive features. Some of them get into these novels. Others elsewhere. The essence of the matter is that these novels merely illustrate, in varied detail, local or transient forms of permanent social stresses in English life up and down the country; and that to do so has been a recurrent feature of the English novel. If the heroes have something new in common, they have something old in common too. If the plots centre on details of jobs, money, sex, and success, they centre on what the English novel centred on throughout the nineteenth century.

The surprise, in fact, is not that this should be so, but rather that readers should be surprised and intrigued when they find the details of obscure middle-class provincial life occupying the substance of what make a claim to be serious and ambitious novels (Amis and Wain have standing as poets, critics, and commentators in general upon the current cultural scene).

Why should work of this kind be a source of surprise and intrigue? I can only venture a very long shot at this, because to give the full answer would be to write the history of literature and of thought about it in Britain this century. But several things afford clues. Among them are Virginia Woolf's essay on 'Modern Fiction' (included in *The Common Reader*, 1925), with its attack on Wells and eulogy of Russian fiction. The counterpart of this is Amis's depreciation of Virginia Woolf in a recent issue of the weekly *Spectator*. The best clue to what has been going on, though, may possibly be John Wain's verse. On the surface, this is cool, self-depreciatory, ironical: it follows on from William Empson, and Wain has claimed more than once that he was the first to work the Empson line, as it were. In so far as this is so, it would have its relation to the poetic revolution of Eliot and Pound (largely, as everyone knows, on French models) and would continue their reaction against the English poetic tradition of the Romantics and the Nineteenth Century. Yet in

these characteristic lines from a poem characteristically entitled
Eighth Type of Ambiguity, is that really what one finds?—

> When love as germ invades the purple stream
> It splashes round the veins and multiplies
> Till objects of desire are what they seem;
>
> Then *all creation wears a chic disguise* . . .

'Chic' is an unkind and perhaps unnecessary word in my context, but the words I have italicized bear an illuminating relation to Wain's own verse. Take *Don't Let's Spoil It All*:

> She had to *leave him choking in his fear* . . .
> The lesson is that *dying hearts must die.*

Or take *Reasons for Not Writing Nature Poetry*. One can imagine
Pound, or conceivably Eliot, endorsing that subject. But treated
this way?—

> Content, without embellishment, to note
> How little beauty *bids the heart rejoice*,
> How little beauty *catches at the throat*.
> *Simply, I love this mountain and this bay*
> With love that I can *never speak* by rote . . .

This is exactly the reason against writing nature poetry which
would have least appealed to them. We know, however, where
to look for poetry which sees the cosmos essentially as fringe for
the ego, or which claims that there are thoughts (especially
about mountains and what goes with them) that lie too deep for
tears or words. It is not in the work of Eliot and Pound, it is in
what they reacted from.

My last port of call would be, with Virginia Woolf's praise for
the Russians and depreciation of Wells in mind, the well-known
letter of D. H. Lawrence (June 5th, 1914) in which he expresses
his new conception of personality as it concerns the novelist
('you mustn't look in my novel for the old stable *ego* of the
character'), and starts by saying that this is something he has
partly learnt from Marinetti. Everyone is agreed, I suppose,
that literature in England, in the two decades after 1910, received the biggest impact of avant-garde ideas, interests, and

techniques from the continent of Europe that it had had since the later seventeenth century. This relates not only to Pound and Eliot, but also to Joyce, to Lawrence ('I believe that, just as an audience was found in Russia for Tchekhov, so an audience might be found in England for some of my stuff': letter of February 1st, 1913), Yeats, and (one should have Bergson in mind besides the Russians) Virginia Woolf.

The present fact is that in Britain this great impulse has largely spent itself; just as the not altogether dissimilar impulse spent itself by the mid-eighteenth century. One could go even further, and say that rather as mid-eighteenth century writers were veering round towards Spenser's and our other early poetry, but at the same time were inclined to patronize these things, so there are writers today who disparage Romantic poets while standing far nearer to them than they think.

Here I revert to provincial young men who grow up, get grants and girls, and struggle to climb up in or out of the career stream. What John Wain's verse shows so clearly, his novels and those of the others show not much less so. The Great Continental Impact (we were in for it when two American college teachers got off their boats around 1910) is no longer the decisive force; and English writing, for good or ill, is reverting to some of its more indigenous traditions. In poetry the situation is complex by virtue partly of the fact that the continental, Symbolist influence was deeply and in large part rightly linked with a recovery of what had been forgotten in our own Elizabethan–Jacobean period. In the novel, we are reverting to our well-established nineteenth-century preoccupations: the detail of our provincial and local life; our elaborate and multiple gradations of money, influence or power; and what has perhaps always been intimately linked with these, our processes of sexual selection. To be surprised or especially intrigued by the Angry Young Man school (to speak in labels for a moment) is merely to take the admirable, but special and indeed esoteric fictional preoccupations of the last thirty years as not special, but normal; and to find the familiar unfamiliar when one sees it again after, in more than one sense, a Period.

That the Continental Injection has worn off seems to me to be a plain fact. True, the work I have been discussing makes one say that this is a major loss and very little gain with it. Whether that must always be the verdict remains to be seen. What may even now be added, though, is that the fully effective recovery of some of the indigenous resources of our literature, and at the same time the enrichment of them with at least something from the last forty years, is one of the major tasks now confronting the writer in Britain.

PART THREE

XI

MATTHEW ARNOLD
AND THE MODERN DILEMMA

IT HAS BEEN WIDELY THOUGHT (T. S. Eliot has done something to bring this about, and something to correct it) that Arnold
is superseded as a critic, superseded in his particular judgements
because his central insight into poetry was defective. If so, it is
unfortunate; for the defects, if they exist, remain uncorrected.
To say this is not to say that 'a criticism of life' adequately sum-
marizes what poetry is. But Arnold himself did not say so or
think so. Later critics have added their riders to the phrase;
Arnold added the same riders first. Perhaps two of the most distinctive tenets of modern criticism are that poetry is an imaginative fusion, and that it fuses not few but many elements into
a single complex with an organic unity. But consider two pairs
of quotations. First Eliot, in his essay on *The Metaphysical Poets*,
explaining the source of complexity in literature:

Our civilization comprehends great variety and complexity, and
this variety and complexity, playing upon a refined sensibility, must
produced various and complex results;

and then, in *Tradition and the Individual Talent*, describing how
this complex material is integrated:

It is not the 'greatness', the intensity, of the emotions, the components, but the intensity of the artistic process, the pressure, so to
speak, under which the fusion takes place, that counts.

Now Arnold giving his account of the same source and the same process:

> . . . our present age has around it a copious and complex present, and behind it a copious and complex past . . . [it] exhibits to the individual man who contemplates it the spectacle of a vast multitude of facts awaiting and inviting his comprehension.
>
> (*The Modern Element in Literature*)

So far, we might argue, Eliot's word 'sensibility' makes or at least hints at a point that Arnold's 'comprehension' misses. But this is how Arnold goes on:

> . . . it is to the poetical literature of an age that we must look, in general, for . . . the performance of a work which demands the most energetic and harmonious activity of all the powers of the human mind. Because that activity of the whole mind, that genius, as Johnson nobly describes it, 'without which judgement is cold and knowledge inert; that energy which collects, combines, amplifies, and animates', is in poetry at its highest stretch and in its most energetic exertion.

Perhaps intentionally and perhaps unintentionally, Eliot has exactly reproduced Arnold's style in the first of these passages, and in the second has used almost his very metaphors to describe the mark of the genuinely poetic synthesis. Moreover, what Arnold says here is no isolated oddity, but runs through the body of his work as the essential first point about poetry, though not the last. It is what lies behind the key phrase 'the imaginative reason' in *The Study of Celtic Literature*. It reappears in the essay on Maurice de Guérin: 'the grand power of poetry is its interpretative power; by which I mean, not a power of drawing out in black and white an explanation of the mystery of the universe, but the power of so dealing with things as to awaken in us a wonderfully full, new, and intimate sense of them'. Above all it comes out in Arnold's letters to Clough, to whom he wrote of 'a growing sense of a deficiency of the *beautiful* in your poems, and of this alone as being *poetical* as distinguished from rhetorical, devotional, or metaphysical'.[1] From the standpoint of poetry, he finds fault with 'trying to go into and to the bottom of an object (i.e. abstraction) instead of grouping *objects* (i.e. particulars)'.[2] Perhaps the clearest expres-

[1] *op. cit.* (ed. H. F. Lowry, 1932), p. 66.   [2] *ibid.*, p. 99.

sion of all is in a letter to his sister: 'more and more I feel bent against the modern English habit (too much encouraged by Wordsworth) of using poetry as a channel for thinking aloud, instead of making anything'.[1]

An alleged critic who missed this basic principle would have to be brushed aside as something other than a critic. Arnold deserves defence from the charge only because it has sometimes been directed at him. If Eliot was tilting at Arnold when he wrote (*Tradition and the Individual Talent*) 'how completely any semi-ethical criterion of "sublimity" misses the mark'—and one is a little inclined to suppose that he was—he tilted at an Arnold remade to measure. Yet that Eliot was not first with what is surely the bedrock of all sense in criticism does not detract from what he did in directing our attention to the poetry of the seventeenth century, and it does not excuse Arnold's silence about that period either; though better that than the 'Marvell's amatory poems are cold; probably he was passionless' of Arnold's contemporary Goldwin Smith.[2] There is no need, however, to rate a critic's sins of omission too high. If Arnold does not direct his insight into the nature of poetry where we should most like him to, he does explain, better than his successors, why having this nature makes poetry uniquely important.

Oddly enough, modern critics, if they do not treat this as self-evident or *de fide*, or do not simply paraphrase Arnold, tend to make his account dangerous by so explaining it as to create either or both of two false impressions. Of these the first is that poetry has value because it is a kind of compendious shorthand, packing an unusually large number of 'meanings' into a small compass, or 'integrating' an unusually numerous or finely differentiated set of 'responses'. The second is that although it makes a contribution to fuller or better living, this can be explained without reference to what it says, can be put in terms of therapeutics, of healing verbal massage—poetry, in a sense, being a soother, though of course a special one. Except along these erroneous lines, modern criticism has tended not to relate

---

[1] *Unpublished Letters*, ed. A. Whetridge (1923), p. 17.
[2] T. H. Ward's anthology, *The English Poets*, Vol. II, p. 383. It was to this collection that Arnold contributed his essays on 'The Study of Poetry', 'Gray' and 'Keats'.

its two basic truths: that literature can add something important to the general pattern of life, and that it is an imaginative, not intellectual, synthesis from complex material. Arnold, in the more polished and less technical language of his time, gives a simple but essential line of guidance. He avoids the first false impression because he is willing to talk about beauty, and can therefore emphasize those aspects of form which depend on a works' general contour, and are in a large part independent of its simplicity or complexity. And he avoids the second because he is willing, as modern critics and their readers usually are not, to make assertions about the parts of human personality and to make clear value-judgements about their respective importance.

Perhaps this is clearest in the essay called 'Literature and Science'. Arnold is attacking the exclusively scientific education: 'Those who are for giving to natural knowledge, as they call it, the chief place in the education of the majority of mankind, leave one important thing out of their account: the constitution of human nature . . . when we set ourselves to enumerate the powers which go to the building up of human life, and say that they are the power of conduct, the power of intellect and knowledge, the power of beauty, the power of social life and manners . . . this scheme, though drawn in rough and plain lines enough, and not pretending to scientific exactness, yet gives a fairly true representation of the matter. Human nature is built up by these powers; we have the need for them all.'[1] Literature, Arnold goes on to say, makes its contribution exactly because it is an organic unity, a fusion, that has this broader front of our personality as both its origin and its target. 'In other words, poetry is interpretative, both by having *natural magic* and by having moral profundity.' ('Maurice de Guérin'.) There is much to be said for this plain-language account, drawing attention, as Arnold himself says, to vital but simple truths that the scientist does not deny but easily forgets. For there has been a strong tendency in modern times to *arithmetize* criticism; to turn it, that is, into a science, concerned somehow only with quantities. This may be traced in recent attempts to define 'imagination', or to explain the difference between major and minor art, and elsewhere too; and one suspects that it is based

[1] *Works* (Macmillan's Edition, 1903), Vol. IV, pp. 330–1.

on ignorance of the distinctive use to which words like 'beauty', 'imagination', 'charm', 'power', and so forth, are put. For their distinctive use (of course they have others) is to draw attention to something that moves or excites or pleases us, when the reasons why it does so are obstinately obscure to us. We may be able to say a great deal; but exactly why, on a given occasion, the writer has not failed but succeeded, is something which we cannot wholly explain; and we shape our aesthetic vocabulary for exactly these occasions which resist complete elucidation. Consequently this is the field where measured, bold simplicity may help, but enthusiastic ratiocination is likely to do harm. No analysis may well be better than any; because there is a standing danger that analysis, sooner or later, may switch to what is perhaps best described as a false dimension.

Arnold himself, incidentally, had a clear insight into just this use of language. Some of his best remarks about it are in *Literature and Dogma*, where he suggested that those who are insensitive to poetry in particular are likely to be insensitive to language as a general means of expression, and to fall into error about it. He had in mind a certain perspective, a 'tact' as he called it, that can scarcely come at all if not from the discipline of letters; and once again, he was thinking of the wider contribution made by literature, and its quite new importance—even unique importance—in his own time. This idea of literature determined his idea of criticism: above all, he thought, it tells us where and how and in what measure literature makes its wider contribution. Arnold was meticulous in directing his own criticisms to this end, partly by assessing what was already well known, and partly by introducing his readers to what, though important, was relatively unfamiliar.

Critics today often forget this second task. They argue again and again over well-known ground, until readers weary of their esoteric squabbles. But exploration was a genuine and important part of Arnold's work. He did not watch the contemporary scene abroad hour by hour, and when he does write of Flaubert or Zola he may not be without insight; but he certainly omits what today one most wants to hear. Yet the whole body of his critical work, with its essays on French literature from Joubert to Eugénie de Guérin, on Heine, Spinoza, Marcus Aurelius,

Tolstoi, Homer, Welsh literature, and the Persian drama—all this displays that lively and genuine curiosity, that varied equipment, without which a critic cannot after all be taken very seriously. 'It is the critic's first duty—prior even to his duty of stigmatizing the bad—to welcome everything that is good'. ('Last Words' on translating Homer.) Can the modern reader help a nostalgic sigh? 'Criticism must not lose the occasion offered by Mme de Guérin's journal being the first time published . . . of *directing notice* once more to this religious and beautiful character'. An admirable consciousness of function! This can be traced too in a comment which shows his own sense of what was valuable in his first *Essays in Criticism*: 'In going through them I am struck by the admirable riches of human nature that are brought to light in the groups of persons they treat.'[1] Some of his observations in these more or less exploratory essays seem also to be very just: especially his opinion of Amiel, which is a bulls-eye, and (for its subtlety and sense of proportion) the difference he finds between the work of Eugénie and of Maurice de Guérin. All the time he remembers his informing purpose: literature contributes to something beyond itself, and the critic shows what the contribution is. He is struck not only by the riches of human nature brought to light, but also by the 'sort of unity that as a book to stimulate the better humanity in us the volume has'.

But introducing the new or familiar is not, after all, the critic's central task. The crucial operation, for Arnold, is to distinguish the major work from the minor, the merely entertaining. This controls what he does far more thoroughly than has always been realized. 'In poetry the distinction between excellent and inferior, sound and unsound or only half sound . . . is of paramount importance . . . because of the high destinies of poetry' ('The Study of Poetry'). The essay on Sainte-Beuve begins with a justification for writing about Saint-Beuve at all: he is within the charmed circle, he is 'first-rate', though only in the minor branch of the critic. In the major branches Homer, Shakespeare, Milton, Goethe, Tolstoi, even Heine qualify for greatness; Chaucer, Dryden, Pope, Gray, the English Romantics, in varying degrees and for various reasons, do not. Sooner

[1] Letter to his mother, January 21st, 1865.

or later, each time, Arnold answers his own central question. Even when he denies greatness to a man's work as a whole, he pursues the strand of greatness. Joubert was a little precious, a little short-winded; but his desire for insight, for *light*—that was as real as it could be. Amiel as a philosopher cannot really be taken seriously at all, but his flashes of literary insight are true gold. Or Coleridge—'how little of his poetry, or of his criticism, or of his philosophy, can we expect permanently to stand! But that which must stand of Coleridge is this: the stimulus of his continual effort . . . to get at and lay bare the real truth of his matter in hand'. Much that critics praise in Burns is really lightweight, but there is a vein of boisterous zest, and another of delicacy—they at least are genuine. Much of Byron, much of Keats is adolescent, but there was a sincerity, a hatred of cant in the one, and in the other an integrity and shrewdness, as well as a sense of beauty, that were unimpeachable.

Sometimes it seems important to Arnold to stress not the strand of greatness present, but the absence of such a strand: an absence of high seriousness in Chaucer, an absence of sensuous directness and strong emotion in Dryden and Pope, an absence of artistry and poetic sense in Clough. The same ultimate purpose underlies his use of single lines as touch-stones: they test whether the poem 'belongs to the class of the truly excellent' ('The Study of Poetry'). And it underlies his historical interest in literature: 'to ascertain the master current in the literature of an epoch, and to distinguish this from all minor currents, is one of the critic's highest functions'. If he denied *porro unum est necessarium* in ethics, he came near to asserting it in criticism. This is what sometimes led to a schoolmasterish touch—and may also excuse it.

In claiming something for Arnold's approach and method, one is scarcely obliged to defend his detailed conclusions. But as some modern critics have turned Arnold into an Aunt Sally— or father figure—the situation invites this kind of irrelevancy. He has been attacked for 'what a set!', said of Shelley. What he wrote was 'What a set! What a world! is the exclamation that breaks from us as we come to an end of this history of "the occurrences of Shelley's private life" ', and he was arguing that Dowden's newly-published biography, so far from serving, defeated its author's pious ends. If we prefer, we can choose instead Eliot's 'sometimes almost a blackguard'[1]—there is, at all events, nothing exclamatory about that. As for Dryden and Pope, Arnold did not refer to them except in passing. Undeniably, he is insensitive to some of their qualities; but does not 'classics of our prose' elliptically make a point (though very elliptically) that in the end must be made, if we are to compare these poets with Marvell, say, or Vaughan or Wyatt? Arnold himself diagnosed this method of distorting a brief passing comment that is really dependent for its meaning on its context: 'terms are detached and employed . . . not in the fluid and connected way . . . for which words are really meant, but in an isolated, fixed, mechanical way, as if they were talismans'.[2] And when Arnold asserted that the quality of high seriousness was lacking in Chaucer, he was in the main (not, to be sure, entirely) right; though his belief that this quality was essential to great poetry is another matter. Perhaps his worst mistake, underrating the *Chanson de Roland*, has received little comment.

Modern criticism, if it rejects Arnold's opinion that the critic is essentially a winnower, separating wheat and chaff, tends to run in a quite contrary direction. It holds instead that criticism is sensitive and sympathetic interpretation, and that selecting among what is actually good is a kind of impoverishment. To think this the staple of criticism is to make one of two assumptions: that there is no hierarchy within what is good, or that that hierarchy is so easily and familiarly known to all that it need not be insisted upon. The point is less that the first assumption is false, as that unfortunately the second is false too; and that because of this the criticism of sympathetic interpretation is unduly optimistic. It is criticism for readers in Heaven. Yet Arnold shows one of the qualities of mind most his own in refusing to be a winnower-critic and nothing more. He explores, interprets, sympathizes, within a fairly wide range of qualities; and within what is mediocre he finds it worth while to identify even a slender strand of the really good. The titles of his essays prove this by themselves; and *A Persian Passion Play* reveals most clearly, perhaps, how much pleasure he takes in giving an account of

[1] *The Use of Poetry and the Use of Criticism* (1933), p. 89.
[2] 'Culture and Anarchy' (*Works*, Vol. VI, p. 151).

what he is quite sure is minor art. Gently but firmly, he insists that this is not Sophocles: perhaps it is rather like the sacred play at Oberammergau, he adds. Then, even so, he writes one of his most sensitive and sympathetic essays. Criticism, for him, includes several quite different activities, though among them there is an order of importance; the idea that to do one of them well you must abandon the rest would have seemed to him a crotchet.

There is a further aspect of Arnold's concern for the contribution of literature. It had better not be mentioned today without first recalling how he knew that literature integrates its material uniquely, and stands in contrast to religion or metaphysics. Having said this, however, Arnold adds something that by now is out of fashion: he adds that the importance of poetry is also determined by what it says. 'More and more mankind will discover that we have to turn to poetry to interpret life for us, to console us, to sustain us' ('The Study of Poetry'). Minor art may, like the *Scholar Gipsy*, fill us with melancholy, but it will not animate:[1] or like Horace's

> Damna tamen celeres reparant coelestia lunae:
> Nos, ubi decidimus . . .

be 'exquisite—but . . . not interpretative and fortifying' ('The Modern Element in Literature'). These two words are not idly associated. Arnold clearly believes that when literature really interprets, when it reveals the governing truths of life, it fortifies necessarily; it brings 'that noble serenity which always accompanies true insight' (*ibid.*). Whether noble serenity does indeed always accompany true insight may well be questioned; but what is important for the moment is simply the stress which Arnold puts here on literature as *having* insights to convey; and those, it is clear, being not trivial but profound and central ones. Some modern critics overlook the fact that when they make truth—or significance of truth—irrelevant to poetic merit they are not discovering anything: they are creating the truth of what they say by an illuminating, perhaps salutary, but distinctively strict use of the work 'poetic'. This may be legitimate, but they have still (or others have) to distinguish, in some other terms,

[1] *Letters to Clough*, ed. Lowry, p. 146.

the poetry that affords us central insight from the poetry that
does not. Anxiety to insist that poetry is not prose has tempted
us to forget that it is, after all, language. Its aspirations (if it has
any) to the condition of music are unrealized. The attempt to
assess it *fully* in abstraction from what it says is another attempt
to evaluate without making value judgements; it tempts us today because we handle values uneasily. Arnold is perfectly clear
that no work of literature can be fully assessed save by reference,
in part, to the insights into life which are to be found in it, as
well as to the organization which these receive, because literature is art. He makes both demands. In the end no one, unless
confused either by timidity or by language, can do anything
else.

I mentioned that Arnold thought the wider contributions of
literature particularly important in his own time. He thought
this because he was convinced that religion (which in previous
ages had provided the wider pattern) was doomed before the
advance of the scientific temper; while science alone could provide no pattern that would be complete. Hence literature had
the brunt to bear by itself. But also—perhaps inconsistently with
this—he attempted to show that Christianity could be understood, and was indeed properly to be understood, in a way
which made it accord with science. This part of Arnold's work
contains some of his most interesting ideas, and because it has
been first attacked, then misrepresented, and then neglected, it
needs attention. Arnold wishes to purge Christianity of what
there is in it that is unprovable. He begins his argument by
drawing on his sense for language, arguing that the conventional theologian's reading of scripture is too rigid and—odd as
it may sound—materialistic. What he does is comparable with
what a child does when he thinks that abstract qualities are real
people. Arnold claims that the Bible is like, not the child, but
the adult, who knows an abstraction for what it is. The Bible
sees God as not a real person, but an 'Eternal Influence':[1]

the stream of tendency by which all things strive to fulfil the law of
their being, and which, in as much as our idea of real welfare resolves itself into this fulfilment of the law of one's being, man rightly

[1] 'Literature and Dogma' (*Works*, VII, p. 200).

deems the fountain of all goodness, and calls by the worthiest and most solemn name he can, which is . . . God.[1]

By the time of Christ, Arnold goes on, the Jews had lost their genuine religious intuition. They had lapsed into a crude super-stition (or 'Aberglaube') of nationalist success. Christ attempted to lead them back by means of three things: a *method* of inward self-examination; a *secret* of self-renunciation; and a *mood* of 'sweet reasonableness' or ἐπιείκεια. Christianity is the true re-ligion because it takes us immeasurably further than any other.

Eliot's comments on these suggestions of Arnold's have exer-cised more influence than they deserve. 'The books about Christianity . . . their aim is to affirm that the emotions of Christianity can and must be preserved without the belief . . . the effect of Arnold's religious campaign is to divorce religion from thought'.[2] Arnold gives an account of his aim, but it is not Eliot's account:

our one object is to save the revelation in the Bible from being made solidary, as our Comtist friends say, with miracles; from being at-tended to or held cheap just in proportion as miracles are attended to or held cheap. In like manner, nay far more, our object is not . . . to pick holes in the apostles and reporters of Jesus. But much which they say cannot stand; our one object is to hinder people from mak-ing Jesus solidary with this.   ('Literature and Dogma', p. 250)

So much for the negative part of Arnold's endeavour, the divorcing process. There was also a positive part. He would have denied wanting to preserve the emotions of Christianity without 'the belief'. But what, one may ask, is essentially 'the belief'? Arnold thought that the theological or mystical dogmas which had so far been its usual form would in the future simply not *be* beliefs. An age trained in science would let them go: it would refuse to take unverifiable dogma seriously. Yet the emo-tions associated with Christianity were the source of good con-duct, and therefore the main source of good life. There was one hope, and one only. Could the power of Christianity to in-fluence conduct be rooted—as rooted somewhere it must be—not in *Aberglaube*, but in something provable? Arnold thought that it could:

---

[1] 'St Paul and Protestantism' (*Works*, IX, p. 9).
[2] In Eliot's essay on *Arnold and Pater*.

If . . . they ask: 'How are we to verify that there rules an enduring
Power, not ourselves, which makes for righteousness?' we may answer . . . 'How? *by experience!* . . . You can try it . . . disbelieve it,
and you will find out your mistake' . . . But they may go and say:
'Why, however, even if there *is* . . . should we study the Bible . . .
will not other books do as well?' And here again the answer is
'. . . there is infinitely more of him there, he is plainer and easier
come at, incomparably more impressive' . . . and here again it is
experience we invoke: *try it!* . . . take a course of the Bible first, and
then a course of Benjamin Franklin, Horace Greeley, Jeremy Bentham, and Mr Herbert Spencer'.   (*ibid.*, pp. 325–6)

Arnold does not, as Professor Trilling suggests,[1] want apo-
deictic certainty of God. 'We get a much firmer, nay an impreg-
nable, ground for the Bible', he goes on, 'if we put the construction on it that we propose.' But that it is the right construction
must be proved by 'the same test which we have employed
throughout . . . reason and experience', by which, as the context shows, he means reason *from* experience. Our interpretation must come from a trained sense of how mankind always
uses language when trying to express such truths as the Bible
expresses: 'a tact which letters, surely, alone can give'.

Arnold's discussion of language outside the field of the sciences
was remarkably acute. The basic error, he argued, was to treat
expressions of 'common discourse' or 'eloquence and poetry' as
if they had the fixed and rigid significance of terms in science:

The word 'God' is used . . . as . . . an idea about which everyone
was agreed, and from which we might proceed to argue and to make
inferences with . . . certainty. . . . But, in truth, the word 'God' is
used in most cases as by no means a term of . . . exact knowledge,
but a term of poetry and eloquence, a term *thrown* out so to speak,
at a not fully grasped object of the speaker's consciousness, a *literary*
term, in short.   (*ibid.*, pp. 12–14)

Under certain circumstances, this is the natural and best kind
of language. 'If the object be one not fully to be grasped, and
one to inspire emotion, the language of figure and feeling will
satisfy us better about it, will cover more of what we seek to express, than the language of literal fact and science. The lan-

[1] Matthew Arnold (1939), p. 358.

guage of science about it will be *below* what we feel to be the truth.'

Arnold's religious views can easily be attacked. We could argue that whether intrinsically sound or not, they had nothing to do with the Bible. We could argue with a good chance but not certainty of success, that he is unduly optimistic about the empirical evidence. We might perhaps argue that even if true, what he said was trivial because its influence could not be enduring. But Eliot's assertion that it could not endure seems to be based on a failure to detect what Arnold thought might make it endure; and if it is a question of who is divorcing religion from thought, we might very well select not Arnold but his accuser. For when we read 'The religious habits of the race are still very strong, in all places, at all times, and for all people' ('The Humanism of Irving Babbitt': 1927), can we avoid being reminded of some of Eliot's own most telling and influential phrases? Can we avoid the suspicion that a *dissociation of sensibility has set in*, whereby there are certain experiences which Eliot himself is not able to *devour?*—that no one could credit such a view who had not *thought and felt by fits?* that, in short, for once, Eliot had *ruminated?* Whose *sense of fact* (these are all Eliot's phrases) are we to trust?—that of Eliot?—or that of Arnold, who in 1865 wrote: 'Heaven forbid that the English nation . . . should remain as it is. If it does it will be beaten by America on its own line, and by continental countries on the European line.'[1]

Arnold, after all, made clear who was to read his work and who was not.

The reader whom the present work has in view is not the man still striving to be content with the received theology. With him we do not seek to meddle . . . it is meant for those who, won by the modern spirit to habits of intellectual seriousness, cannot receive what sets those habits at nought . . . but who have stood near enough to the Christian religion to feel the attraction which a thing so very great . . . cannot but exercise.[2]

By now one may doubt whether we have not moved too far for Arnold's attempt to have much contemporary impact; but

[1] Letter to Miss Arnold, May 14th, 1865.
[2] 'God and the Bible' (*Works*, VIII, p. xxxiv).

there is no doubt that he saw a profound need of his time, and was brave enough to set about solving it in not a backward-looking but a forward-looking way. At the present day, we turn wistfully sometimes to the Elizabethan World Picture or beyond, and wish we had something which we really know we do not want. Arnold touched on the Elizabethan synthesis in 'The Modern Element in Literature'. He compares the *History* of Thucydides with Raleigh's *History of the World,* and simply points out that (at least as regards cosmology) Raleigh 'wanders helplessly and without a clue'. Thucydides's phrase 'the charm of the uncritical half-fabulous narratives of earlier writers' would make a good summary of Raleigh's merits and demerits; whereas Thucydides' critical, scientific sense still has a contemporary note, and can still genuinely instruct us.

Perhaps, indeed, this willingness to speak out, and with decision, is the best thing in Arnold. We see it when he gives his interpretation of Christianity, when he declares his faith about the aspects of man's personality and their relative importance, and when he distinguishes major and minor literature and insists that what literature *says* helps to decide how good it is. He also has qualities without which this willingness might be troublesome. Of these, perhaps the most vital is a certain breadth of intellect, whereby he can see more things than one at a time, and make concessions generously or do justice to his opponents' case without impairing his own. He wants no nostrum. 'There is no *unum necessarium* or one thing needful, which can free human nature from the obligation to come to its best at all . . . points.'[1] Much of what has been said above illustrates this, and perhaps the major part of his work either argues for or exemplifies it. At his best, he gives us the sense of a strong, clear, calm intelligence that can be trusted to have in mind more than it is engaged for the moment in expressing, and that trusts itself to put secondary points firmly because its own grasp of the primary is firm once for all. 'The Function of Criticism at the Present Time' is, from beginning to end, a plea for this spirit.

This quality is not easily to be separated from another that is less one of intellect than temperament: that urbanity, that amenity of thought and style for which he is so widely known.

[1] 'Culture and Anarchy' (*Works,* VI, p. 148).

'The critic of poetry should have the finest tact, the nicest moderation, the most free, flexible and elastic spirit imaginable' were his words.[1] But Arnold has an important essay—the well-known 'Literary Influence of Academies'—that shows conclusively how urbanity or poise of style is not a linguistic trick, but the inevitable consequence of, and only thing tolerable to, a genuine balance of mind. Many-sidedness can cohere with urbanity only through a basic integrity of outlook. Towards the end of *Culture and Anarchy* Arnold brings these qualities together when he speaks of 'our best self, which is not manifold, and vulgar and unstable, contentious, and ever-varying, but one, and noble, and secure, and peaceful'; and the dignity of this ideal pervades the whole of his work.

At the present time, literature and criticism are frequently called upon to make that wider contribution which Arnold thought it was their chief purpose to make or to indicate; and yet writers are to some extent in a dilemma, because there is also, at the same time, a strong tendency to make literature more sophisticated or *recherché*, and criticism more specialized. These tendencies spring partly from good; a particularly clear understanding of what distinguishes literature as an art having the characteristic technique of an art; and partly from bad, in that there would be no demand for the wider contribution if we were not all somewhat embarrassed to give it.

We should consider whether Arnold's approach and temper do not offer us help.

[1] 'Last Words' on translating Homer (*Works*, V, p. 267).

XII

THE CRITICAL
INTIMIDATION

I

WHEN PHILOSOPHERS turn to criticism, critics sometimes give them a cool reception. They often deserve one. They hope, perhaps, and the critics fear, that by some ingenious line or argument they can turn the flank of what critics have been doing by themselves: in face of this, critics are both uneasy and sceptical. They are right to be sceptical. The discipline of one activity of thought may give useful or even illuminating hints to another; but, as in every discipline, the exact, the *exact* course of the right approach to art—rightly directed criticism in its full sense—can be learnt in approaching art and cannot be learnt in approaching anything else whatever. This for the simplest of all reasons: that art is, in Bishop Butler's well-known words (already borrowed by T. S. Eliot), 'what it is, and not another thing'.

Yet this truism seems to be the most elusive of all important critical truths—so that it not only eludes philosophers (which is excusable) but plenty of critics too. They cannot, as it were, believe their good fortune—that the only place to learn fully about what they do is where they do it, within the field of art. And philosophy can rarely do more to help criticism than free it from errors, or crudified truths, that perhaps in fear, it has allowed in from outside itself—errors deriving sometimes from philosophy, sometimes from science or psychology or even just the general climate of thought of the time.

The purpose of this essay is to locate, and confiscate, some of these borrowed mistakes. It may save some readers the trouble of going further, and help to retain those I should like to retain, if I emphasize that nothing will be done to transmogrify criticism by any philosopher's abracadabra, or suggest that something in the latest philosophy provides criticism with its first proper basis. There will be no parallel to Mr Wellek's breathtaking discovery that a poem is a system of systems of norms of intersubjective ideal concepts.[1] There will be nothing like this, because if recent developments in philosophy suggest anything about such formulations, they suggest that those who want to solve problems outside philosophy are not normally obliged to solve problems inside it first. For example, philosophers have discussed whether or not a chair is (somewhat like Mr Wellek's poem) really a system of systems of intersubjective hypothetical sense-data: but the question is not obligatory for those who wish to identify, say, Hepplewhite chairs, or handsome ones. Of course, it is possible that the principle of which this is an illustration may not be true after all; or perhaps it is possible that, though true, the literary work of art (especially if it is what Mr Wellek says) constitutes an exception to it. But there seems to be something more urgent to do than find out.

II

It is now thirty years since criticism received a really large injection from philosophy, for it has not done so since Richards based the principles of literary criticism on (broadly speaking) the meaning of meaning. In fact, of course, what he did had its roots deep in the intellectual soil of the time: he was accommodating the study of literature to an outlook for which science was the dominant mode of intellectual activity. Art was being found a place in a world of Fact. Richards' varied and fertile mind led him in passing to say many striking things not always along this one line, but this clearly is the main line. Keats is a

[1] R. Wellek and A. Warren, *The Theory of Literature*, pp. 151–2, 157.

more *efficient* poet than Wilcox; states of mind are valuable as they reduce waste and frustration; art can be justified in serious terms because it is a stabilizer and organizer; above all, the very texture of literature (or at least poetry) tends to satisfy the scientific norm, though in a somewhat unexpected way; for its distinctive feature is to be a kind of encyclopaedic suggestive shorthand. It is not to 'appeal to the imagination' or any other special faculty, and not (like pseudo-statements) to evoke emotions; but essentially it is to be a complex though implicit texture of detail; of apparent fact, indeed, though this was odd enough, since Richards emphasized too that the statements which constituted poetry were falsehoods. Certainly, for Richards, the integration of this detail is what enables the poem to have its unique integrating and appeasing effect on the individual; but in the first place the difference between good integrations and bad ones is simply in the number of units that they integrate.

This account is extremely brief, but so it should be, for the ground is familiar. Perhaps less familiar, is the fact that when Richards met the objections to his view, he did not weaken but emphatically confirmed his allegiance to science as a norm. He took two further steps (in retrospect they were plainly gestures of desperation) to make that view adequate; and they are precisely the steps that J. S. Mill took seventy years before, when he was trying to rescue utilitarian ethics from the rigidly scientific model on which his father had formed it. Seeing how unlikely it was that anyone would think goodness identical with mere quantity of pleasure (whatever that is), Mill the younger explained that some pleasures were lower than others—pushpin, in spite of Bentham, being lower than poetry. Richards in his turn connected good art not simply with 'the fine ordering of responses', and the 'appeasement' or sense of 'reconciliation' that this brings, but with 'the level of organization' at which the appeasement or reconciliation takes place. In both cases equally, there is behind the first difference between good and bad a second difference, and it is this which is apparently decisive. Only apparently: behind the second difference there is in each case a third. Mill, challenged to prove his claim that poetry was 'higher' than pushpin, could only reply that those with equal acquaintance with each were all sure it was; and Richards, looking for something that could prove one integration more adequate than another, in the end had to say that those with adequate experience of both—Keats and Wilcox were his examples—could be relied on to choose the one we all know is right anyway.

All this happened thirty-five years ago; it has been modified by Richards himself; and its errors have by now been abundantly pointed out. There is no need to lose more time on it, provided that within the complexity of the theory and all its qualifications we hold to the central fact: that Richards, working through a philosophical theory about statements and value-judgements, and a speculative-psychology theory about comprehension, was finding a place for poetry in a scheme of things where science was the norm. This shows itself in at least three ways. First, it shows in Richards' conviction that literature is not to be judged by the *statement* it makes—by the truth of what it says. Probably it says nothing; if it does say something, that is probably false; and since true statement is the prerogative of science, criticism must have no concern with it. Second, it shows in his unconcern for the ethical views and judgements sometimes implicit in literature (pseudo-statements to Richards) and in his denial of any aesthetic sense—for to assert such a sense is one way (though a naïve one) of justifying direct judgements of value in art and these, for Richards, are also pseudo-statements. Last, and above all, it shows in what he tried to provide as the proper method of criticism: a poem, for example, being rather like a scientific specimen, the complex structure of which needs to be laid bare, and a critic requiring the detachment, fine discrimination, patience, persistence, and sharp cutting-edge of a biologist—with the underlying suggestion that *that is all*. For under this progressive dissection, the good poem turns out to have a delicate and subtle organization, and the bad one to have, not another kind of organization, but no organization whatever. Evaluation need not take place. Analysis veritably disintegrates the bad; the good is proved good by standing up to it.

III

Now comes the crucial point. This same bias towards a scientific norm of statement and method shows very widely in modern criticism; and it shows, moreover, not just in the work of critics like Richards who were avowed sympathizers with the scientific outlook, but also, more insidiously, in critics of a kind exactly opposite. In particular, it shows in T. S. Eliot's early essays, although these were written well before *The Meaning of Meaning*, and although Eliot soon came to disagree wholeheartedly with Richards. This is a not often stressed aspect of the poet and critic who has done more than anyone else to diagnose what literature and society have lost through the encroachments of the narrowly scientific mind; and clearly it was never a dominant aspect. But when Eliot wrote 'In matters of great importance the critic must not coerce, and he must not make judgements of worse or better. He must simply elucidate' (*The Perfect Critic*), one sees a clear though slight trace of the same attitude to value-judgements as Richards'. When in *The Function of Criticism* Eliot wrote 'the most important qualification which I have been able to find . . . is that a critic must have a very highly developed sense of fact', or 'interpretation . . . is only legitimate when it is not interpretation at all, but merely putting the reader in possession of facts which he would otherwise have missed', he was displaying how he also inclined to think of scientific statement as the norm. Finally, when in the first of these essays we discover 'the scientific mind . . . there is no other intelligence than this, and so far as artists and men of letters are intelligent (we may doubt whether the level of intelligence among men of letters is as high as among men of science) their intelligence is of this kind', there is no need to argue the point further.

Other critics, of course, have been far more inclined than Eliot to think that science has established a new norm of authenticity, and that this new norm has discredited criticism of the older kind and obliged the critic to come to terms. John Crowe Ransom's statement in the Preface to *The World's Body* (1938) is one illustration: referring to science, he asserts that we must find a poetry which does not deny 'what we in our strange

generation actually are: men who have aged in these pure intellectual disciplines, and cannot play innocent without feeling
very foolish'. Another is Herbert Read's homage to psychology:
it 'impinges directly on the province of the literary critic—raids
it and despoils it and leaves it a sorry desolation of unconscious
prejudices . . . in this situation the critic must retaliate, and
pick from the science of psychology his brightest weapons'.[1] But
Read's observation, though more outspoken, is incomparably
less significant than Eliot's. One is the overt act of allegiance
which has largely created Read's contribution to modern criticism; the other is an incidental concession to the opposing camp,
and it did not create, but runs counter to the main direction of
Eliot's achievement. For if anything is central to Eliot's earlier
criticism it is what he said was central, 'the problem of the integrity of poetry, with the repeated assertion that when we are
considering poetry we must consider it primarily as poetry and
not another thing'.[2] And of this attitude—from which modern
criticism has enormously benefited—conceding any sort of hege-
mony to science is a distortion.

IV

From the dominant side of Eliot's work, more than from anywhere else, has come the widespread contemporary grasp of
poetry as something that is significant by having the texture and
the structure of a distinctive thing and a thing of art. This insight—perhaps it is fair to call it a telling and emphatic restate-
ment of a perennial insight—has brought with it its own *method*
of coming to a full comprehension of particular poems: that
close, scrupulous attention to texts which is to be seen in the
'New Criticism' as practised in the United States by Allen Tate,
or John Crowe Ransom, or Cleanth Brooks. In the wider diffu-
sion of this method the influence of Richards, at least in Great
Britain, is far from negligible; which is a significant fact. It
means that this new method is not a homogeneous creation, but
has combined two radically opposed trends. It has combined
Eliot and Richards; or if you like it has drawn upon both the
science-influenced undercurrent, and the independent main

[1] Introduction to *Selected Essays*, 1938.
[2] Preface to the 1928 Edition of *The Sacred Wood*.

current in Eliot's work. Predominantly, it has come from a keener sense of what is distinctive of poetry, and of the fine contour of its organization of language. As far as this has been the impelling power, it has been nothing short of an illumination. But hidden away in that movement, though leading paradoxically to a very similar kind of detailed analysis, has been the quite opposite notion that scientific assertion is the norm, and that poetry is reputable at bottom because, in a quite peculiar and unexpected manner, it actually satisfies this norm—satisfies it by being (though cryptic) denser than prose, fuller than prose, with a subtle order of complexity that superficially departs from the kind of reality that science finds acceptable, but is really an example of it. These two quite opposed attitudes seem to have brought it about that modern criticism, and especially the 'New Criticism' of America, has often come much closer to its poetry, and occasionally been driven erratically from it.

It is not fanciful to see Eliot's celebrated essay, *Tradition and the Individual Talent* (1919), which did so much to inaugurate the whole movement, as an emblem of this two-sidedness. It is in this essay that Eliot described poetry as 'a concentration, and a new thing resulting from the concentration, of a very great number of experiences', and the hint for a new critical method is plain. It is here too that he rejected two of the common confusions about poetry, its being either a personal effusion of soul, or an undifferentiated loftiness: 'the poet has, not a "personality" to express, but a particular medium . . . in which impressions and experiences combine in peculiar and unexpected ways' . . . 'it is not the "greatness", the intensity, of the emotions, the components, but the intensity of the artistic process . . . that counts'. Yet in elucidating these impeccable statements, Eliot surely revealed how deeply all the time the norm of science had occupied his mind. The intensity of the artistic process is 'the *pressure*, so to speak, under which the fusion takes place'. Elsewhere chemistry, not metallurgy, supplies the metaphor. The poet is a catalyst; and his mind is a 'receptacle for seizing and storing up numberless feelings, phrases, images, which remain there until all the *particles* which can unite to form a new compound are present together' (my italics). The more these metaphors are thought of in the way that we have

learnt from Eliot to think about metaphors, the more they lead
the mind away from a sensitized idea of poetry as Eliot revealed
it, and towards a notion of something on the lines of an elaborate scientific construct, a tour-de-force linguistic protein molecule, of which we can come to an understanding by the mode of
attention of the scientist. And when so profound and urgent a
tension exists between the substance of an argument, and the
imagery that vivifies it, are we not justified, if not in suspecting
an uncertainty in the author's own mind, at least in looking for
a mixed and to some extent confused impact on his readers?
Yet here we have perhaps the most influential prose that Eliot
has ever written.

V

The present argument, then, is that the lineage of 'close reading' as a critical method is impure; deriving in part from a
keener sense of the distinctiveness of poetry, which was an asset;
and in part from excessive though perhaps half-conscious respect for science, which was a liability. The particular form that
this hindrance seems to have taken, is a notion that the un-
ravelling of complexity is the one and essential and characteristic form of close reading, and that therefore you cannot have
too much of it. The time has now come (and perhaps came some
while ago) to illustrate these disparaging generalities.

When in *Tension in Poetry* Professor Allen Tate writes 'the
meaning of poetry is in its "tension", the full organized body of
all the extension and intension we can find in it',[1] one senses,
perhaps, that this invitation to apparently unlimited ingenuity
might prove dangerous. It proves dangerous at once. For Professor Tate goes straight on in the same essay to discuss these
lines from Donne's *A Valediction, Forbidding Mourning*:

> Our two soules therefore, which are one,
> Though I must goe, endure not yet
> A breach, but an expansion
> Like gold to aiery thinnesse beate.

—and his comment runs: 'the interesting feature here is the
logical contradiction of embodying the unitary non-spatial soul

[1] *The Limits of Poetry*, p. 83.

in a spatial image: the malleable gold is a plane whose surface can always be extended mathematically by one-half towards infinity; the souls are this infinity. The finite image of the gold, in extension, logically contradicts the intensive meaning (infinity) which it conveys'. Surely it is fairly clear, on Professor Tate's own principles, that this has got somehow away from the poem; for *infinity* of extension is not at all what the beaten gold, once it is given exact and scrupulous attention, can convey either intensively or otherwise. And there is something in the poem—the 'aiery thinnesse' of the gold—that brings this point emphatically before the reader's mind; bringing also, one may add, through this very thinness, and this inability to be expanded indefinitely, its own very definite enrichment of meaning. It brings this enrichment through hinting at the fragility (for all that Donne overtly says to the contrary) of the lovers' separated existence; and the tenderness, like a gold-beater's delicate strokes, with which the speaker is bringing about this unavoidable separation. And perhaps it is in things like these, rather than in any logical contradiction, that the 'interesting feature' of the comparison resides. But for the present discussion what matters is what led Professor Tate to analyse these lines as he did; and it is difficult not to believe that it was because the image appeared to offer a structure of meaning as precise as any structure that a scientist finds in a molecule. 'Extended mathematically by one-half': this quasiscientific precision, one may suspect, intruded itself because it deceptively seemed just the kind of thing to find. And if this was so, it was because Professor Tate (of all people) momentarily allowed the analysis of poetry, as if by an enharmonic change, to revert to the analytic norm of science.

Consider a parallel example from an essay by Professor Cleanth Brooks. In *Irony as a Principle of Structure*[1] he examines Randall Jarrell's controlled and eloquent *Eighth Air Force*:

> If, in an odd angle of the hutment,
> A puppy laps the water from a can
> Of flowers, and the drunk sergeant shaving
> Whistles *O Paradiso!*—shall I say that man
> Is not as men have said: a wolf to man?

In *Literary Opinion in America,* ed. M. D. Zabel.

The other murderers troop in yawning;
Three of them play Pitch, one sleeps, and one
Lies counting missions, lies there sweating
Till even his heart beats: One; One; One.
O murderers! . . . Still this is how it's done:

This is a war . . . But since these play, before they die,
Like puppies with their puppy; since, a man,
I did as these have done, but did not die—

—and so on. The comment begins with stanza one:

These 'murderers', as the poet is casually to call the airmen in the next stanza, display a touching regard for the human values. How, then, can one say that man is a wolf to man, since these men 'play before they die, like puppies with their puppy'. But the casual presence of the puppy in the hutment allows us to take the stanza both ways, for the dog is a kind of tamed and domesticated wolf, and his presence may prove on the contrary that the hutment is the wolf-den. After all, the timber wolf plays with its puppies.

There is a basic and surely final objection to this as a model of critical method: that it means there is nothing the poet can definitely *not* say, definitely decline to say. His complexities are explored with a gusto and unreserve against which he cannot hope to exclude anything whatever from his poem, however much he might want. It is doubtless true that Randall Jarrell, if he had chosen, could aptly have explored how airmen playing with a pet puppy are like timber-wolves playing with their own puppies; but the fact is that his poem does not do this. At the particular point in it when he writes of playing with the puppy, he focuses attention on quite different aspects of his airmen— aspects no less necessary to the main trend of the poem, and not developed at all, *but denied*, by likening them to timber-wolves (unless of course a wolf is shown to be very different from the idea of a wolf, as this comes in the first stanza). He has, in fact, said that the airmen play 'like *puppies* with their puppy'; and, short of rewriting the whole poem just to frustrate this particular critic, it is hard to see how he could have done more to exclude the idea that they were like timber-wolves. Once again, it looks as if a certain kind of solution—in this case 'to take the stanza both ways'—as Professor Brooks says—seemed so much on the right lines that for a moment it took control.

But why, it may be asked, does this exemplify criticism distorted by a norm appropriated from science? Because the notion that there will always be some new complexity, some new hidden inter-relatedness of structure to discover, that certain methods of inquiry can be applied over and over again, and that if they yield anything, then what they yield is really there, is a characteristic of what science takes as its objects; while poems are entities of another kind, and (though they may contain more than their creators deliberately put into them) contain what the text offers and emphatically do not contain what it excludes. But the *cult* of complexity, the notion that a critic always adds to what we see in a poem, and never diminishes or restricts it, appears in criticism because the patterns of scientific thought surreptitiously extend themselves beyond science. It has, perhaps, some slight analogy with a card-game that goes by the homely name of *rummy*. The object of this game is to acquire cards so as to make various combinations with them; but for this purpose it is much easier to acquire the cards than to discard them once acquired; and the over-enthusiastic player usually collects with such gusto that he soon has far more than the state of the game will justify. What is required, both here and in criticism, is a principle—or a tact—that will equip one to collect just what it is proper to collect, and to leave exactly all the rest. And to return to Randall Jarrell's poem and Professor Brooks's analysis of it, one cannot help feeling that, as with the example taken above from Allen Tate, in the pursuit of an ingenious linkage the critic passed over a simple one. For Professor Brooks asked 'how, then, can one say that man is a wolf to man. . . .' Yet Randall Jarrell's uncertainty is about something tellingly different—'shall I say that man Is not *as men* have said: a wolf to man?'; and the irony in this self-discrediting judgement is exactly what Professor Brooks knows best how to elucidate, save when the foreign body in the body of his critical theory leads him off into doing something else.

VI

These tinkerings are trivial, unless they can be made to create a clear sense of the tact or principle that they seem to hint at.

But what is this tact or principle? Remembering all the time that it will be no ingenious importation from some other discipline, but must emerge from the practice and mis-practice of criticism itself, consider another of Professor Brooks's critical analyses: his account of Tennyson's poem 'Break, Break Break'[1] Here is the poem:

> Break, break, break,
>   One thy cold grey stones, O sea!
> And I would that my tongue could utter
>   The thoughts that arise in me.
>
> O well for the fisherman's boy,
>   That he shouts with his sister at play!
> O well for the sailor lad,
>   That he sings in his boat on the bay!
>
> And the stately ships go on
>   To their haven under the hill;
> But O for the touch of a vanish'd hand,
>   And the sound of a voice that is still!
>
> Break, break, break,
>   At the foot of thy crags, O Sea!
> But the tender grace of a day that is dead
>   Will never come back to me.

Professor Brooks compares this poem with Tennyson's lyric 'Tears, Idle Tears' in *The Princess* and claims, with justice, that the latter is the more interesting poem of the two. Yet it seems as if the more varied, complex, and paradoxical poem established itself at once in Professor Brooks's discussion as the poetic norm; and his preference for it is justified by comments on 'Break, Break, Break' which are strikingly and unexpectedly generic. That 'stately ships' is 'idle and finally irrelevant' is almost the only point of detail; the main comparison between the two poems, and depreciation of 'Break, Break, Break' is merely:

Memory in this poem does not become a kind of life. . . . The poet makes no attempt to connect this activity with its former 'actual' life . . . the elements of 'the tender grace of a day that is dead' remain

[1] In *The Well-Wrought Urn.*

175

frozen at the conventional prose level . . . we are not encouraged to take the poignance of his present memory of it as a ghost from the tomb. The poet does not recognize that his experience represents such an ironical resurrection nor does he allow the metaphors buried in 'dead' and 'come back' to suffer a resurrection into vigorous poetical life. Of course, the poet need not be concerned with them; I should agree that we have no right to demand that this poem should explore the nature of memory as 'Tears, Idle Tears' explores it. At moments, men are unaccountably saddened by scenes which are in themselves placid or even happy.[1] The poet is certainly entitled, if he chooses, to let it go at that. Yet it should be observed that in avoiding the psychological exploration of experience, the poet risks losing dramatic force.

The central point of criticism is clear. Both poems explore something, but 'Break, Break, Break', is much less alive, less vigorously searching in its conduct of the exploration. And three phrases in the passage quoted above—'his experience'; 'the nature of memory'; and 'the psychological exploration of experience' indicate what is being explored. But there is something about these which makes it easy to overlook an important point, for only the first really emphasizes that each poem explores not 'memory' in general, but some one concrete situation which the poem defines and specifies through its whole texture; and there is no doubt that in doing this defining, this specifying work, the two poems move, not in the same direction to different lengths, but (however far either goes) in quite different directions. 'Tears, Idle Tears' creates for the reader a situation arresting because it shows a memory rising paradoxically into a strange and moving vividness that almost surpasses waking life: small wonder if its texture of expression notably satisfies Professor Brooks's characteristic demands. But does not 'Break, Break, Break' define a situation where memory persistently refuses to spring into a paradoxical life?—a flat, a heart-rendingly *un*exceptional situation where the dead are not only dead, but cannot even be remembered except with a barren and frustrating inadequacy? And if so, is it not the least likely thing in the world that this poem, even if it contains *some* element of paradox

[1] It is virtually certain that in its context this sentence refers to 'Break, Break, Break'; though surely it would fit 'Tears, Idle Tears' more closely still.

and double meaning, should be *as* ingeniously paradoxical, *as* intellectually elaborate, as the other? To doubt this is to take complexity as the essence of poetry, not as (at most) its method; and this, once again, is to supplant what may be discovered about poetry in poems themselves by a norm from an alien, a scientific mode of thought. Or, to put the point in terms not of poetic technique but of poetic subject-matter (a vivid but risky way of putting it), it is to make, in a new direction, the very mistake about poetry that elsewhere Professor Brooks himself has effectively diagnosed. It is to give a preference to a certain kind of *situation*—to that which is fullest of striking contrasts, which is most directly and readily specified through modes of expression that are paradoxical and complex. But it cannot be right to free poetry from the limited range of experience that lends itself to picturesque romantic lyricism, only to shackle it again to another limited range, that which lends itself to 'paradox, ambiguity, and ironic contrast'.

Struck by the fact that in some sense 'Break, Break, Break' is indisputably an 'easier' and 'thinner' poem than 'Tears, Idle Tears', Professor Brooks seems to have treated the issue between the poems as settled, and hardly applied his characteristic method to the thin one. But—though I hesitate very much, after criticizing Professor Brooks, to use his own weapons—there seems to be much in the easier poem that invites just his kind of analysis. For the vainly breaking tide is not only, perhaps, what Tennyson is looking at; its ambiguity is to be also an image of the memory that for all its nagging recurrence, never floods properly into the mind; and the quality of this reiterated but useless movement seems to be emphasized through contrast with the casual spontaneity of the children's play and song on the one hand, and the long uninterrupted motion of the ships to their goal on the other. If so, not only does 'stately' have work to do after all, but the ambiguity of the memory that, for all its insistence, is a dead memory, is exactly the ambiguity that does reside in 'dead' and 'come back'. And is there not, unmistakably, an irony in the condescending 'O well for . . . but . . .' that indicates sharply how Tennyson valued these trivial pleasures of the seaside, against the companionship, or love, or both, that he has lost even beyond proper recall?

If any of this is right, it is partly because Professor Brooks, in analysing other poems, has shown one how to find it. And if there is (which I fear) something faintly ridiculous in thus trying to push a method of analysis so much further than it was taken by its virtual originator, there is also something salutary, because the question of *where to stop* becomes absolutely inescapable; of which—one recalls with surprise—Professor Brooks and other 'New Critics' seem to have said nothing at all. If there are *no* limits, though, in using the method, surely this is a fact so important and surprising that it should be established beyond all doubt?

But instead, it is to be refuted beyond all doubt. For suppose that, encouraged by some or all of the suggested paradoxes, ambiguities, and ironies advanced in the last paragraph, one attempts to push further still by exactly the same method. Suppose one argues that the poem, through its whole length, constructs a metaphor defining the kind of influence exerted on Tennyson by whomever he is recalling, rather as the metaphor latent in the breaking tide helps to specify Tennyson's condition of mind as he stood beside the waves. Is there not an ambiguity in the 'still voice' that Tennyson tries to catch among the fishermen on this sea-shore? Is the comparison that this begins to hint at not taken further by the other things he mentions—a touch of the hand (with a magic gift of healing?); and the 'tender *grace*' that (ambiguously) seems to have been an influence as well as a way of behaving? Do we not anyway know how Tennyson felt about Arthur Hallam, who died overseas? Finally, is there not, in view of all this, an ironic second meaning when Tennyson laments that he cannot utter his thoughts?—that, though inexpressibly precious as far as they are memory, they are inexpressible in another sense—too deeply despairing for words—because Tennyson feels he is cut off forever from his Redeemer?

No. It is an entertaining game to play, and it is by no means over even for this one poem; but a game is quite obviously what it has become. Yet the game was not without its instructive side. For its extravagant results come from precisely the same methods as served at first for legitimate analysis of the poem, and along the same general lines, I think, as make up the staple of Professor Brooks's analyses of other poems; and if the method gives, in this way, sometimes admirable and sometimes wild results, it becomes, as I said, urgent to trace what can indicate when to take it further and when to stop.[1] This means, to trace the principle underlying, and confirming, the tact mentioned earlier on; a tact that usually stops 'close-reading' critics well on the hither side of wildness, but that is more fallible than it need be, because the heredity of close reading is a heredity of hybridism.

The answer, of course, everyone knows. It is that same boring truism which is also the most elusive of critical truths. The principle is simply that the poem decides. There is no *deus ex machina*, no ingenious theory from psychology, philosophy, semantics, semasiology or any other external thing, which can make the critic's work a drill. The poem—the successful poem, that is—decides because, being not an object for quasi-scientific routines of dissection, mechanically applied, but a work of art, it progressively shapes and prescribes its own interpretation. It requires, and indeed can tolerate, no supplementation from outside, no external clues. As the work of comprehension proceeds, the poem creates a fully defined reality which is what it is; and it is this which progressively shows, more and more clearly, what still waits to be added to reach that full and final definition, and what is alien to it. And the situation with 'Break, Break, Break', I take it, is simply that as one comes to terms with this poem as a whole, its rhythms, the static quality of its reiterative structure, and the almost myth- or fairytale-like selectivity of its detail, lead one to see that the poem prescribes by its mood a certain fairly definite level of intellectual play, and more and more strongly resists any progressively greater degree of it. The *exact* line to be drawn depends on a tact for which no principle can substitute. It may even be that nothing but the basic analogy between what Tennyson is watching and how he is feeling can be admitted into the organization of this poem without overloading it with a complexity that turns it from what it is. But the

[1] And historical considerations are insufficient. It is not anything historical that *rigidly* excludes the well-known ambiguity in the word 'die' from the last line of Goldsmith's 'When lovely woman stoops to folly', or Keats's 'Bright star! Would I were steadfast as thou art'.

general point is clear: a poem is a unified experience of which, as we come to know it better, we see that certain ideas are parts, and certain others are emphatically not.

VII

The encroachments of science as a norm show also elsewhere in the 'New Criticism': in that important part of it which is concerned to stress the integrity of poetry, and to argue that this integrity significantly restricts the critic in trying to discuss the content or subject-matter of a work, and in particular makes its morality or doctrine plainly not his business. Valuable as this insistence has been, it too seems to contain error and truth mixed; and as the error is diagnosed, it comes to look more and more like an alien element brought in through the influence of a foreign discipline. No one is going to say the last word on the perennial topic of form and substance. The rest of this essay will try only to diagnose, and then trace to its source, one single particularly important confusion.

This is the confusion, in the New Criticism, of two theories about the content-form or subject-language issue—two theories that have been falsely thought of as virtual twins, to choose between which was a matter of only trivial importance. John Crowe Ransom puts a version of the first when, having defined the moralistic critic as one who wishes 'to isolate and discuss the "ideology" or theme or paraphrase of the poem', he goes on to say that in his view 'the business of the literary critic is exclusively with an aesthetic criticism'.[1] Professor Tate sometimes says the same: 'As literary critics we must first of all decide in what respect the literary work has a specific objectivity . . . from my point of view the formal qualities of a poem are the focus of the specifically critical judgement because they partake of an objectivity that the subject-matter, abstracted from the form, wholly lacks'.[2] Theme or subject-matter, that is, may be abstracted from the whole texture of the literary work, but the act of abstraction leaves criticism behind. About these formula-

[1] 'Criticism as Pure Speculation'. See *The Intent of the Critic* (1941), pp. 101–2.
[2] *The Limits of Poetry*, p. 57.

tions there are only two brief points to make at present. First, Professor Tate may be right that the formal qualities are the focus (indeed, are they not on his view, the whole field?) of the *specifically* critical judgement—the judgement, that is, which is distinctive of the critic, which he makes as of right, and others make if at all only by encroachment. But this 'specifically' does not clinch Professor Ransom's 'exclusively'. Second, Professor Tate's change from 'the literary work' to simply 'the poem' is going to look more significant later on than it does now.

At bottom, the second theory is rigidly incompatible with the first, and its implications are quite different. Yet strangely enough, it can be so phrased as to seem merely a more forth-right version of the first; and that is how, in another of his essays, Professor Tate presents it. 'The important question goes further. It is: What is the relation of language to the "subject" . . .? The question may be *pushed even further*: Is it possible finally to distinguish the language from the subject? Are not language and subject one?"[1] (italics mine). But this second theory is by no means a more forthright alternative; and it *wrecks* the literary critic's chance of limiting his attention to formal qualities, thereby leaving the ideology or idea or subject over for the 'moralistic' critics. It does so because, if language and subject are one, nobody can have possession of the subject (as opposed to some attenuated ghost of it) unless he has the critic's expertise with language. The 'specific objectivity' of the literary work does not free the critic from consideration of subject or ideology, but is precisely what constrains him to it. No one else can do the job. Professor Ransom's argument why the critic could leave 'moral criticism' on one side was different from Professor Tate's; he argued that we can rely on having it with us always. So we can. But unless language and subject are finally distinguishable (and even this first step, notice, must not require the critic's expertise) we shall have it with us always done badly—unless critics do it.

This second view, that the form-subject abstraction is a myth, is fairly clearly the better view, and the view that means most to Professor Tate: it is behind some of his best accounts of the distinctive achievement of art in words. 'The poet . . . is

[1] *The Limits of Poetry*, p. 20.

responsible . . . for the mastery of a disciplined language which will not shun the full report of the reality conveyed to him by his awareness.'[1] Sometimes Professor Tate even emphasizes how the writer's subject matter (or whatever we call it) gets its full report only through the things in writing that make writing art: 'In the long run, whatever the poet's "philosophy" . . . by his language shall you know him; the quality of his language is the valid limit of what he has to say.'[2] Commenting on Yvor Winters' remark that Babbitt never understood how the moral intelligence gets into poetry, Professor Tate says 'it gets in not as moral abstractions but as form, coherence of image and metaphor, control of tone and of rhythm, the union of these features. So the moral obligation to judge compels us to make not a moral but a total judgement.'[3] But this is to yield the whole case. The 'us' deserves italics; it can hardly be stressed too much; for this total judgement must be a caricature, or it must be controlled by the critics, whose special skill is with the things that appear in Professor Tate's catalogue.

'Miss Emily and the Bibliographers', which contains this discussion, was addressed mainly to those who do not even recognize the existence of critical categories like image, tone, or rhythm. For those who do recognize them, they not only constitute a field of inquiry within which the critic moves alone (except for the artist, whose path he follows), but at least with literature they enable both artist and critic to make a special and indeed irreplaceable contribution outside their own field. One can put this another way by pointing out that Professor Ransom's 'moral abstractions' bring no one much nearer to morality—to a real comprehension of virtue or sin—than they do to a comprehension of literature. They are the merest bones of morality, they must be made to live, and among many other things literature *can sometimes* powerfully do this. And it should be emphasized further that (what it is not perhaps a part of the critic's expertise to know) this real comprehension of virtue or sin is not any familiarity however detailed with principles and rules; what lies at its heart is a deep and humane understand-

[1] The Hudson Review, Autumn 1951, p. 333.
[2] *The Limits of Poetry*, p. 85.
[3] *ibid.*, p. 56.

ing: wisdom that has grasped 'the quality of experience, the total revelation'—Professor Tate's phrase for what the literary art essentially reveals. Certainly that grasp of the total revelation may be come at otherwise than through literature; and perhaps the contribution of much or even most literature to a specifically moral wisdom is relatively oblique. But at least, the revelation of literature and the wisdom of the moralist do not diverge, they converge.

VIII

Once again, then, it seems as if the New Criticism had hardly demanded enough for itself and for literature. In its anxiety to locate and defend what is distinctive of the literary art, it underestimated how other branches of humane thought must have regard to what that art reveals. The last part of this essay is going to suggest briefly that this timidity sprang once again from a strand of deference to the norm of science, a strand that survived all these critics' vigilance against scientific encroachments. The timidity seems to have taken the form of a halfnotion that, save in some special sense, literature might turn out to be either false or meaningless; and another half-notion that, save again in some special sense, it might turn out to be useless.

According to the first of these, what is true properly is science; and poetry must be made to stand on its formal qualities, because ultimately, anything it may state will be shown up by science. When Macbeth says 'Out, out brief candle! Life's but a walking shadow ...', Professor Tate comments 'The lines ... are certainly not "true": we know that life is not a shadow, it is a vast realm of biological phenomena.'[1] He allows that they are 'true' as a stage in Macbeth's development, but once we bring their truth anywhere near scientific truth, it collapses. One sees at once how odd this is. It is almost like Professor Tate writing ironically, and at his best. Again, in speaking of allegory he says: 'there is nothing true but fact. About this fact science alone can instruct us, not with a fundamentally different kind of instruction from the allegorist, but with the same kind, more systematic and efficient ... mere allegory is a vague and futile

[1] *The Limits of Poetry*, p. 109.

The Critical Intimidation

kind of science.'[1] This same view that the norm of statement is
the scientific statement seems to underlie both Professor Tate's
and Professor Ransom's preference for speaking only of poetry,
and for that significant change, in a passage by Professor Tate
that was quoted earlier, from 'the literary work' to 'the poem'.
Prose, at a pinch, is expendable. If the critic has nothing to say
about a poem's texture, says Professor Ransom at one point, he
'is treating it only insofar as it is prose'[2]—as if prose never had a
texture, was never itself literature, was essentially bare science.
Professor Tate's retreat from prose is even clearer: 'For Arnold
the subject is what we commonly call the prose subject—that is
to say, as much of the poetic subject as we can put into ordinary
prose. The poet takes it up at the level at which the scientist—
or Arnold's simulacrum of him—takes it (=leaves it?): the level
of observation and description. The poet now puts it into language that will bring the inert facts to life and move us.'[3] Professor Tate has taken, here, too easy and also too dangerous a
way to expose the defective notion of poetry that he inflicts on
Arnold: for a moment, he uses the same defective notion of
prose, and aims only to show that poetry is different. In the face
of what he calls, on the very next page, 'that remarkably ingenious and dynamic fellow', the modern scientist, with his
scientific mode of expression, he makes a present of prose, so as
to bring out the essential otherness of poetry. This, of course, is
far from Professor Tate's real and settled notion of prose; but
the point is that, when he really feels the edge in the scientist's
attack, he is accommodating enough to fall back on it for the
moment. Here is the basic concession: 'ordinary' prose is scientist's prose.

Yet this notion of what is ordinary in truth or in prose is
wrong; and again, philosophy ought to confiscate what has perhaps been wrongly borrowed through philosophy's wrong influence. 'Ordinary' language—so far as we can identify such a
thing at all—is very different from scientific description. It is
full of remarks like 'he is an ass' (compare *Life is a shadow*), 'I

[1] *The Limits of Poetry*, pp. 95–6.
[2] *The Intent of the Critic*, p. 111. Compare: 'the straight ethical consideration would be prose; it would be an act of interested science' (*ibid.*, p. 103).
[3] *The Limits of Poetry*, p. 20.

am really in love with her', 'we live in unhappy times', and so on, which may or may not employ metaphors and therefore be true only as a metaphorical statement is true (this is a simple point), but which all go definitely beyond 'the level at which the scientist takes it' because they all try to record an impression, to be a vague but full report, to catch the total revelation, the quality of experience. In other words, the mode of utterance in which literature is straightforwardly true is perfectly familiar— more so perhaps than the mode of utterance of science—and nothing can make us in the least hesitate to see literature as capable of one straightforward kind of truth, and not supplanted by science but proceeding along a path divergent from it; nothing, that is, save a theoretical homage to a dominance by the scientific mode that our practice conclusively rejects. Literature, of course, is more highly organized, more animated, more subtle than anything in ordinary speech—sometimes incomparably so —and it both demands a more intent, trained attention, and can penetrate the quality of experience with greater, with even explosive force. But its germ, its monocellular prototype (to use a scientific illustration myself for a moment), is one of the familiar modes of ordinary speech.

The other half-notion was that, save in some special sense, literature would on investigation prove useless; and it is not difficult to show that this idea comes in turn from the idea that the normal mode of action is the normal (or rather, I should think, one occasional) mode of action of the scientist. The work of literary art, says Professor Tate 'proves nothing; it creates the totality of experience in its quality; *and it has no useful relation to the ordinary forms of action*'.[1] These italics are my addition; but it is only when they are added that one notices how two very different points have somehow come, in this sentence, to look like one. The same difficulty shows elsewhere: Shelley's

> Life like a dome of many-coloured glass
> Stains the white radiance of eternity

(an utterance which it is no part of my purpose to defend) 'is an explanation of "life" that seems laden with portent and high significance, but *as explanation* it necessarily looks towards possible

[1] *The Limits of Poetry*, p. 113.

action, and it is there that we know that the statement is meaningless. Practical experimental knowledge can alone fit means to ends.'[1] It is a mistake, to think that the only mode of 'explanation' is that which fits means to ends; and it is another, that shows in both these examples, to think that ordinary action draws only on the explanations that do fit means to ends. A mere glance at what actions actually occur outside the laboratory proves this. It would not perhaps be an exaggeration to assert that every ordinary action of any importance (choosing careers, partners, houses, even books or clothes) is ultimately directed, though perhaps in a most fitful and telescoped way, by whatever glimpse of 'the totality of experience in its quality' we may have acquired; and if we have any such glimpse, the chances are that in part it is a residue of the various full reports of samples of it, proffered by what we have read. Indeed, action that owes nothing whatever to such glimpses is not only confined to science, but a non-scientist would suppose that it was confined even more closely—to the subordinate and more mechanical parts of science. And what is the upshot of this deference to a distinctively scientific mode of action? It is that the full claim for literature is not made: the full scope of criticism is mistakenly disallowed.

All these points add up to the general conclusion that the New Criticism has achieved most when it has given an absolutely single-minded attention to its own subject-matter, and achieved less whenever it has paid any service to disciplines outside itself. If so, the moral is obvious: New Criticism must be even more ambitious, even more itself. That is surely a moral which no critic can find discouraging.

[1] *The Limits of Poetry*, pp. 92–3.

XIII

THE NEW AND THE
NEWER CRITICS[1]

—————

I

THE 'CHICAGO' GROUP of critics, R. S. Crane, Elder Olson, Richard McKeon, Norman Maclean and others, drew together in the mid-nineteen-thirties; thus only by a head do they deserve the title of 'newer' over John Crowe Ransom, Allen Tate, and Cleanth Brooks. They probably constitute the first critical movement to be born entirely on the American side of the Atlantic, and to have developed there for two decades without a counterpart here. The fact is a striking one. Let us hope that it is to be accounted for solely by the Chicago critics' imperfections, and not by our own inertia or parochialism. The second striking fact is that this group's leading ideas have been developed through concern for humane education as a whole and for 'the current decline in the prestige and effectiveness of humane studies'. Space prevents my discussing either of these points. They can only be saluted, the first apprehensively, the second with cautious satisfaction, and passed over.

[1] This essay discusses the following works: the collection entitled *Critics and Criticism*, edited by R. S. Crane, University of Chicago Press, 1952; R. S. Crane, *The Languages of Criticism and the Structure of Poetry*, University of Toronto Press, 1953; Elder Olson, *The Poetry of Dylan Thomas*, University of Chicago Press, 1954. References to 'CC' and 'LC' are to the first and second of these books respectively.

187

The Chicago movement is by origin a theoretical one; and proud of it:

I am encouraged . . . by what has happened in other fields . . . the notable advances of the present century in physics, genetics . . . have all been preceded and accompanied by theoretical revivals; and in any university the subjects which are now most alive are those in which there is the least indifference to general ideas and the least inclination to find an incompatibility between a concern for them and the pursuit of particular facts. (LC, p. xiv.)

This attitude has dangers, and the critics sometimes fall victim to them. An intolerable style, for example, is common to them all. For savagely thorough avoidance of any form of intellectual concession, and sometimes for plain clumsiness and prolixity, this style is the despair of even the philosophically trained reader. But the danger may not be all on the side of those who theorize. 'Practical criticism', fortunately no doubt, is now more or less the established practice: but about its basic justification and principles, or its method and range, fundamental thinking has become stagnant, and taking-for-granted rampant. 'It's just a method, you can't really investigate it,' a critical acquaintance said to me recently. Faced with that blithe credulity—every critic a *bodhisattva*—one welcomes even an overdose of theory.

Thinking about the fundamentals of criticism naturally brings (as practical criticism did in its formative days) destructive analysis of the existing kinds of criticism. Professor Crane uses the phrase 'criticism of criticism' in the first of these books, and a large part of *The Language of Criticism* is taken up with destructive, or rather, with restrictive analysis of two conspicuous modern critical 'schools': the New Critics, and the myth-ritual-psychoanalysis critics (among whom Crane mentions Northrop Frye, Maud Bodkin, and Edmund Wilson). The comment on this second school is brief and telling. What is it, Professor Crane asks, to explain *Oedipus Rex* as the winter–spring ritual, Ahab in *Moby Dick* as a *shaman*, *Henry IV* as an Id-Ego-Superego myth, or *The Ancient Mariner* as a synthesis of spiritual disintegration and reintegration? It is, he answers, simply to state a resemblance. Myth and written work are alike. If this, however, is all that the mythologizing critics wish to say, then there is no need for us to be surprised at their mutual disagreements. Each thing is like many other things. Crane's implicit point is the radical incompleteness of this approach. By now it needs no explicit reference. His comment, by the way, or something like it, receives interesting confirmation from a recent article by Northrop Frye himself.[1]

II

Now for the other sort of criticism. Two modes of inquiry issue from the method of 'close reading': analysis of the short lyric or extract (the keywords would perhaps be 'complexity' or 'ambiguity' or 'inter-animation') and analysis of the extended works, especially the whole verse play (where the keyword is perhaps 'theme'). Both William Empson and Cleanth Brooks would represent the first of these; and G. Wilson Knight the second. It is this second sort of criticism which most interests the Chicago writers, but an essay by Olson (CC, pp. 45–83) makes some good points about the first. To begin with, it brings out how, despite passing disclaimers, Empson's critical method assumes that what is interesting or significant in substance lends itself *naturally* to what is complex and ambiguous in treatment. This is a telling comment, and the first of many points (which it is largely the purpose of this essay to indicate) where to review the approach of the Chicago critics is to challenge current presumptions among ourselves. Empson is not the only modern critic whose work assumes that to trace complexities, associations, and inter-animations was a method valid for the criticism of every kind of good work, and therefore a conclusive index of good work.[2] Yet this seems the strangest of dogmas, as soon as one thinks it over.

In the second place (Olson continues) full meaning simply does not come from the interactions of words and their dictionary possibilities taken by themselves. It is largely created by, and therefore also controlled and restricted by, the full dramatic or (in a poem) poetic situation in which the words are used. 'What [Empson] misses is the governance of metaphor by

[1] *Hudson Review*, Winter 1954, p. 616.
[2] See above, p. 171.

thought, of thought by character, of character by action . . . a
metaphor is not simply a figure of diction in poetry . . . it is the
thought . . . of a certain character in a certain situation' (CC,
p. 56). There is no need here to revert at length to Empson's
books; but there is still a point in suggesting that Olson's essay
will help to prevent their misuse. To have meaning is to mean
several things, or perhaps more often, even in poetry, to mean
just one thing. It is also, however, to not mean others. The range
of the meaning, and also the limits of that range, are prescribed
by the whole nature of the work it comes in, and the local
nature of the phase in that work at which it comes.

Olson's essay is followed by Crane's 'The Critical Monism of
Cleanth Brooks'—not the only Chicago document which pro-
vokes both agreement and disagreement in startled contiguity.
In summarizing Brooks, for example, Crane writes 'It is not,
therefore, any special principle of unity derived from the nature
of the "experience" or object represented in a given kind of
poem that determines poetical structure; . . . rather it is the
presence in poems of poetical structure . . . that determines,
and is the sign of, the unification of experience.' With this Crane
wishes us to disagree. But do we disagree? To my mind, we do
not. Unity does come from the poet's unifying power. It does
not come from the mere experience. There is no situation which
cannot but run into the form of an integrated poem. Agreed, complex situations are not a guaranteed stock-in-trade for the poet.
Neither, however, are unified ones. Indeed, it is far from easy
even to indicate what reality we wish to speak of, unless we
either provide, or refer to, some description of that reality; and
this, simply through being a description, is a made version,
where unity is controlled or even imposed by the mind of the
'maker', the poet. One's misgivings here have something in
common (it is not hard to see why) with misgivings at Olson's
reference (CC, p. 55) to 'the finest diction', or Crane's (LC,
p. 157) to the writer's 'beautiful rendering . . . in words' of the
activity or state of feeling he deals with. These are old dangers,
however, and they have been succumbed to and also sur-
mounted often enough. Rashly perhaps, I propose to ignore
them for the sake of other questions.

If Brooks has the best of it here, that is partly because Crane did himself less than justice. This, at least, is what his work suggests as a whole. The method of the New Critics, he argues, is to approach every kind of poem in the same way. They look each time for one and the same structure: paradox, irony, complex meaning. Thus they assimilate 'poems so obviously different in the special kinds of pleasure they give us' as *Who is Sylvia?*, *The Rape of the Lock*, and *The Waste Land* (CC, p. 96). Moreover, they are pre-occupied with content of an intellectual kind. They seek for structure exclusively in terms of thought, rather than of that 'anything whatever' which may prove to be the distinctive unifier of a given poem. In Crane's view, the two errors are ultimately one. To concentrate upon simply the units of language is nothing other than to concentrate on meaning; therefore (in practice if not theory) on intellectual content rather than the distinctive emotions and pleasures of the work; and it is thus that Brooks gives Gray's *Elegy*:

'an outline, to be sure, but an outline of the kind that any sermon might have, or any serious familiar essay. The "reading" gives us, in short, not a poem but simply a moderately subtle piece of dialectic' (CC, p. 99).

The obvious retort is 'What on earth would you have us concentrate on, if not on meaning?' It will be seen that Crane has his answer ready.

This interesting argument plays a significant, in fact a disturbingly significant, part in Crane's work; and I shall revert to it at a crucial point in the present discussion. Whether or not it is wholly fair to Brooks is a question: that critic's performances being often more perceptive and alive than his critical assumptions need be expected to guarantee. But Crane is touching here upon certain highly important though perhaps elusive defects in what much modern criticism takes for granted. Has, for example, the now common quest for themes and patterns been fully thought out? After all, to discover in a work the things which make it a masterpiece is to discover what has a supreme importance. Does a pattern of moral attitudes, or the exploration of a moral theme, have supreme importance? If so, does it have this supreme importance in a great play or novel because the great play or novel conducts a moral exploration more searching, comprehensive, and informative than the classics of philosophy, religion, or casuistry? The question is never examined comparatively by the critics who beg it, and many of them would admit or boast that it was a question half of which lay outside their competence. But even were we to answer it affirmatively, a difficulty would remain. Were superiority to the *Phaedrus* or the *Timaeus* or Book IX of the *Republic* or the *De Consolatione*, in the same kind of excellence, to be what constituted the greatness of *Lear*, then the philosophers might always hope that sooner or later one of their number would write with such moral informativeness that he would catch up with Shakespeare and even excel him. Yet we know that, however good a discursive work may be, it can no more surpass a literary masterpiece than improving the quality of food can make it a substitute for drink.

Moreover, it is very much open to doubt whether the real and supreme excellence of the literary masterpiece can lie simply in its moral pattern, however this may be defined. W. R. Keast makes the point well in his devastating analysis of Robert Heilman's book on *Lear*:

When the wonderful imagery of King Lear has been reduced to sense . . . what shall we discover? That man, though he is liable to damnation, may yet achieve salvation . . . [etc. etc.]. That these principles are profound and important no one is likely to question— so is the Golden Rule; but that the assertion of them, even through the details of a particular case, is likely to be powerfully moving, as the play has always been felt to be, is manifestly improbable (CC, p. 124).

Crane expands this. 'What we are committed to, if we want to write this kind of criticism, is the discovery of conceptual equivalents of the concrete relationships of elements discernible in poems.' He then reminds us, that since these equivalents *cannot but* be discoverable, it is very much an open question whether in tracing them we have really traced a work's chief merit:

It requires no great insight to find an inner dialectic of order and disorder or a struggle of good and evil in any serious plot; or a profound dialectic of appearance and reality in any plot in which the action turns on ignorance or deception or discovery . . . and what is true of plots and characters is true also of language and imagery. Perhaps the most striking thing about the essays on Shakespeare of Mr Wilson Knight is the facility with which he has been able to subsume the wonderfully varied images of the plays under his favourite simple oppositions of 'death themes' and 'life themes', conflict and order, war and love, 'tempests' and 'music' (LC, p. 124).

This is of real importance. Imagery may be ranged comprehensively under many schemes of categories, and a writer would have to contort himself with ingenuity in order to frustrate the efforts of critics who wish to riddle his work with moral themes and preoccupations. But the further question always remains: admitting the *presence* of these things, what exactly is their *importance*? Thus there are two different objections to the moral-theme-and-pattern kind of criticism, when it is employed without restraint: first, the moral informativeness often consists only of traditional commonplaces; second, even when it is impressive, it does not, as normally discussed, add up to the full impressiveness of the work.

Crane puts his own objection in a polemical and not altogether satisfactory way. He says that it requires us 'to assert something akin to allegory' in 'all poetic works that seem to us to have "relevance to life" '. As it stands, this does not catch the practice of the moral critics. It does not, for example, meet the point made with conspicuous reiteration in F. R. Leavis's *The Great Tradition* by phrases like 'the real in its concrete fulness', 'realizing imagination', 'firm and vivid concreteness', or 'concretely rendered' (*op. cit.*, pp. 91, 167, 195, 196). But this is not quite the end of the matter. Vividness and concreteness are not, one may presume, assets merely as servants of something else, merely as means for transmitting the ethical content in easily-remembered form. They are not superior substitutes for good paragraphing or neat syntax in a philosophy-book. If they were, we should always have to fear that really superlative paragraphing might make the philosopher surpass the creative writer in his own field: and that fear, as we have seen already, is absurd. But if vividness and concreteness have their intrinsic value, we must then inquire whether they are always one and the same, simply present or simply absent (like electric light in a room, simply on or not on); or whether on the other hand they may significantly vary, and therefore be sometimes trivial, sometimes good but not more than good, and sometimes masterly. More than this, we must inquire whether their intrinsic value might be great, wholly or in part regardless of moral-attitude-patterns or of quasi-discursive themes. Once these questions are raised, we see that they are quite new questions, and that much depends on them.

Keast does not analyse the idea of 'concreteness', but he has some telling comments on Heilman, who excuses the bareness of the moral insights he traces in *Lear* by saying that they are 'complexly', not simply, asserted (CC, p. 125). I cannot agree with Crane (LC, pp. 125–8), in his assertion that since the 'heads of interpretation' (order, disorder, etc.) which the moral-pattern critics employ 'can be made to fit without too much difficulty almost any poem we have in hand', arguments in favour of them can therefore be made plausible only through some kind of special pleading. The point is rather, I think, that some literary masterpieces clearly do have these moral patterns as their predominant reality, but that it is (at the present stage of the inquiry) quite an open question whether all masterpieces do so, and whether to trace them is therefore the only critical approach; or failing that, at least the best one; or failing that, an approach which will be always illuminating and never confusing (for I can see the insistently 'moral' critic retreating to these positions one by one). However this may be, Crane's work has real value in showing that much contemporary criticism is quite arbitrary, quite begs the question; and it may remind some readers that we are in danger of falling into criticism where moralizing and theme-detecting have become intransigent and mechanical routines. Moreover, it would be easy to find evidence in the whole body of Crane's work of a much more moderate attitude than he expresses in the pages I have been discussing (e.g. LC, p. 192, and CC, p. 646, where he stresses that there is a place for rival modes of criticism).

III

What do the Chicago critics offer as a positive critical approach? One may answer, vividly and not quite innocently, by saying that their positive approach is what is suggested by a certain quite distinctive way of reading a book. They offer a new 'How to Read'. We know already, of course, that the kind of criticism they reject issues also from a distinctive way of reading. Indeed, this fact is stressed by its champions. The proper approach to Shakespeare, writes L. C. Knights, is 'an exact and sensitive study [how but by reading?] of the quality of the verse, of the rhythm and imagery, of the controlled associations of the words and their emotional and intellectual force, in short by an exact and sensitive study of Shakespeare's handling of language' (*Explorations*, p. 10; quoted by Crane, LC, p. 15). Another similar critic, Mr Raymond Williams, directs us to Shakespeare's 'finalized organization of words', to 'the particular sequence of words which conveys an experience' (*Drama from Ibsen to Eliot*, pp. 14, 15). This distinctive kind of reading (too familiar to need further comment) has often been misunderstood. It in no way removes or even reduces the obligation on a reader or a critic to give attention to the plot or to the characters. The only things it definitely instructs the reader to ignore are those things about the contents of a written work which he might learn about not through its language but from some other source; and what these are, no one has ventured to explain. On this recipe for reading a work, therefore, it remains a perfectly open question whether the characters of the *dramatis personae*, or the plot, might in a given case deserve our chief attention. One begins to wonder whether this whole mode of criticism does not rest upon half-thought-out foundations. It remains true, however, that Knights' or Williams' recipe for reading directs our attention to many other things beside character or 'plot': things which earlier criticism often ignored but which do often prove of great importance. Herein, of course, lies its great and indisputable value.

What of the distinctive mode of reading of the Chicago critics? They are frequently referred to as 'Aristotelian' critics, but there is no really essential reason why they should have linked themselves with that philosopher. It has given them an opportunity to stress how works of literature are wholes (LC, pp. 85–6, etc.), but this is what everybody has been stressing. It has made them use Aristotle's distinction (*Poetics*, Chapter I) between differences in imitative works of means, objects, and manners; but it is perhaps a question whether these tidy distinctions have not given some of their remarks an unreal, or perhaps real, appearance of elementariness. It has made them draw attention to the relevance, for understanding the nature of a work of art, of what Aristotle says in *The Parts of Animals* about the distinctiveness of a *couch*, or in the *De Anima* of an *axe*; but these partial parallels, though (rather to one's surprise) genuinely illuminating, are by no means irreplaceably so. To be able to point to Aristotle's distinction between literary kinds has perhaps helped their arguments; but against this must be set their perfectly explicit and indeed perfectly necessary admission (Crane, LC, p. 65; Olson, CC, p. 558) that the number of the kinds is indefinitely large, and that the writer creates the new kind in advance of its differentiation by the critic. They certainly draw more essentially on Aristotle in their insistence that the principle of individual order in a work is somehow connected with its *cause*; but this might have been taken from Coleridge—indeed, Crane quotes Coleridge's distinction between poetry and prose 'in consequence of a different object being proposed' (CC, p. 87)—and, moreover, it proves to be an assertion by no means entirely free from obscurity.

I have still, however, to suggest the distinctive mode of reading which underlies the critical work of the Chicago school. It is that a legitimate and significant way to read a work is to begin at the first page and advance page by page to the end. Further, these critics argue that with a good book the ensuing experience is of a wholly individual, of a unique sequence of interests, sympathies, concerns, excitements, and the rest, which (whatever their objects) have it as their essential characteristic to be sequential: to be aroused and then subsequently to be resolved. Finally, the essence of this kind of experience is that it should be a kind of pleasure—in a way that it is not of the essence of reading a work of say geography that it should be a pleasure, because it is of the essence of this kind of reading that it should be informative; and if the geographer so organizes his work that it is also a sequence of excited and then resolved interests, that is because he is an artistically-inclined geographer who is embellishing his book in an incidental and perhaps even embarrassing manner.

This Chicago account of reading is a not wholly innocent account, of course; because it is not an account of one way to read a book at all. It just is how people do read. It is, one is inclined to say, *the* way. It is a vastly more central and significant conception than that of reading by turning to and fro the pages of a book (one we have already read the Chicago way several times) in order to complete a 'spatial analysis' or to find out what words 'take up' or 'anticipate' others. It ought, seemingly, to sweep the board with the criticism of its opponents. Why it does not do so will prove a vital question.

The central claim of these critics is thus not simply that written works are wholes, but that they are unique wholes and therefore require and justify a unique approach. This seems to be the point behind Crane's reference to 'the forming principle or immediately shaping cause of structure in individual poems' (LC, p. 140); and behind Olson's

Epic, tragedy, and comedy . . . are ordered, not to a doctrine, but to a plot. A plot is not a string of incidents, but *a system of incidents so constructed as to give us a specific pleasure by arousing and allaying our emotions* . . . It does not engage our interest and emotions in particulars of the action in order to instruct us generally; on the contrary, it instructs us about particulars of the characters and actions in the poem in order to engage our emotions and interest in behalf of these very characters and actions (CC, p. 67, my italics; compare also an explicit passage by Keast, CC, p. 127).

It seems also the point of Crane's reference to 'the emotional "working or power" ' which is the 'controlling form' of a poem or book (LC, p. 159), as he amplifies this in his essay on *Tom Jones*. Here he demands a criticism which

takes the form of the plot as its starting point and then inquires how far and in what way its peculiar power is maximized by the writer's invention and development of episodes, his *step-by-step rendering* of the

o 197

characters of his people, his use and elaboration of thought, his hand-ling of diction and imagery, and his decisions as to the order, method, scale, and point of view of his representation (CC, p. 623, my italics).

These remarks are useful. Far as one might be from accepting every detail of their formulation, they equip critics to draw an essential distinction: that between the religious, ethical, mythical, or philosophical concepts and attitudes which may be traced in a work on the one hand, and the *running preoccupation of the reader's interests*—in the most serious and significant sense, be it added—as he goes through the work following its central organization of excited and resolved concerns on the other. There is little doubt that ethical or indeed any other kind of material may be present in a work which nevertheless gives that material a subordinate place. Examples of treating this sub-ordinated material as the main centre of interest could be found, perhaps, in recent discussions of *Sir Gawain and the Green Knight*, and perhaps also of *Measure for Measure*. This is not to say that in other works these matters do not genuinely predominate. Nor, in arguing against the analytical method used to excess, ought one to forget the hard fight which had to be fought to get it used at all, and the valuable results which it has achieved.

It is this insistence upon the idea that a work has as its central organizing principle what is essentially a principle of sequence, that leads for example to the shrewd remarks of Crane and Mac-lean on Shakespearean tragedies (LC, p. 170; CC, p. 601). But now comes the crux. One cannot easily extract, either from Crane's own work, or from that of his colleagues, a quite explicit account of what this 'working or power' is like. Crane insists that criticism ought to trace not merely the signs of order in a work but the *cause* in an individual poem from which that order springs (LC, p. 145). At one point he implies that criticism ought to receive 'some sort of verification in terms of what was actually put into the poems by their poets' (LC, p. 33). Else-where he writes that 'the problem, in any given poem, is what actually was, *for its poet*, the primary *intuition* of form which en-abled him to synthesize his materials into an ordered whole' (LC, p. 146; my italics). Elsewhere again he admits the unanswerable force of 'the common objection to criticism based on "inten-

198

tion" ', and states that the only relevant sense of 'intention' must be 'the hypothesized form' of a work. One would suppose, then, that 'intention' was a construct in the critic's mind out of what the work itself was like, had Crane not just written that it had nothing to do with 'saying that [the poet] must have intended to write this work because this is what he had written' (LC, p. 182). Finally (LC, p. 166) he says:

The question . . . is primarily one of fact and cause . . . answered, for a given work, when we have made intelligible as we can the fashion in which its material elements . . . are made to function in relation to a formal whole . . . the actual final cause of its composition. By 'actual final cause' I mean simply a cause without the assumption of which [the presence and order of the parts] cannot be adequately understood . . . hence the causes that centrally concern us are the internal causes of which the only sufficient evidence is the work itself as a completed product (LC, p. 166).

How this hypothesized cause of order is a cause at all, or how tracing it is anything other than tracing the signs of it and the inter-relations between them, seem to me to be nice philosophical problems which I shall certainly not attempt to solve. But that this part (of course the crucial part) of the theory has not been put quite explicitly does not mean that it could not be so put; one inclines rather to suppose that it could.

IV

Unfortunately, one cannot do much to clear one's mind about the Chicago theories by turning to see how they work out in practice; for by contrast with their history, theory, and criticism of criticism, these critics have written very little criticism proper, and what they have written is disappointing. It is unfair to assert this without proper argument; but I do so (noting, at the same time, the many subtle and interesting points which do occur in their handful of critical essays) because I think it may perhaps be possible to identify the real defect in theory which has led to the allegedly defective practice. I must admit that the attempt, for an outsider, is a rash one.

Sometimes one's objection to the practice would have to take the form simply of claiming that the Chicago critical method had not been fully deployed. This is true for example of Olson's book on the poetry of Dylan Thomas. Much of this very short work is elementary exegesis or comment of a general kind. This is welcome enough, as is any real help in comprehending Thomas; and it is certainly better done here than it has been done before. But the most interesting pages of the book are those on the 'altarwise by owl-light' sonnets, where Olson has shown in detail how this sequence attempts to treat of the whole human situation through an account of the earth's apparent seasonal journey through the constellations. His remarkable discussion makes the whole sequence clear; to me, for the first time. But, exhausted perhaps by these unprecedented exegetical labours, Olson has not brought out the real upshot of his discovery: which is, that Thomas wrote these poems in what was quite literally a *code*, which the critic has now (with the help of Flammarion's *The Wonders of the Heavens*) broken. But, in terms of the Chicago theory, it is to say the least of it very much a question whether this code, with its fake gentleman and bagpipe-breasted ladies and the rest, comes anywhere near to a full development of the 'peculiar sequence of emotions' which we might have from the organizing principle of the poem and its six-fold symbolism. It is very much in question, on the Chicago critics' own terms; but it is not a question which Olson raises.

'Peculiar sequence of *emotions*.' It is Crane's phrase (LC, p. 179), but the notion that this is the final outcome of reading a work of literature seems common to these critics. Olson puts this view plainly enough (CC, p. 554), and in doing so speaks of emotion specifically as the end-product of literature, and of emotions as mental pains, pleasures, or impulses. Another relevant passage is by Maclean (CC, p. 598): 'We may ask for many other things from poems [besides emotions]—biographical information, or political or theological wisdom—but, in making any of these further requests, we should recognize that we are asking for what only certain good poems give, and then generally not so well as something else.' Maclean then brings the point out into the open by referring to 'a high order of distinctive *pleasures*' (my italics) as 'what is here taken as ultimate in poetry'. That such views have a current timeliness has perhaps

by now transpired; but surely they are incomplete. One thing
that we ask for from literature is a heightened, an unusually
comprehensive vision of an imagined situation or a train of
events. This vision (it can certainly not be analysed away
merely into emotions) may well be something that all true
literature provides, and it is certainly something which is not
done better in some other kind of writing. We feel, to put it
briefly, because we grasp. To interpret the experience of reading as a sequence wholly or even primarily of *emotions* is a dangerous simplification. If I am right in seeing this as a Chicago
tendency, then it is very noteworthy that it is the exact converse
of the error—attention only to the *intellectual* side of literary communication—which Crane detected in Brooks (see above, p. 191).

Perhaps this is the source of what looks like a plainer error
still.

This comes out in Crane's:

What distinguishes all the more developed forms of imitative
literature is that . . . they give us plots of which the effects derive
in a(n) . . . immediate way from the particular ethical qualities
manifested in their agents' actions and thoughts . . . When this is the
case *we cannot help becoming . . . emotionally involved; for some of the
characters we wish good, for others ill,* and, depending on our inferences
as to the events, we feel hope or fear, pity or satisfaction (CC, p. 621,
my italics).

and it comes out also when Olson writes:

The basis of our emotions towards art may be explained as follows: We
feel some emotion, some form of pleasure or pain, because our desires
are frustrated or satisfied; we feel the desires because we are friendly
or hostile to, or favour or do not favour, the characters set before
us . . . and we are friendly or hostile to the characters because of
their ethical traits; in brief, *we side with the good against the bad* or . . .
with the oppressed against the oppressor . . . etc. (CC, p. 555, my
italics).

'The basis of our emotions towards art,' one is inclined to reply,
may by no means be so explained. To speak in this way is to
speak of those who boo the stage villain and cheer the hero.
There are certainly readers whose emotions stop here; but we
do not normally think that they grasp either the seriousness, or

the real potentiality for giving enjoyment, of the literary masterpiece. No doubt the same reactions, controlled and qualified,
may still be traced in those who comprehend what is going on in
a great work of literature; but they are at least as far from what
is central in one's experience of literature as tracing imagery-
patterns or the last refinements of verbal complexity. There is
no simple sense in which our desires are frustrated when Desdemona is killed or Oedipus found out, or satisfied when the
traitor Macbeth is beheaded. We do not 'side with' Lear in that
we 'wish good' for him in the shape of military victory or the
rescue of Cordelia. So far as these things go, our sympathy for
the characters somehow co-exists with a detachment in which
we accept—no, more than that, we demand—whatever is
brought by the fable in its entirety. Our emotions of concern for
the individual characters to help to make possible other and
more important emotions, those which come directly through
comprehension and contemplation, as we grasp the total reality
which is the tide of events carried through to its end. From a
great literary work we receive insight, illumination, richer comprehension of what existence may bring; it is only in our coming
to possess these things, which are cognitive things, that we may
enjoy the more impersonally directed emotions which transpire
from them. What I am saying may almost be said by means of
Crane's own words: 'The peculiar power of any plot . . ., as it
unfolds, is a result of our state of knowledge at any point in complex interaction with our desires for the characters' (CC, p.
622). But the knowledge is other, and the complex interaction
vastly more complex, than he seems to have meant.

The end of an essay is not the place to pursue these points;
but one may venture the suggestion that they could be pursued
to the disadvantage, and also to the advantage, of the Chicago
critics. In the first place, it looks as if in tracing the growth and
resolution of this more extended sort of comprehension and insight, one would find that in order to complete even the Chicago
critics' kind of inquiry, one was obliged to give attention to
imagery, general poetic texture, and the themes that emerge
therefrom, after the manner of the Chicago critics' main opponents. In the second place, however, to give these matters their
due weight would so greatly extend the scope and power of the

Chicago critics' search into the unique *sequential* experience of the given work, that there might then be no need for them to say (as Crane modestly does say) that their method is 'better adapted . . . to the appreciation of success or failure in individual works than it is to the making of comparative judgements based on criteria of literary "greatness" or "seriousness" that transcend differences of kind' (CC, p. 646); which if correct is an admission of no mean importance.

These critics are difficult writers. I should not be surprised, on further acquaintance with what they have written, to find that incomplete understanding of it has caused me here to do them either less, or more, than justice. To discover, though, that their work does not have a real, provocative interest, would indeed be a surprise.

XIV

THE NEW 'ESTABLISHMENT'
IN CRITICISM[1]

I

DURING THE LAST THIRTY YEARS there has been a revolution
in literary criticism. I said 'has been', and that is the point. The
revolutionaries—or, as is usual, their sturdy henchmen—are in
office. It is therefore time to be careful: this is when revolution-
ary, emancipatory ideals are silently transformed—and no one
notices until a generation later.

I am speaking as one who has been a ranker, anyhow, on the
victorious side; but a new battle now confronts us. Literary analysis, close reading, 'taking a poem to pieces', talk about imagery, ambiguities, associations, poetic texture—this is the new
critical establishment. And we can watch this new establishment
changing, in its turn, into a new pedantry; transforming what
was once a new and keener and fresher vision into a grinding
routine, where one or two skills are operated at the expense of
everything else. If I am right about this, there is no need to be
surprised: on the contrary. We shall only be watching here the
characteristic fate of new ideas forged in the first place by the
bigger men as a vital tool for richer living, and then blunted

[1] The first and third parts of this were given as broadcast talks in Septem-
ber 1956. Some readers may wish to consult the correspondence, varying
much in interest and relevance, which ensued in *The Listener*.

down by the smaller ones to preserve routine security and cosy limitation.

I am going to refer, later in this talk, to passages in the work of several well-known critics where the dangers now confronting us can be seen, I think, in their small beginnings. But this is merely to indicate more or less isolated weak points in work which as a whole has brought us notably forward. These are of interest rather as points of origin for dangers which now occupy the critical climate. How can I hope to diagnose something so intangible? I can do so, perhaps, by referring to two recent experiences of my own. The first is this. Not long ago I went to a meeting of a literary society, and listened to a paper—a skilful one too—analysing a certain poem by Marvell, 'The Definition of Love'. This poem has been regarded as a major one of its century since Mr Eliot and Dr Leavis wrote of Marvell a generation ago. Scores of acutely critical readers, I suppose, have tackled the poem in the last two decades, and have agreed to admire it; now it has begun to be referred to, in the literary guides and histories, as a classic of the period.

This agreement was what the speaker at the meeting wanted to challenge; he analysed the poem anew, and claimed that 'better than Cowley' was what could most properly be said for it. He called his paper 'Second Thoughts on Marvell'. What neither he nor anyone in his audience seemed to think of was that, if he was right, 'Second Thoughts on Analysing Poems' were even more urgently called for. Here is a mode of investigation which is widely applied, and by now moreover confidently applied, over a period of twenty years. In a certain case it has given a certain answer many times. Then, one day, it gives almost the opposite. How drastically this would discredit, say, statistical sampling! I am no kind of scientist, but I believe that something of this kind happened when scientists tried to measure the velocity of light through the ether, on the analogy of a man swimming across a river as against one swimming up and down it. Their hitherto reliable method suddenly gave a wildly odd result. The consequence, in that field, was an absolutely fundamental re-thinking of the whole problem. On the evening I am speaking of, the audience was confronted by this kind of situation: but the need for fundamental re-thinking did not seem to be glimpsed. The well-known, familiar, reliable approach was being followed, and it led to a certain result. That was that.

The other experience I have in mind is this. An acquaintance of mine recently said in conversation that criticism of the novel must necessarily be based, in the end, on detailed analysis of a few short extracts: because, he said, 'after all, one must *inspect something*'. That brings out a central assumption of the whole modern critical technique. The great contemporary discovery, or re-discovery in criticism, is that any worthwhile critical opinion must spring from concentration of the whole mind on the object. Vague impressions, worked-up emotional responses, simply will not do. Of course not. But there was a concealed yet vital assumption behind that remark about inspecting something: that one could only inspect, only concentrate the whole mind on, the short passage taken, as it were, word by word.

We ought, at this point, to remember how practical criticism developed historically. In large part it emerged with the detailed rediscovery of Donne, the Metaphysicals, and Hopkins; with Richards' famous set of short poems in his book *Practical Criticism*: and above all, with the filtering into English critical and poetic thought of the ideas about poetic texture of the French *Symbolistes*. In such poems as these, the things we may find in longer works will barely have time to develop; on the other hand, a single image may pervade a short poem from beginning to end. Again, short poems invite complexity of texture, because it is easy to read them several times over before one understands them. This is the field in which 'close reading' was learnt. But now we assume that it is relevant, and indeed decisive, everywhere: that the narrative work, for example, raises no fundamentally new problem. We think it is still the old choice between inspecting verbal texture, and inspecting nothing at all. What an odd view, once you look at it!

My two experiences prove nothing, but what they do, I hope, is bring out the way in which a critical system is rigidifying all around us. Here is the new 'establishment': it turns up in after-dinner conversation, on the railway bookstall, in the sixth-former's homework, at the teacher's weekend conference.

Now to get closer to what it is that is being taken for granted.

First of all, the new establishment has a certain general notion of the poetic texture. The points of origin of this are now familiar. There is T. S. Eliot writing of Marvell's 'succession of concentrated images', or of his 'wit fused into imagination'; or Eliot's essay on Massinger with the well-known 'words perpetually juxtaposed in new and sudden combinations'; a little later, there is Dr Leavis writing about Eliot himself: 'psychological subtleties and complexities in imagery of varied richness and marvellously sure realisation. The whole body of the words seems to be used'. These are simply pointers towards the now received ideas.

This received idea brings with it two assumptions. In the first place, that poetic texture of this close kind is a decisive merit; not just a quality, one kind of writing; not even, at least sometimes, a mere minor embellishment; but a sure winner every time. On the other hand, if it is absent, the poem is in the dock straight away. These notions are now so much taken for granted that it is hard not to see them as self-evident truths. Yet it has not always been like that. Walter Bagehot, writing nearly a hundred years ago, saw in Milton's verse much the qualities seen in it by some modern critics. 'We have a superficial complexity in illustration and imagery and metaphor,' he said, 'and in contrast with it a latent simplicity of idea'; or again, 'the words of some writers are said to have "hands and feet"; they seem, that is, to have a vigour and animation which belong only to things which live and move. Milton's words have not this animal life.' Bagehot, however, saw himself here as engaged in literary diagnosis; not in evaluation. Milton's verse lacked this —what a modern critic has called 'muscular quality'—because it was verse of another kind. Here we may, or may not, have a valid account of *Paradise Lost*; I think, in fact, that we have not. But what is at issue is that Bagehot did not see his comment as condemnation. Too many of us today would think that of course it was.

As a matter of historical fact, a taste for 'tentacular roots' did not grow up from an exclusive concern for good poems, but largely from a more ambitious and wide-ranging interest: for general cultural health. Mr Eliot's admiration for the new and sudden combinations in the verse of Tourneur and Middleton is in the context of his reference to 'a period of high development of the senses, a development of the English language which we have perhaps never equalled'. I dare scarcely venture, myself, to use those ambitious categories of thought. Yet, I wonder: might such an extraordinary development sometimes work as a kind of hypertrophy of language; one that could, as it were, swamp a poem? That is very much what Arnold said did happen in a good deal of Elizabethan, even Shakespearean, verse. Again, he may or may not have been right: but to recall his view opens up a question which was being closed for us; by now, I fear, not for given poems individually, but on general grounds. No attention at this exact point can, in present conditions, be too sharp, too stringent. When we discover a new refinement of texture, we need to ask always whether this actually makes the poem any better; and, if it does, whether it makes it much better or only a little.

An insufficiently sharp recognition of this has led to two different kinds of critical defect. One is stressing the small point as if it were a large one; and the other, arguing as if subtle poetic texture were something you could not have too much of. There is a passage in one of Dr Leavis's books which neatly illustrates the first of these points: it may be right as it stands, but the reader has to think quickly if it is not to lead him into error. This passage is about Lady Macbeth's words of welcome to the king as she receives him at her castle:

> All our service,
> In every point twice done, and then done double,
> Were poor and single business, to contend
> Against those honours deep and broad, wherewith
> Your majesty loads our house . . .

In that word 'contend', says Dr Leavis, we feel an unusual physical force, related ultimately to the implicit image of a 'full-flowing and irresistible river' which is 'realizing' the conventional metaphor of the king as the fountain of honour. Let us concede, for the moment, that this piece of analysis is complete and accurate. The question remains: how much better does it make the actual passage? How much more shall we value that, enjoy it, feel it contributes notably to the play, because of the

metaphor of the fountain of honour as irresistible river in it? To
my mind, not much. But when Dr Leavis goes on to speak of
Shakespeare's 'marvellously sure and subtle control' here—
something that manifests his 'genius' as much as his most striking imagery does—a distinction has to be made. We have to
notice how exactly Dr Leavis has expressed himself. If this
means that here Shakespeare displays, in passing as it were, a
power which elsewhere really does bring marvellous results, all
right. But we certainly ought not to jump to the conclusion that
this is marvellous poetry itself, or wonderfully illuminates the
play, because of the incipiently realized metaphor. This would
be, as I said earlier, to take the presence of one quality of poetry
as a routine guarantee of superlative merit. Yet how often do
critics today diagnose this kind of texture, and then merely
assume, or dogmatically assert, that the poem is outstandingly
good? If this goes much further, we may have a divorce between
genuine poetic merit and mere complex texture just as rigid and
stultifying as the divorce in minor criticism of a generation or so
back between genuine poetic merit and 'verbal music'.

Almost everyone nowadays has reacted from the other defect
I spoke of: the cult of unlimited complexity—what one might
call the 'more-the-merrier' school. But this reaction, for the
most part, is justified by a vague standard of what is reasonable:
one must not be extravagantly ingenious. That misses the point.
There is usually a much more powerful argument against the
over-ingenious critic. Consider some lines from Marvell's poem
'The Garden':

> Mean while the Mind, from pleasure less,
> Withdraws into its happiness:
> The Mind, that Ocean where each kind
> Doth streight its own resemblance find.

A good while ago now, Professor Empson discussed these lines;
and he argued, among other things, that 'from pleasure less'
meant not only 'from smaller pleasures', but also that the mind
itself grew less, grew smaller, from its pleasures (I think he said
that country pleasures made the poet less intellectual). Further,
the word 'streight' did not only mean 'at once', it also meant
'closely packed together' in the mind, which was, after all, a

little world, a microcosm. Both these, I believe, illustrate an undue confidence in the idea that complexity guarantees merit. For the idea of mind as ocean is a prominent one in those lines; it protrudes; and how inept Marvell would have been to say that something made the mind shrink, and then go straight on to liken it to an ocean! What ineptitude, again, for him to say that it is like an ocean, and go straight on to say that things are closely, straitly packed together in it! These complexities would not make the lines better, but worse; they would wreck them. The critic is offending here, not against some vague general idea of what is reasonable, but against the poem; which by that word 'ocean', condemns these interpretations; condemns them stringently and directly.

One may generalize. A poem may include a wealth of meanings; it also, just as much, excludes a wealth of other meanings. The main part of the close reader's task is to be conscious of what poems do not mean. But this now goes almost unrecognized; because complexity itself, once an exciting discovery, has become a routine object of search, almost the only thing we know how to look for.

Almost the only thing: perhaps that is the most important point of all. As against the full variety of literature itself, the present critical establishment often seems to move, as if by inner necessity, towards a narrower and narrower range of interests. Here I must be brief and crudify and caricature, but behind this caricature there is an impoverishing reality. An early example of this narrowing-down occurs even in Mr Wilson Knight's *Wheel of Fire*—even, that is, in one fructifying source-book of the modern movement. In discussing the plays *Julius Caesar* and *Macbeth*, Mr Knight notices, rightly, certain 'imaginative similarities'. 'Imaginative', notice; a word apt for the full range of the literary impact. But this, he goes on, will be evident to us only if we are 'submerged in the *poetic* quality of the plays'. Can 'imaginative' thus suffer a reduction-process, without comment, to 'poetic'? No. But the process is not yet over. The reference to poetic quality leads Mr Knight straight on to poetic symbolism or imagery; as if poetry were the same as symbolism and imagery.

The essential point at issue is that Mr Knight's discussion, while preserving an air of comprehensiveness, is really becoming narrower and narrower. And when one reads, 'The word "blood" or "bloody" appears seventeen times in Act III, Scene 1 alone', one can see, if I may put it this way, the full scale of the narrowness ultimately threatening us. All this, remember, in the context of a classic first chapter which offers to open the reader's eyes to wide fields to which he was blind before.

Another, later, and clearer example may be seen in an essay by Mr Traversi on the proper way to read and criticize Shakespeare. This comes in Volume 2 of the recent Pelican *Guide to English Literature*. Mr Traversi begins his essay by saying (what is already controversial in the extreme) that with Shakespeare's early plays—not, the passage implies, with his others—we ought to begin by looking first at the occasional striking turn of phrase or individual word. From this it is natural, he says, to pass to the run of the verse expanding into images: images 'which are eventually seen to bear significant repetition . . . (and) form a more subtle and suggestive unity'; though he notes, much in passing, that character and action are 'correspondingly developed' as well. But in the next sentence, Mr Traversi virtually drops these qualifying remarks: 'To proceed from the word to the image in its verse setting, and thence to trace the way in which a pattern of interdependent themes is gradually woven into the dramatic action, is the most fruitful approach'. This fruitful approach, which was offered at first for the early plays, now seems related to what he calls 'Shakespeare's art' generally. It is, in fact, the method which Mr Traversi uses himself whenever he writes about Shakespeare. So, with nothing more than this most perfunctory discussion about approach, we find ourselves committed to an approach which commits the critic to look mainly at one thing: the image-pattern.

What I have tried to do so far is to suggest how the now dominant critical system is threatening to rigidify, to freeze silently up on us. This is still not the sharpest of our present critical dangers.

II

What is sometimes loosely termed 'moral criticism' affords a very clear illustration of how certain important general insights about literature have come, in the recent proliferation of criticism, to be applied mechanically, insistently, in the end fruitlessly. Consider, in the first place, certain general remarks by Dr Leavis; to me they seem well-directed and important, and their point of weakness is not the gist of what they say, but a certain cryptic quality in them, something which is not lucid in spite of much that is emphatic, which could lead others, if not their author, astray. Thus in *The Great Tradition* we read:

The dramatic imagination at work is an intensely moral imagination, the vividness of which is inalienably a judging and a valuing (p. 30).

Serious readers of literature ought to warm to this; and yet on reflection to wish that one who could say this much so clearly could have said a little more. For what does the word 'inalienably' mean? Everything hangs, if we are to give weight to this generalization as a general guide, upon exactly how it is to be understood; and here there is much room for uncertainty. Does 'inalienably' mean, for example, something as whole-hearted as 'nothing other than'? Or would it be more exact to understand the phrase as going not quite so far; meaning instead, say, '. . . always predominantly, though not always exclusively, (a valuing and a judging)'? Or would something which went even less far be right?—for example, that judging and valuing were always an important part of the vividness of the moral imagination (and hence of the dramatic imagination), often a predominant part, and quite often, or sometimes, the whole of that vividness? Some readers may think these distinctions tedious; but they will not be those who are well advised to discuss or stress critical generalizations, and they should rely as critics on native flair, if they have it. If we are going to formulate generalizations, and allow them to influence us, it is essential that we know how to take them. Once this is brought to mind, indeed, we begin to wonder (or so I think) whether the word 'inalienably' is really the right word, in any sense, in Dr Leavis's pronouncement. This is because, unless our minds are closed or closing, we are likely to recall something like George Eliot's comment on *The Mill on the Floss*: 'the exhibition of *the right on both sides* (on Tom Tulliver's, that is, and on Maggie's) being the very soul of my intention in the story'.[1] This ought to lead us to remember that the seeing of the good (and the evil) on both sides, or on the several sides, of a human situation is itself an achievement of the imagination, and necessarily of the moral imagination, of a high order; that in principle this can go with 'judging' and ideally it should do so, but that in practice it is often precluded by judging and fostered by deliberate though temporary suspension of judgement. At this point we ought to begin to notice that much great literature, beyond question, is great because it offers vastly to enlarge our moral imagination, and its achievement is in the direction of insight, understanding, entering into human predicament—not of course in opposition to 'judging' (to think that would be a queer kind of moral *fainéance*) but certainly not just as a mere preliminary to it, valuable not for itself but only as means to something else. Then it is, that a doubt should enter our mind whether 'inalienably' was, whatever exact sense we give it, really the right word for Dr Leavis to have used. For 'inalienably' cannot mean 'usually' nor 'very often' nor even 'nearly always', and if one of these would be right, it is a pity to accept what conceals that from us.

I have just quoted a remark by George Eliot on the moral concern of one of her novels. Henry James commented on what might be called the 'moral dimension' in her work, and to see what he said, and also what Dr Leavis has said about that, will advance the present discussion a stage further. James wrote (the italics are mine) of George Eliot's

general attitude with regard to the novel, which for her, was not primarily a *picture of life*, capable of deriving a high value from its form, but a *moralized fable*, the last word of a philosophy endeavouring to *teach* by example.

Even the keen admirer of George Eliot will sense that James is pointing to a genuine limitation in her work, save when it is at its best. At the same time he will see, implicit in how James

[1] Letter of 4th April, 1861.

expressed himself, certain dangers. Dr Leavis was not blind to those dangers, and he wrote:

> . . . Not much to the point is said about a work of art in calling it didactic—unless one is meaning to judge it adversely. In that case one is judging that the intention to communicate an attitude hasn't become sufficiently more than an intention; hasn't, that is, justified itself as art in the realized concreteness that speaks for itself and enacts its moral significance.

One could sum up the difference between these two writers by saying that James has suggested a certain excessive didacticism in George Eliot, and Dr Leavis has replied that didacticism, when it warrants adverse comment, is not so much excessive as imperfect. It is bold of Dr Leavis to speak of his formulation as the only available one ('in that case *one is judging* that . . .'); and it is also fair to observe that words like 'realized' and 'enacts' depend very heavily upon their detailed context, if they are to have any definite meaning. For all that, this formulation is not one which it is necessary to deny. The same may be said of another remark of Dr Leavis's, one which appears earlier in the same book:

> Is there any great novelist whose preoccupation with form is not a matter of his responsibility towards a rich human interest, or complexity of interests, profoundly realized?—a responsibility involving, of its very nature, imaginative sympathy, moral discrimination, and judgement of relative human value?

The value of a remark like this as counter to preponderantly 'aesthetic' notions of form is obvious. Again, one may regret a certain lack of explicitness: to imply that a great novelist's preoccupation with one thing is 'a matter of his responsibility towards' another, is inexplicit enough. One would like to know more about the nature of the involving ('involve' is a notoriously vague word), and about the differences between two things so clearly distinguishable as imaginative sympathy and moral discrimination, or so conspicuously similar as moral discrimination and judgement of relative human value. But to find that this assertion leaves much to be desired is one thing, and to have to take issue with it is another. One is surely so far from wanting to take issue with it that one thinks it (insofar as it is precise) quite true. Moreover, both these remarks are useful as

correctives to critical attitudes or presumptions which have
been influential at various times in the past.

Both, however, have one thing in common: a very emphatic
stress which they lay on the immediate relevance of moral attitudes, and moral discriminations, to outstanding achievement
in literature (what is 'great', what warrants no judgement 'ad-
versely'). This very emphatic stress was of value, as I said, in
aiding a critic to avoid some of the dangers which encompass
him. The question now is, whether such a stress can create (if
not in Dr Leavis's hands, then in those perhaps of someone less
dexterous) dangers of its own.

To seek an answer to this question in Mr Derek Traversi's
essay on Shakespeare's last plays in the Pelican volume on *The
Age of Shakespeare* is soon to find oneself in a state of mournful
enlightenment. Perhaps the most famous passage in *The
Winter's Tale* is Perdita's speech on the flowers of spring, and
what Florizel says when she has finished:

Camillo: I should leave grazing, were I of your flock,
　　　　　And only live by gazing.
Perdita:　　　　　　　　　　　　　Out alas!
　　　　　You'd be so lean, that blasts of January
　　　　　Would blow you through and through. Now, my fair'st
　　　　　　friend,
　　　　　I would I had some flow'rs o' th' spring that might
　　　　　Become your time of day—and yours, and yours,
　　　　　That wear upon your virgin branches yet
　　　　　Your maidenheads growing. O Proserpina,
　　　　　For the flowers now that, frighted, thou let'st fall
　　　　　From Dis's waggon!—daffodils,
　　　　　That come before the swallow dares, and take
　　　　　The winds of March with beauty; violets, dim
　　　　　But sweeter than the lids of Juno's eyes
　　　　　Or Cytherea's breath; pale primroses,
　　　　　That die unmarried ere they can behold
　　　　　Bright Phoebus in his strength—a malady
　　　　　Most incident to maids; bold oxlips, and
　　　　　The crown-imperial; lilies of all kinds,
　　　　　The flow'r-de-luce being one. O, these I lack
　　　　　To make you garlands of, and my sweet friend
　　　　　To strew him o'er and o'er!

Florizel: What, like a corse?
Perdita: No; like a bank for love to lie and play on;
             Not like a corse; or if—not to be buried,
             But quick, and in mine arms. Come, take your flow'rs.
             Methinks I play as I have seen them do
             In Whitsun pastorals. Sure, this robe of mine
             Does change my disposition.
Florizel: What you do
             Still betters what is done. When you speak, sweet,
             I'd have you do it ever. When you sing,
             I'd have you buy and sell so; so give alms;
             Pray so; and, for the ordering your affairs,
             To sing them too. When you do dance, I wish you
             A wave o' th' sea; move still, still so,
             And own no other function. Each your doing
             So singular in each particular,
             Crowns what you are doing in the present deeds,
             That all your acts are queens.
Perdita: O Doricles,
             Your praises are too large (etc.)

Perdita's speech is made, according to Mr Traversi, 'as she
offers her pastoral flowers to Florizel':

Beautiful as (Perdita's) speech is, . . . the love it expresses still
lacks *the necessary maturity* . . . the emphasis laid, in the imagery, upon
Spring, that is upon birth, inexperience, virginity, is subtly balanced
by an implicit sense of death; the flowers to which Perdita refers are
'pale' and 'dim'; they 'die unmarried', in unfulfilled promise, having
failed to 'behold Phoebus in his strength'.

I am unsure who it is here who is going to explain what degree
of maturity is the necessary degree—whether Mr Traversi, I
mean, or Shakespeare; and I am also unsure which of them it is
who asserts that 'Spring means birth, inexperience, virginity':
I think it is Mr Traversi, because there is no reference whatever
to 'birth' in the passage under consideration. But these points
aside, Mr Traversi writes as if he were simplifying and crudify-
ing Dr Leavis: were able to snap up such a phrase as the 'Com-
municate an attitude' which appeared in the quotation from
Dr Leavis on page 214, but not able to carry effectively in his
mind the qualifications at which, in both the remarks I quoted,
Dr Leavis hints.

It is inexact to say that the flowers are 'pale' and 'dim'. Only the primoses are the one, only the violets the other; and the violets are 'dim, but *sweeter* than the lids of Juno's eyes or Cytherea's *breath*'—this, rather than their dimness, is what receives the emphasis. As for the oxlips, they are 'bold'; and the daffodils seem bold too, coming before the swallow dares. The other thing about them is simply that their beauty 'takes' the March winds; March winds being bold enough in their turn, and the 'taking' being an amorous one. The crown imperial is a fine robust plant; and 'lilies of all kinds, the flow'r-de-luce being one', which Mr Traversi leaves out of his quotation, do not convey an implicit sense of death either (lilies were symbols not of death but of virginity). What about the primroses, the only one of the flowers which seems to offer clear, unequivocal support for the moral interpretation which this critic has put upon the whole speech? In respect of this last remaining scrap of supporting evidence, something else is relevant. It comes at the beginning of the speech, and (like the lilies of all kinds) Mr Traversi left it out of his quotation. Perdita has been speaking to the middle-aged Camillo, and then she says:

> Now my fair'st friend,
> I would I had some flowers o' the spring that might
> Become your time of day; *and yours, and yours,*
> *That wear upon your virgin branches yet*
> *Your maidenheads growing . . .*

Not Florizel! Then at the end, after the lilies, she concludes,

> O these I lack,
> To make you garlands of, and my fair friend
> To strew him o'er and o'er.

In other words, the remarks about the flowers are to Mopsa and Dorcas, the two country maids, as much as or even perhaps rather than to Florizel; and the reference to dying of a malady most incident to maids is far from unconnected with this. Mr Traversi's whole discussion seems to result from seizing upon one phrase in the speech, misunderstanding that, and then letting loose his own pre-occupation with the communication of a moral attitude.

Mr Traversi next examines Florizel's speech. It is not quite right to call this a 'reply' to Perdita's, as he does; but it certainly follows soon after. Florizel says that Perdita does everything she does with such grace that it seems to have a kind of finality; whatever she does, she does it with such beauty that he wants her never to stop. It is a passage which one might well quote, as illustrating how a few lines by a true poet enable us to see part of experience with a new and fresh keenness, and to realize that life is so far richer and better than perhaps we should have been able to grasp for ourselves. ('O brave new world, that has such people in it,' Shakespeare makes another of his young lovers exclaim elsewhere.) Mr Traversi does not concern himself with the way in which Florizel's speech—which is a beautiful compliment, of course—illuminates what Perdita is like. He is interested in the desire it allegedly expresses:

a 'desire to live outside time, to hold up the course of mutability in a way that is ultimately impossible . . . nostalgic, . . . an attempt to evade the pressure of mutability, to escape from the problems presented by maturity into a permanent dream of first love. The conclusion is, inevitably, the same as that implied in Perdita's speech . . . Spring needs still to pass over into summer . . .'.

Here the critic is interpreting somewhat boldly. The 'conclusion implied' in Perdita's speech seemed on close examination not to be there at all; but at least Mr Traversi could point to imagery —in his view much of the imagery, but anyhow one phrase— as conveying that conclusion. The primroses did die unmarried; there was something, anyhow, to suggest that the attitude they stood for (if they did stand for an attitude) was implicitly being condemned. What is there in Florizel's speech? Mr Traversi points to nothing; and I can find nothing. 'The conclusion is, inevitably . . .' seems here to express nothing but his own judgement upon the alleged attitude of Florizel. Then comes the next step. 'This love is not yet mature; in order to become so, it needs to be reinforced by the deeply spiritual penitence of Leontes.' Where do we see this penitence specifically reinforcing the love of Perdita and Florizel, or being explicitly treated as something which makes good a lack or defect in that love? Mr Traversi does not say, and I can find nothing to say for him.

Perhaps, in a way, this is unjust, and he has tried to point to something: 'This love is not mature . . . in order to become so, it needs to be reinforced by the spiritual penitence of Leontes. *That is why* (Mr Traversi goes on), at this moment of idyllic celebration, Polixenes enters to cast across it the shadow of aged, impotent anger. . . .' That Polixenes entered 100 lines before; that he displays his anger nearly 300 lines later; that it is then very far from impotent; and that it is very much an open question whether to cast the shadow of aged impotent anger over young love is to show that it needs to be reinforced by the spiritual penitence of Leontes;—all these points are barely worth making any longer. Mr Traversi seems to be writing his own play, a moralized fantasy on *The Winters Tale*. What is ostensibly an insistently responsible approach to the play proves on close examination to be the opposite.

Mr Traversi's phrase, 'the problems presented by maturity' is significant and I think disquieting. Perhaps it underlies all the vagaries of his analysis, because in that analysis he is hurrying forward so as to reach something which he himself needs to reach: what will, in Arnold's phrase, 'console' and 'sustain'. 'How to live', in another of Arnold's phrases; guidance which will help one face 'problems'. But maturity does not chiefly bring problems; these arrive easily first. Maturity (insofar as I understand that word) brings serenity, confidence, breadth of vision, a capacity to apprehend and comprehend (and thereby, incidentally, to assess) the whole range of life. Mr Traversi's discussion seems less to reveal the maturity of Shakespeare's (or the critic's) vision, than to show how important critical guiding ideas of the recent past, becoming established, becoming readily or perhaps automatically accepted, have lost their value in their application.

III

How far has the new régime in criticism equipped us to discuss not the short passage or poem but the longer literary work, the full-length play or the novel? The new régime provides us with two main concepts for this. The first of these is the idea of 'imagery' or 'image-patterns'; as the main part, at least, of language texture generally. The second is 'theme'. In my view, this word is what really bedevils us at present. Before I come to it, however, I want to say something about 'imagery'.

In this matter, the new criticism argues from two contradictory principles. One is that true criticism must be based on response to the total work: not mere neatness in the plot, not mere anything, but the total work. That is unimpeachable; it has unquestionably increased the whole imaginative depth of our critical grasp. The last thing to do would be to go back on it. But so far as I can see, some critics have no sooner glimpsed this wider view than they have drawn the curtains on it. They have turned away to another principle of criticism; one which is so much narrower than the first that it contradicts it. They have not openly repudiated the idea of a total response: they have begun to repudiate it, in effect, unconsciously. Mr Raymond Williams, in *Drama from Ibsen to Eliot*, writing about our response to a work in its entirety, says:

> Literature, in its most general definition, is a means of communication of imaginative experience through certain written organizations of words . . . a controlled product of the author—the control exercised by being exerted in the *finalized organization of words*.

Next, Professor L. C. Knights, in an important essay of 1933 which was a point of origin for the modern movement:

> The total response to a play can only be obtained by . . . in short . . . an exact and sensitive study of Shakespeare's language.

Here we are, back at linguistic texture again; and I entirely agree. But the question is: would this kind of approach, studying the language, exclude *anything* from our consideration of a play; or would it even tell us that some things were unimportant, others specially important? Certainly not: there is nothing whatever in a play—not plot, not characterization, not the Girlhood of Shakespeare's Heroines, even, which we could conceivably study in any way save by a study of the language of the play. There is nothing else to study. Whatever aspect of a play we study—relevant or irrelevant to true criticism—where we have to study it is in the language. If we study the language loosely and vaguely, our results are loose and vague; an exact and sensitive study gives exact and sensitive results. So this general principle gives no guide at all as to what things will be important in a play. It leaves every question completely open. In fact, it is a truism.

But the critics who have put forward this principle of studying the language have drawn an inference from it. They have written as if it turned the critic's attention one way at the expense of another. Thus, when Professor Knights said we needed 'in short' an exact and sensitve study of language, what that 'in short' summarized was something highly selective and tendentious: merely, 'the quality of the verse, the rhythm and imagery, the controlled associations of the words and their emotional and intellectual force'. (Elsewhere Professor Knights sums up what he calls 'all the resources of poetic drama' as: 'action, contrast, statement, implication, imagery and allusion'. One sees at once that, again, this is highly selective, and heavily weighted on the side of the close readers.) Similarly, Mr Williams' conviction that, as he puts it, 'language is the central medium for communication', makes him disparage form, and action, and character, as conventions. Both he and Professor Knights seem to dislike these aspects of drama; both of them write as if they were secondary, derivative aspects. That may well be true, in this or that play. But the critics argue for it not solely by direct contact with the plays; they do so by their general preambles about the right way to read any poetic drama. I am now making the same kind of point as I made previously: the question of whether form, plot, character, or verbal texture are major or minor is a completely open one, until one starts to read a play. These critics have written as if they had closed it; and closed it with a general argument; one which in fact proves nothing at all.

Now for 'theme'. This is a hard-worked word in contemporary criticism: so hard-worked, in fact, that it is given at least three different meanings. Sometimes it looks as if the 'theme' is a topic or an idea; just something which comes into the work. Sometimes the alleged theme looks more like a kind of statement embodied in the work; and sometimes it actually looks like that old out-of-work, the plot. Thus, when Professor Knights says that the theme of *Macbeth* is 'the deceitful appearance', or 'the reversal of values', I think this is theme as topic. Similarly with

Mr Wilson Knight's 'madness-theme' in *King Lear*; or the theme of sexual nausea which Mr Speaight traces in Hamlet. But when Dr Leavis says that the theme of Lawrence's *The Rainbow* is 'the urgency, and the difficult struggle, of the highest human possibilities to realize themselves', these are not just topics: the point seems rather that the novel as a whole is displaying something, is conveying how urgent and difficult that struggle really is. Mr Speaight, in his book on Shakespeare, says that the tragedies have a recurrent theme: 'the lust of the flesh which dislocates the reason and blasphemes against nature in nature's name'. This looks as if the plays express an attitude to lust, as if they place it in the scheme of things.

Thirdly, the word 'theme' is sometimes used pretty much as a synonym for plot: a critic recently said, for example, that the theme of Trollope's novel *The Way We Live Now* was 'the collapse of standards and of social order before new methods of finance'. This obviously cannot be a statement about social order and new finance in general, because standards and social order sometimes collapse and sometimes do the opposite, under these circumstances. On the other hand it is more than a mere topic: it is the whole story of the book.

Can we not rule out the first of these meanings—theme as topic—immediately, as irrelevant to criticism? Every intelligible work, however abysmally bad, has several or many themes in this sense, and they probably cannot help becoming interrelated unless it is a very short work indeed. Could one not, if one tried, be sure of finding interrelated themes in the first short story in the pile of magazines at the dentist's? It is the same point as I made about metaphors in my previous talk. The mere presence of the thing is without interest, unless it can be shown that its presence makes the work better. The whole problem lies there.

Is the theme of a work, then, some statement—implicit, needless to say; some point of view embodied in the work? Sometimes the critics are cautious, and they talk about 'vital problems' or 'obstinate questionings'; as if the great masterpieces of literature went in for these things, but not the answers to them. When they do come out into the open and do indicate the main point of view which they detect as theme, I cannot help thinking that, normally, the result is disastrous. For example, one critic says that for Shakespeare the chief meaning of the history plays was 'that political capacity and moral sensibility tend necessarily to diverge'. We do not need Shakespeare to convey the truth of this, because we know from history and experience that it is false: sometimes those two things diverge, sometimes they converge.

Another critic speaks of 'the revelation' of *Macbeth*: that it 'suggests . . . the true nature of evil—the dissociation from all external phenomena of the individual soul'. Again, if we confront this assertion with our experience of evil, we recall the fact that life is an elaborate thing; evil is sometimes like that and sometimes like the opposite. A third critic says that the fundamental insight embodied in *Coriolanus* is 'that political and social forms cannot be separated from the human and moral qualities that shape them, and that they foster'. If this means 'cannot be separated as a matter of fact', this would not be a fundamental insight, because it would be an elementary mistake: we know from experience that they are separated all too often. The critic clearly meant that they ought not to be separated; that we ought, morally, to judge political and social forms by their moral qualities. And that is not a fundamental insight either, but a truism.

What is needed, at this stage in the problem, seems to me to be common sense. However much one is an idealist, one knows that general truths about life are learnt, and proved, from one place only: life itself; experience—either our own experience, or real events which are related to us by history or otherwise. That is a laborious way to learn; and moralists have sometimes thought that they could abridge this labour by abstract proofs— Spinoza's geometry of the emotional life, for example; perhaps Plato's discussions of pleasure and freedom. This is now unfashionable; nowadays we hope that literary, imaginative works will abridge experience for us instead. They will not: the literary work takes and develops one particular situation—or a small handful—two, say, as in *Women in Love*, three as in *Anna Karenina*. It cannot possibly prove any general truth. In knowledge about human beings there is no such thing as a crucial experiment.

Much more to the point, there is never such a thing as an

imaginary crucial experiment. Try the idea on a physical or social scientist, and see what he says. Certainly, literature can help one to see new facts in experience when one turns back to experience; that is another matter. But by itself it cannot establish a single general or universal truth about what human affairs are like or how they develop; and thus when one of these critics says that the play *Macbeth* 'defines a particular kind of evil—the evil that results from a lust for power'—he must be mistaken. That is defined for us by experience, extended perhaps by knowledge of history; and what these two things do establish is that there is no one evil resulting from lust for power: lust for power leads in different cases to an indefinite variety of evils (or exceptionally, of course, even to good: which makes it no better in itself). What *Macbeth* does, I suppose, is to depict for us, in great and remarkable detail, one imagined case and one only.

This view may exasperate some people. 'English ought to be kept up', they will say with Keats. If one can talk about fundamental insights and universal truths in literary works, literature sounds important. Does not the train of thought I have been following make it unimportant?

On the contrary: if—to put it baldly—literature is general moral insight, plus concreteness (that is the stock word), we have only to find that we do not need concreteness and imaginative writing is expendable: we could manage with moral reflections instead. This view makes 'concreteness' the absolutely vital link in the chain. Yet the present critical régime has hardly discussed this idea; uses it frequently but almost in passing. This is why I think the word 'theme' the real villain. It is—perhaps this will sound surprising—tempting us to accept a surreptitious transformation of imaginative literature into what I am inclined to call a non-imaginative dimension, the dimension of general moral reflections on life—save, that is, for a difference which we hardly think about but which we pay lip-service to by that catch-phrase 'in the concrete'. To say that a literary masterpiece is 'a studied explication of the moral nature of man', done in the concrete, is not much better than saying something like 'poetry is music but played on a dictionary'; or 'sculpture is drawing but you can walk round it'. A radical, the total transformation, is hidden away in a phrase. It is as if we got in such a muddle that we called the dog its tail, and the tail the dog.

What is this radical, this total transformation, when we turn from discursive reflections to great imaginative literature? I turn to the third sense of the word theme: theme as story—the least fashionable but I suspect the only fertile one. In ordinary conversation, we tell anecdotes along two fundamentally different lines. Sometimes we tell an anecdote which is meant for typical. 'Here's a case,' we say; 'this kind of thing goes on every day.' At other times we tell a story because it is not typical but the opposite: because it is amazing and exceptional. Nor does that make it any the less informative. Life is not chemistry: being informed about it is not knowing about the general nature of man, or life's necessary tendencies, or what, according to the natural order, is the consequence of what. Men whose knowledge is only of this kind live in shells. Besides all this, real knowledge of life is knowledge of the exceptional: of how near the exceptional always is; of how easily it can come; and if it does come, how elaborate, or astonishing, or disastrous it may very well be.

There is no elementary parallel to this in the physical or social sciences: though there are, I believe, some fairly recondite ones. But this is the way in which many, perhaps most, literary masterpieces extend and enrich the reader's grasp of life. Seldom or never in experience does one encounter a divergence from the norm, an aberration of nature, which is as fully developed in every detail, and above all as complete, as what is depicted in the literary work at its most ambitious. Which is not to deny that such works have a universal relevance, nor that we can sense a norm within the extraordinary; but to come closer to how this universality and normality really enter our experience as we read.

It is this completeness through to the end with which a particular case is depicted that distinguishes imaginative writing; this is what it does that no other kind of writing begins to do, and is thus what makes it irreplaceable. There is a speech by Anna Karenina which brings this out with beautiful exactness. She is half way through her disastrous affair with Count Vronsky. In speaking of it to her brother she says: 'No, Stiva; I'm lost:

worse than lost: I'm not lost *yet*—I can't say that all is over: on the contrary, I feel that it's not ended. I'm like an over-strained violin string that must snap. But it's not ended yet . . . and the end will be terrible.' Anna's was, we might say, the perfect case of the disease, wonderfully complete and intensified—which is to say, highly exceptional—and she had to go right through to the end of it: there is its completeness and finality.

This 'going right through to the end', neglected as it is, seems the central feature of imaginative literature in the full-length work. Which brings me back to the current critical establishment. A pattern of imagery, a set of interdependent themes, could run through a group of unrelated short stories; or a discursive work like an essay by Montaigne or a long selection of *pensées* from Pascal. We do not, by these means, even glimpse the really decisive quality of the play or novel; or, in general, of the work which is a unity in the imaginative order. What is that decisive quality? It is what demands that the work be read and seen from beginning to end as a single organic thing; something that, as we read it, pervades and controls and extends our whole experience throughout a period of time; and that, whenever we recall it, lives in our minds again with that unique temporal coherence. In most cases (though not in all) what is really distinctive of this kind of writing, what it does that nothing else does, is start off a narrative, a story, and carry it through to a point where that narrative appears to complete itself, to run decisively to a halt.

Hence the basic, the final inadequacy, of close reading of the isolated passage, when it is transferred to the longer literary work. No reading of isolated passages can locate this unity; it is what operates from one to the next, what integrates them. There must be something else to 'inspect', some other dimension in which the critical scrutiny can operate. 'Plot', no doubt, is a useless word here: it has become tied to the mechanics of story-telling—is the time-table of the book all right? are things always found where they were lost?—detective-story stuff. But it seems to me that to find a way of seeing and discussing the narrative itself, as normally the fundamental quality of the full-length work, as its essential principle of imaginative order, is the key idea for a truly 'literary' criticism.